For every marketer who ever had the guts to challenge assumptions and believe in themselves.

'What would we do if we had no courage to attempt anything?'

Vincent Van Gogh

Teach®
Yourself

Make a Difference With Your Marketing

J Jonathan Gabay

For UK order enquiries: please contact Bookpoint Ltd,
130 Milton Park, Abingdon, Oxon OX14 4SB.
Telephone: +44 (0) 1235 827720. Fax: +44 (0) 1235 400454.
Lines are open 09.00–17.00, Monday to Saturday, with a 24-hour
message answering service. Details about our titles and how to
order are available at www.teachyourself.com

Long renowned as the authoritative source for self-guided learning –
with more than 50 million copies sold worldwide – the **Teach Yourself**
series includes over 500 titles in the fields of languages, crafts, hobbies,
business, computing and education.

British Library Cataloguing in Publication Data: a catalogue record
for this title is available from the British Library.

This edition published 2010.

Previously published as *Teach Yourself Marketing*.

The **Teach Yourself** name is a registered trade mark of
Hodder Headline.

Copyright © 2010 J. Jonathan Gabay

In UK: All rights reserved. Apart from any permitted use under UK
copyright law, no part of this publication may be reproduced or
transmitted in any form or by any means, electronic or mechanical,
including photocopy, recording, or any information, storage and
retrieval system, without permission in writing from the publisher
or under licence from the Copyright Licensing Agency Limited.
Further details of such licences (for reprographic reproduction)
may be obtained from the Copyright Licensing Agency Limited,
of Saffron House, 6–10 Kirby Street, London EC1N 8TS.

Typeset by MPS Limited, A Macmillan Company.

Printed in Great Britain for Hodder Education, an Hachette UK
Company, 338 Euston Road, London NW1 3BH, by CPI Cox &
Wyman, Reading, Berkshire RG1 8EX.

The publisher has used its best endeavours to ensure that the URLs
for external websites referred to in this book are correct and active
at the time of going to press. However, the publisher and the author
have no responsibility for the websites and can make no guarantee
that a site will remain live or that the content will remain relevant,
decent or appropriate.

Hachette UK's policy is to use papers that are natural, renewable
and recyclable products and made from wood grown in sustainable
forests. The logging and manufacturing processes are expected to
conform to the environmental regulations of the country of origin.

Impression number   10 9 8 7 6 5 4 3 2 1

Year   2014 2013 2012 2011 2010

Front cover: RT images/Alamy

Back cover: © Jakub Semeniuk/iStockphoto.com, © Royalty-Free/Corbis,
© agencyby/iStockphoto.com, © Andy Cook/iStockphoto.com,
© Christopher Ewing/iStockphoto.com, © zebicho – Fotolia.com,
© Geoffrey Holman/iStockphoto.com, © Photodisc/Getty Images,
© James C. Pruitt/iStockphoto.com, © Mohamed Saber – Fotolia.com

Contents

Acknowledgements

Special thanks to: Jill Birch, Simon Brewster, Alison Frecknall, Pat Mani, Patricia Allan, and Susan Young.

Meet the author

Hi my name is Jonathan. I am really looking forward to helping you make a difference with your marketing. Working with some of the most prestigious marketing organizations, including the world's biggest marketing training body, I have addressed and mentored literally thousands of marketers. I am particularly proud that many students have carved out successful careers with globally admired and respected brands. During three decades in advertising and marketing I have held several creative directorships as well as Head of Copy positions at renowned advertising agencies. My company, Brand Forensics, develops brands, explains core messages and so encourages employees, partners and markets to feel connected with propositions. As a journalist I deliver insights behind brand-related headlines for some the world's most trusted news organizations, including CNN, BLOOMBERG TV, ITN, BBC, SKY, Five News and many others. Major educational establishments and academic bodies feature my books on business, marketing and copywriting. Other Hodder published titles include, *Improve Your Copywriting* and the sister companion to that book: *Gabay's Copywriters' Compendium*. So if you are ready to have fun whilst learning how to succeed in one of the most exciting professions, read on and let's explore your full marketing potential.

Without marketing there is no market – without you there is no marketing

Without marketing, there is literally nothing to be said about enterprise. Communicating your message requires imaginative marketing that doesn't simply comply with best practice standards but exceeds them.

Whatever the size and type of your organization, this book will help you communicate your message clearly and in doing so gain you entry into a proud community of business leaders who belong to a sector of business with a remarkable history and reassuring future.

Marketing is neither convoluted nor academic. It's about real life; getting the most out of relationships. To maximize those relationships, in this book we'll uncover the crucial issues you need to know, from unfolding classic marketing fundamentals to stretching your marketing budget without squeezing its effect. There are also insights on brands and marketing techniques used by some of the world's most powerful organizations – ready for you to adapt and adopt. Throughout 'Put it to the test' exercises put you to the test and remind you of key lessons and insights.

Are you eager to explore your potential, exploit further your own abilities, the marketing function of your organization and, not least, your target audience? Then driven by the momentum of your imagination, like toppling dominoes, one by one I'll guide you towards generating maximum impact in your marketplace.

J. Jonathan Gabay
jj@gabaynet.com

Only got a minute?

Imagine you have less than a minute to sell (position) your company to me.

- ► Who is your company aimed at?
- ► What, specifically do you do?
- ► How and why are you qualified to do it?
- ► Why do you do it better than anyone else?

Or to really get to the point:

For   _____

It is   _____

Only we can   _____

Because _____

When it comes to marketing yourself, you must be convincing rather than clever.

5 Only got five minutes?

Consider this. You manufacture mobile phones. Advertising – perhaps on the radio, in the cinema, on television – raises the notion that rather than watching TV at home, we could be watching TV while on the move. This establishes a brand positioning which strengthens the motive that watching on a mobile is worth pursuing.

Next, a preference for your particular brand needs to be established. So you further explain – by direct mail or e-shots perhaps – why your mobile phone is particularly appropriate. Following this, you persuade the potential buyer, that having opted for a mobile phone, yours has the edge over the competition. This could be demonstrated by a promotion through a discount or value-added campaign – a great way of dispelling any 'last minute' change of mind on the part of your customer.

The customer buys your mobile and is happy – but it's not enough for you as an imaginative direct marketer. You want to encourage loyalty to your brand, so you may follow up the purchase with incentives rewarding continued allegiance. Once all done, thanks to the recommendations by your existing customers, prospects for your mobile are better targeted. Plus, in recognition of your awareness advertising, you are already further up the list of customers' preferred brands.

An integrated approach to marketing, such as this, adjusts itself to the age and reputation of your brand. The greater the market maturity, the less the need to invest in the awareness and positioning – and the greater the need to invest in loyalty (unless of course you are re-positioning your brand).

1

The tools of the trade

In this chapter you will learn about:
- *the roots of marketing*
- *marketing definitions*
- *the Boston matrix*
- *product life cycles*
- *Pareto*
- *demarketing*
- *implementing your marketing plan*
- *global markets*

Marketing is really about common sense. Sun Tzu, the fourth-century Chinese military strategist said, 'the most difficult things in the world must be done while they are still easy'. Open the marketing kit of simple business tools and you'll find four neatly divided sections, each featuring distinctive processes:

1 *Strategic marketing analysis*
2 *Communications planning*
3 *Marketing implementation*
4 *Marketing control.*

The essence of marketing is understanding, supporting, appreciating and being empathetic towards people connected with your organization. Just as a river meanders, so your marketing adapts and blends into a commercial landscape.

There is a marketing lesson to be learned from the tragedy that befell the cruise liner *Titanic*. The key issue was the hidden depths of the deadly iceberg. Urged to make 'marketing' headlines, the ship's captain, Edward J. Smith, ordered full steam ahead to reach New York in record time. The ship had received a total of seven iceberg warnings. But the sea was calm and the Officer of the Bridge, William Murdoch, decided eyesight rather than foresight would suffice.

Marketing is about getting things right by keeping a watchful eye on the horizon as well as an ear to what's happening below, around as well as above the 'deck' of your business. Approaching midnight on 14 April 1912, a mountainous iceberg was spotted and Murdoch desperately tried to turn the ship around. His action was in vain. The iceberg gnawed a row of gaping tooth marks into the ship's structure. Within two hours, along with its invincible promises, the 'unsinkable' *Titanic* sunk.

Only 20 lifeboats were on board. The wives and children of dignitaries were saved first. Over 1,500 men, women and children perished. The marketing lesson? Protocol comes second to marketplace vigilance to enable those in charge to protect and safeguard those in your care.

The evolution of marketing

Contrary to popular belief, marketing is the oldest profession. The marketing process forms part of the progression of exchange. That is, giving up something in return for something else which has some perceived value. Humankind's original idea of supply and demand was pretty much a self-centred affair. The hunter made a crude weapon to kill an animal. If a vessel was needed to carry the food, the hunter improvised. Then came the task of gathering wood for a fire. Once again, someone had to come up with the goods. So it was that humankind floated along in this lonely, self-sufficient existence, getting nowhere fast. Instead of clobbering as many wild boar as possible, the hunter spent energy and time dealing with related aspects. The same could be said for the people who could have been profitably concentrating on their own jobs such as flint sharpening or wood gathering. There had to be a better solution. So the process of *decentralized exchange* was evolved. In this economy, the hunter, the flint maker, the wood gatherer and the rest of the clan started to see each other in a different light. Each was a potential buyer. Collectively, they formed a *market*.

The hunter's life became more structured. After a good day's clobbering, the hunter visited suppliers to trade the best rump steak. Everything seemed to progress reasonably well. Yet, after ambushing wild boar all day, would hunters really want to drag carcasses around, calling on different traders?

Enter the *merchant* who established a centralized *marketplace*. Along with the other hunters, the hunter brought meat to the merchant who acted as a catalyst for the exchange of services and goods. So the hunter established a profitable point of contact, dealt with the market as a whole and even gained time to clobber bigger game.

This formed a solid foundation for a market in which:

1 *'Producers' could assess the value of their goods or services.*
2 *Buyers knew what they were prepared to exchange for those goods or services.*
3 *For a percentage of the transaction, merchants acted as intermediaries between established or likely buyers and sellers.*

The marketplace's profitable reputation grew. Further deals were struck. Specialist merchants traded in particular items. New markets developed. Humankind evolved, as did its needs. Eventually all kinds of markets grew: job markets, money markets, commodity markets, web markets …

There have always been several options for exchange. Our original hunter bartered meat. However, he could have added value to his services by offering his time and experience to show others how to hunt and prepare meat. Once a value of some goods has been established and a currency of exchange agreed, each of the parties can accept or refuse the proposed 'trade'. Finally, they need skills to communicate what they want, when they want it and how it will be delivered.

THE 'NOW' AGE

Today, sellers and buyers don't always meet face to face. Merchants transport goods anywhere. Distribution has embraced the web, email has superseded direct mail and microblogs like Twitter are superseding email. Even the sound of money has changed from the clinking of loose change to the 'click, hum and swipe' of electronic gadgetry and smart cards. Nationwide, Europe-wide or worldwide, imaginative marketing lifts products off a page, website and, of course, shelf. Mobile PDAs record the golden digits of your credit card. Sophisticated stock control technology moves goods out of a warehouse, whilst delivery services, supported by ingenious stock database technology, places them into a customer's hand.

It is an economy where anything, including the bones of extinct prehistoric creatures, has its place, price and market.

What is marketing?

Or rather, let's immediately dismiss what marketing isn't.

- ▶ *It* isn't *about producing pretty brochures or websites.*
- ▶ *It* isn't *about obsessing over logo colours and style.*
- ▶ *It* isn't *about knowing classical theories by heart without having the courage and conviction to apply them in real life.*
- ▶ *It* isn't *about 'cutting and pasting' tired looking marketing material.*

Marketing *is* about exploring opportunities and having the guts to do something with them and about them. Business without marketing is like winking at a girl in the dark and doing nothing about it. An organization's most influential and creative business tool is marketing. Like any powerful instrument, it needs to be constantly reviewed, preened and prepared to meet new challenges.

Danielle Aarons, one of Australia's leading independent marketers, explains:

Marketing managers must become business managers controlling a portfolio of goods and services to maximize profit and revenue. That's tough in a competitive market with few opportunities to hold a unique point of difference for long.

MARKETING ISN'T BLACK OR WHITE

Economists tend to view marketing from a black-and-white sales perspective (as if the sales process was that easily defined). Generally speaking, neo-classical economic theory is led by supply and demand considerations. Most economists would argue that if costs could be reduced sufficiently to benefit consumers, demand for a product or service would follow.

But if that were the case, your only tool would be a series of cost reduction exercises. In a competitive arena where the player still left standing after a trade shoot-out marks 'High Noon', either you or your competitor would eventually be fired out of business.

FOUR UNFOCUSED VIEWS ON MARKETING

The Financial Director
'Do it by the book. Avoid risks. Look at previous research to confirm you are on track and the rest will look after itself.'

The Department Head
'Save money, just add another department. Offer a standardized customer service function. Who cares about expensive specialists?'

The Sales Director
'It's all sales. If you can't sell now, cut the price, sell high later. Trust me on this.'

The Chief Executive

'"Arty" marketing ideas and fine salespeople are wonderful, just make me and the shareholders a dollar, pound or euro, and make it snappy.'

FROM MORE IS MORE TO MORE IS LESS

During the late nineteenth-century industrial boom period, the pure, economic theory of marketing was at its most practical. As long as you could produce enough goods the chances were pretty good that someone, somewhere would buy it. And if the going got tough – you reduced costs.

As the manufacturing process became increasingly sophisticated, product variations became more extensive. This led to greater product-range competition. When product variations ran out of drawing-board space, it was back to cutting prices. Sooner or later, companies could no longer sustain the reductions. As they couldn't slice sales prices, they cut the cost of manufacturing. Companies became more efficient in production techniques. It was an era of time-and-motion studies. Lower production costs led to greater output and keener prices.

Driven by market demands, the wheels of industry again turned out profits.

However, as recessions came and went, and globalization together with technology shrunk the gap between someone wanting a product and it being delivered, service rather than products alone grew increasingly important. Competition from just about everywhere meant a company's offering not only had to be the best in the market, but the keenest, sharpest and so most valued.

KEEPING THE CUSTOMERS SATISFIED

Marketing evolves around satisfying the consumer profitably. Identify their needs and you can ensure your service or product is attractive, appealing and relevant. Theoretically, that secures sales. However, practically sales don't even get off the ground without some kind of promotion. When used intelligently, advertising (which comes from the Latin root *advertere* – 'to turn towards') aims to persuade customers to either fix or adapt buying patterns and behaviour. Through doing so, marketers assume the roles of commercial cupids – nurturing long-term relationships between the customer and a brand.

However, this puts the kibosh on the purely economic-led view of marketing. Some economists consider one of the roles of advertising is to help consumers save time and costs when choosing a product or service.

Value generates demand. This, in turn, influences price. Even during a recession, people actively search for products or services that add value to their lives. Much of that value doesn't come from old-fashioned notions of Unique Selling Points (USPs) alone. It is delivered through emotional triggers such as images, packaging and words that collectively promoted a sense of image in the mind of a consumer.

So, potentially, markets are not just rationally led: but subjectively and even emotionally motivated. Take the perfume business. This deals with fragrance as well as feelings about what scent says about the wearer. Perfume may be positioned to make you feel confident, sensual, chic …

All products and services need to be distinctive and so establish a point of difference. (See page 183.) As the marketplace in general becomes more crowded so, like in a gigantic rave party, the individual brands with the most distinctive personalities will be those that make the biggest impact.

It is all a matter of positioning to influence the way consumers think and feel. (See 'Image is everything', page 189.) Effective brand positioning addressing customer expectations drives the marketing process forward. Once a positioning has been defined and developed, all the intrinsic and extrinsic attributes of the brand amalgamate.

Brands embody all this not just in design but in a company's entire philosophy – one which is associated with an ideal that is shared by both the brand marketer and market alike. Later I'll elaborate on brand positioning. For now, consider a radio interview I heard. A major drinks company planned to merge with its competitor. The interviewer asked the respective chairmen to place a value on each other's companies. They concluded that the greatest value was that of the portfolio of brands.

Did you know?

In the UK, the first alcohol brand to sponsor a series on morning television was Martini Citro. Made in Italy, the series was presented by an Italian chef and chosen to reflect the brand's target core market: 25–34-year-old women.

Branding gives companies the edge over the competition. Consumers search for products and services which initially may be more expensive than a competitor's. Yet, in terms of relevance to longer-term personal aspirations and needs, these products and services deliver greater value.

Put it to the test

What is neo-classical economic theory?

Try two perfumes – what do you believe they say about you? Write down seven words to describe that sense of feeling.

Implementing your marketing plan

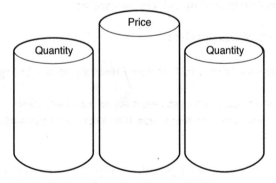

Economically, sell enough at the right price and eventually you'll reach profit targets.

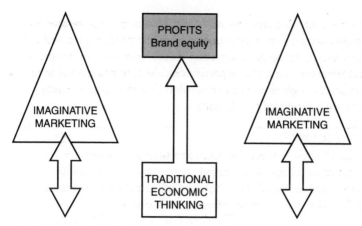

Complement economic thinking with imaginative marketing and you'll spend less time and fewer resources increasing profits and brand values.

LOOK IT UP: MORE DEFINITIONS OF MARKETING – WHICH MAKES THE MOST SENSE?

According to the *Oxford Concise Dictionary of Business*:

Marketing is the process of identifying, maximizing and satisfying consumer demand for a company's products. Marketing a product involves such tasks as anticipating changes in demand (usually on the basis of market research), promotion of the product, ensuring that its quality, availability and prices meet the needs of the market and providing after-sales service.

DEMAND MANAGEMENT

Marketing – as defined by Chartered Institute of Marketing:

The management process responsible for identifying, anticipating and satisfying customer requirements profitably.

(CIM, 2001)

That's excellent, as long as you also accept that different organizations have different expectations from their marketing programmes. For example, charities don't make profits so they could trade the word 'profitably' for 'effectively'. (Providing you are not 'hung up' on grammatical issues like splitting your infinitives!)

Your role isn't just to sell. It includes identifying a demand through research, distribution of your product or service and developing your customer base by continually looking for new ways to satisfy needs.

As an essential business process for the third millennium, part of the function of imagination-led marketing is to formulate targeted strategies that attract an audience for a particular product or service. It's down to you to probe, plan, implement and direct commercial programmes between your organization and the marketplace. In doing so, you can prosper and sustain mutually beneficial trade.

Peter Doyle – from the classic school of marketing – describes marketing as:

> **... the management process that seeks to maximize returns to shareholders by developing and implementing strategies to build relationships of trust with high value customers and create sustainable differential advantage.**

Peter Drucker, a sales and marketing guru, explains that:

> **... marketing is the whole business seen from the point of view of its final result, that is, from the consumers' point of view.**

Marketing – as defined by the American Marketing Association:

> **Marketing is the activity, set of institutions, and processes for creating communicating, delivering, and exchanging offerings that have value for customers, clients, partners, and society at large.**
>
> (AMA, 2007)

Through orchestrating the process by which an organization presents its goods, it becomes armed with compelling reasons for people to choose an organization's product or service in preference to any other. However, marketing is not just about lavishing people with what they want by anticipating, meeting and exceeding their expectations. Like a scrumptious meal, there are times when people can have too much, becoming overwhelmed with a product or service. For example, faddish pop bands often endorse so many products that people become exposed to pop branding fatigue. (As Confucius said, 'To go beyond is as wrong as to fall short'.)

Put it to the test

Which of the above definitions of marketing would you choose?

Demarketing

The more you twist it, the more it turns people on!

Imaginative marketing management can be likened to a tap adjusting the flow of marketing techniques. Effective marketers deal with varying levels of supply and demand. Sometimes the demand is little more than a trickle. At other times it can be torrential. Sometimes, though rarely, demand becomes too great. Demarketing discourages the consumer from buying or consuming something rather than stimulating him or her to do so. A typical example is when people are asked not to hose the garden during a drought.

The trouble with demarketing is that it is a distant cousin of deflation. This often occurs during leads to recessions. When times get tough, too many marketers get hacking prices. Prices fall, however a drop in prices is usually due to a fall in demand. Jobs get cut as do wages, as do house prices ... And the cure? Well, in part, it's to start marketing again – but this time pro-marketing.

Put it to the test
List five reasons for demarketing.

A brief history of marketing

As previously stated, marketing has been around for a very, very long
time. British guildsmen and entrepreneurs are recorded as long ago as
the sixteenth century. There is also evidence of mass consumption in
England during the seventeenth and eighteenth centuries.

Just after the industrial revolution, between the end of the
nineteenth century and first couple of decades of the twentieth
century, marketing went through the *production period*. These
were simple times, concerned with production and demand. If
demand was too great, and production too slow to react, people
just had to wait for production lines to catch up. From the roaring
twenties to the post-war fifties, marketing really took a grip on
business. In America, during the 1930s self-service supermarkets
were launched.

As the decades progressed, marketing became more and more
led by personal selling, research and advertising – including
advertising on TV. Television brought sales people into the home
and with that, the opportunity to market everything from soap
to glamorous cars, directly to the family. All such advertising was
strongly influenced by what customers appeared to want rather
than just by what marketers believed they needed. By the 1960s,
style and fashion were as accessible as switching on a television or

listening to a portable record player. Hollywood 'went for broke' with bigger, more colourful as well as more socially 'aware' docudramas. Presentation was everything. The marketing man was a showman, more interested in 'shine' than product substance.

THE GROOVY SEVENTIES AND ON

The 1970s shook the world into uncomfortable reality. The climate was intemperate. Political scandals shook the credibility of authority. Cold wars gave rise to suspicion. The oil boom dried up. Media costs rose. People became more independent. As marketers assured consumers that their products were good for them, consumers wondered otherwise.

The 1970s was also an era of short-term marketing tactics rather than longer-term stratagems. Many companies distributed their goods via intermediaries rather than direct sales forces. Sales ruled markets. Unions influenced corporations. Profits relied on unit quantities rather than margins. Manufacturers concentrated on marketing their core strengths rather than diversify into product and service related areas.

The market was no longer aimed at consumers as an overall group but at the diverse needs of individuals. So entered direct marketing, leading ultimately to the web and then social network and viral marketing. Thanks to developments in computing, it was possible to compile lists from clubs, geographic areas and surveys to pinpoint the right product for the right person. That information addressed people by their names and so enhanced their customer image.

The eighties saw the rise of the independent businessperson. Marketers become opportunists turning developments such as the rise of personal computers and mass-produced microchips, into the chance to offer people technologies to improve productivity. Everyone believed in his or her potential to become a shrewd business player. Banks encouraged people to spend and invest. Markets boomed and, for some by the 1990s, busted.

The nineties saw industries such as finance imposing tough regulatory rules to protect the individuals who, thanks to the drive for independence back in the 1980s, had disposable income to invest. The more they invested, the more banks urged them to invest more still.

The first decade of the twentyfirst century witnessed political and cultural upheaval throughout the world. Wars led to dispersed communities who would have previously concentrated on their local geographic markets. Yet as the communities spread they discovered advertised hope for improved lives. Looking, often for the first time, beyond their immediate geographic boundaries, they saw mountains of marketing messages made of promises reaching beyond the clouds. Overwhelmed, they had the rights to enjoy the produce from a worldwide bowl of marketed assurances. That required credit. Banks, which had prospered from what would turn out to be reckless lending and investments, collapsed under the strain, businesses folded and, initially at least, marketing, along with anything that appeared to be a short-term cost centre, suffered.

However, before long, the markets realized that without marketing itself, just as in the very beginning of our story, everything would grind to a halt.

By the start of the teenage years of the twentyfirst century, with the Internet firmly in place to help markets gain greater choice and marketers further ways to influence markets on a personal rather than impersonal corporate level, marketing is well and truly in its societal period. It is concerned with social and ethical issues. Car marketers vie with each other to offer the 'greenest' fuel consumption. Food retailers tackle unjust compensation for farmers through supporting producers with Fairtrade products and service companies help boost their ethical messages to employers and customers alike through publishing marketing materials on recycled papers and with vegetable dye ink. Whichever period comes next, it will always still draw on some fundamentals of marketing ...

Box clever (the Boston Matrix)

In the 1970s era of 'medallion marketing man', a company called
the Boston Consulting Group devised an ingeniously simple way
to classify products. It came up with a matrix of four boxes. The
Group suggested that every service or product could be categorized
into one of the quadrants. The vertical axis indicated the growth of
a market, whilst the horizontal indicated market share. Depending
on the requirements and economic conditions, the given value of
market growth could vary.

Companies falling in the best performing part of the matrix had
products with a high market growth and share. These were called
STARS. Those with high market share but low growth were known
as CASH COWS.

In cases of low market share but growing as a whole, there
were PROBLEM CHILDREN (also known as WILDCATS or
QUESTION MARKS).

Products that could manage only a low market share and growth
were DOGS.

According to the Boston Consulting Group, the 'fluidity' of cash
flow was dependent on the box in which a product or service fell.
Then, as now, a common mistake was to confuse cash flow with
profitability. In reality, profits help cash flow but if a business
excessively spends in out-goings like IT, machinery or even
marketing, it could suffer from 'negative cash flow', while still
making a profit. In other words, the money keeps on coming in
whilst the expenses keep draining out.

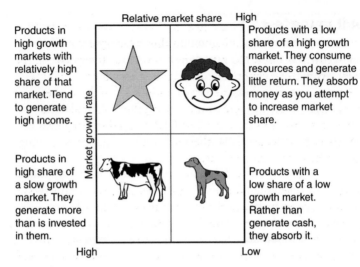

Relative market share — High

Market growth rate

Products in high growth markets with relatively high share of that market. Tend to generate high income.

Products with a low share of a high growth market. They consume resources and generate little return. They absorb money as you attempt to increase market share.

Products in high share of a slow growth market. They generate more than is invested in them.

Products with a low share of a low growth market. Rather than generate cash, they absorb it.

High — Low

The Boston Matrix.

GETTING CORNERED

Virtually all companies share a little bit of every corner of the matrix. Most portfolios of brands cover various sections. Here's what to do if your product or service falls in one of the Boston Matrix's boxes.

Starting at ground level, DOGS produce low (negative) cash flow. Never take DOGS at face value – their bite can be worse than their 'moo'. Let me explain: if a product (or service) falls between a DOG and CASH COW it is sometimes called a CASH DOG. These products roam the twilight zone of low market growth and share. Once a product hits the CASH COW box, it starts to emerge as a market leader, in mature or low-growth markets. The greater the market share the bigger the profits and because the market is relatively mature, you have to spend lots of money investing in production equipment.

If your product or service falls within this sector, consider giving it the marketing equivalent of a pep pill. In other words, re-energize the old by re-launching and looking at extending your portfolio. If you have a more modest enterprise and prefer a less daunting option, maintain your profit source by milking your product or service whilst grazing over profitable pastures.

PROBLEM CHILDREN are just that. On the positive side, products (or services) falling within this category are in a high-growth market. However, they have a relatively low market share. As with all children exploring their world of seemingly unlimited opportunities, the person (adult) left holding the purse strings may suffer a severe drain on cash flow. To make the situation worse, PROBLEM CHILDREN, tend to hang around low-share product areas. So there's not much chance of making significantly high mass profits.

Finally, you can reach for the STARS. If your product (or service) hits this sector, break out the champagne – but make sure you have enough cash to keep the bubbly flowing. This part of the box is equivalent to being a film star living in Beverly Hills. Sure, you are a market leader but everyone else wants to muscle in on your territory. That costs money. You may need to invest in state-of-the-art machinery and you are going to need extra cash tucked up your sleeve to manoeuvre your marketing to 'fight off' any competitors.

Although the Boston Matrix is clever, you are smarter. So by all means refer to it but always remember, the final strategy is still yours and not in a box. In fact, as an intelligent and modern marketer, always take into account your personal gut feeling about marketing campaigns and be cautious of any kind of inflexible planning techniques that may look fine on paper but can't be fully justified in practice.

Even the most respected planners often don't get their predictions right. For example, in the middle of the biggest world financial crisis since the Second World War, a group of eminent economists were compelled to apologize to HM Queen Elizabeth II for failing to predict the financial crisis. During a visit to the London School of Economics the Queen asked why nobody had anticipated the credit crunch. According to newspaper reports at the time, responding to the Monarch by a letter, the so-called 'wise men' of the country said: 'Your majesty, the failure to foresee the timing, extent and severity of the crisis and to head it off, while it had many causes, was principally a failure of the collective imagination of many bright people, both in this country and internationally, to understand the risks to the system as a whole.'

> **Put it to the test**
> Your new social networking site is a CASH DOG. List three
> courses of action.

WHO FITS WHERE IN THE BOSTON MATRIX?

Who	Profile	What you should do
STARS	First on the block. They lead – others copy. They are worth their weight in profits.	Pamper them. Maximize growth by giving total support and commitment.
CASH COWS	They've previously made their mark – everyone knows them – but can they continue to make an impact, considering that everyone has already bought their product or service?	Milk'em for all they've got! With the right management CASH COWS deliver the best profits. Keep an eye on costs – that includes long-term marketing campaigns. To revitalize your sales and maintain interest try sales promotions. Better still, add some extra service or product benefits by extending and so strengthening your line, and then create a bright new star. Ideal ways to achieve this include:

► Adding product functionality to something – e.g. a vacuum cleaner with an added dirt-level indicator.
► Evolving the format of an existing product or service – e.g. MM5 cameras into fully enabled MPEG cameras.
► Adding a new way to deliver added value – e.g. from cash points to Internet banking.
► Merging old technology with new – using toner cartridges from photocopier machines in fax laser printers.

Who	Profile	What you should do
PROBLEM CHILDREN	Growth looks good, for now, however, share is small. If they really are that new on the block, give them time to flourish.	Search deep in your pockets. They'll need your support to make it. That includes promoting them with advertising and/or PR.
DOGS	Real losers. Yesterday's wannabes – who never really made it in the first place.	You could try increasing your prices – might as well make a last-ditch effort to make some money or you could invest the time and money you would have put into a DOG into something more worthwhile (Harvest Strategy).

Product Life Cycles

As we grow older, our outlook on life changes. What appears in one age as a gaping void is bridged in another age. Similarly, another product soon fills the gap created by taking a product off the shelf. All products or services entering the market have a beginning, middle and, near but not necessarily final, end.

Take, for example, old-fashioned long-playing records (LPs). In the beginning, around 1894, gramophones were just a curious fad. The first commercial studio for gramophone recordings didn't open until 1897. Eventually people wanted gramophones to play at home. That spurred demand for more LPs, so the record companies recruited more artists. Eventually, the single came out. Airplay on the newly invented transistor radio generated consumer demand. That created a market for tracks – so the EP hit the record decks – a shorter version of the full LP record with fewer tracks, but more concentrated hits. This generated more sales for LPs, which had now acquired a new lease of life as albums of a band's work rather than single snapshots. The entire process was a perfect example of a Product Life Cycle (PLC) showing a product entering the market, building sales, reaching a peak, declining – developing its stable of products – then letting each product (single, EP...) re-start the whole procedure. Today downloads rule the music waves. The traditional record shops are dying but music sites are booming and tomorrow technology will go even further.

Today PLCs tend to get shorter and shorter in just about every consumer field from mobile phones and players to HI-DEF TVs and recorders. A PLC may endure between six months and a year. The Internet has further reduced PLC through creating online brands virtually overnight.

The changing face of financial marketing

Then	Now
Customer recruitment	Customer retention
Mutuality	Incorporation
Specializations	Generalization
Stand-alone products	Packaged products
Branch counter	Remote/Web
Free services	Charging

Put it to the test
Using the above table as an example, plot out how either the food, car or holiday industry has changed over the last few years.

Did you know?
The first UK Christmas hit record was more of a collection of records marketed by Messrs Perkins & Grotto in London. Costing two guineas, the collection featured tip-top tunes such as 'Twinkle Twinkle Little Star' and that spicy number 'Sing a Song of Sixpence'.

Typically, at the beginning of the PLC, sales are poor. With focused marketing, people get to know about a company and so purchase its products or services. Assuming all goes to plan, your marketing foresight builds up a head of steam and the product is a runaway success. However, steam evaporates. The product or service falls into decline and either you end up with a DOG or look at ways to rebuild, re-assess – rejuvenate or start again.

Did you know?

If you are marketing a non-seasonal household service or product – like a diet plan or magazine subscription – it pays dividends to promote at the start of the year.

Sales teams sometimes refer to something called, 'customer diffusion'. This categorizes consumers into:

- **Innovators** *who will try out any new product.*
- **Early adopters** *or opinion leaders who adopt new ideas early but cautiously.*
- **Late majority** *who are sceptical, buying once everyone else has done so.*
- **Laggards** *who are suspicious of change and buy only when it becomes the norm to do so.*

Researchers often group consumers into life-cycle types. For example, in the UK, a SAGACITY life-cycle grouping divides people by income and occupation.

SAGACITY life-cycle stages are:

- **Dependent** *primarily under 24s, living at home or full-time students.*
- **Pre-family** *under 35s with their own home, but no children.*
- **Family** *main shoppers and chief income earners, under 65, with one or more children at home.*

▶ **Late** *embraces all adults whose children have left home or who are over 35 and childless.*

However you segment your market, make sure that each segment is CIRQ:

Commercial *– so you can turn your efforts into bankable results.*
Individual *– so that you can address it in a distinctive way.*
Reachable *– so that you can use appropriate marketing channels to reach it.*
Quantifiable *– so you can measure how effective your marketing has been.*

If you don't segment your audiences, you will have to rely on an *undifferentiated approach* to marketing. This means having to treat your audience as a mass-market. That can be useful if your product appeals to all kinds of people for all sorts of reasons, such as a chocolate bar.

A *differentiated approach* to marketing occurs when you sub-divide segments. That can be useful if your product or service can be made appealing to different groups through different marketing approaches. For example, a soft drink may appeal to children as a fun party beverage, but also to adults as a refreshing treat.

Niche marketing is ideal if you have a limited budget or want to address a highly targeted audience with a specific interest. For example, a sports clothing company may want to develop a niche marketing campaign for bowling teams.

A *customized targeting* strategy works well for companies offering tailor-made solutions for specific customers. For example, a website designer could offer a one-off complete e-commerce site for a specific customer.

Occasionally companies replace products a little too quickly – just to keep the marketplace fluid. The marketing term for this is cannibalization. That is, when a company sells a new product at the expense of an existing or similar one. An example of cannibalization which tends to annoy a lot of people is when a company brings out a cutting-edge mobile phone and before too long replaces it with a new model that forces people to trade up. In many cases, providing its brand is constantly kept in the consumer's mind as representing innovation, the mobile phone company can go on cannibalizing models *ad infinitum*.

Sales figures can be deceptive. Just as you think that a rising STAR has turned to DOG meat, you spot a wag of the tail – a remote, yet distinctive sign of life. Perhaps your product or service just needed that extra encouragement on your part to succeed. It depends how you manage your PLC.

GETTING YOUR PLC CURVES INTO SHAPE

Product life cycle curves are not as always straightforward as you may think. They may take on many forms. Some are extended waves, whilst others are short and stubby. It's up to you to shape and craft each stage of your PLC curve, from introduction to decline and – with a little imagination – resurrection. Furthermore, you should plan what you want to happen at each stage and how, as far as possible, you can capitalize on your achievements subsequently.

When all is said and done, a PLC model guides you towards building an enduring product or service life. In reality, nobody knows where life leads – but with preparation and research, you can get your house in order to face each stage with confidence. Likewise, as your product or service enters the growth and maturity stage, thanks to focused planning and careful nurturing, your product or service life cycle can be long and prosperous.

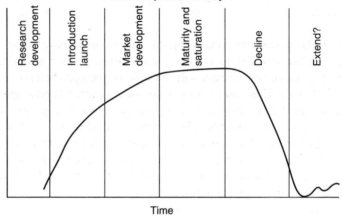

Traditional product life cycle

Research development | Introduction launch | Market development | Maturity and saturation | Decline | Extend?

Time

Traditional product life cycle.

UP CLOSE AND PERSONAL (THE PLC STAGES)

Let's consider each stage, step by step.

Introduction

You've got a great product or service – you know it, but as yet, the commercial world, more particularly your prospect, doesn't. Time to make a big splash. In addition to advertising the right pricing, you have to tempt the ideal people into your business (see Chapter 4). A special introductory price set quite low for a limited period would attract a wide audience. This is sometimes called a *penetration pricing strategy*. If you opt for this approach, gradually you can increase the price.

At the other end of the spectrum you could set your price really high. This reduces the size of your overall marketplace but targets a discreet group of people willing to pay a premium for getting something others who are not at 'the top' of a market simply can't afford. This is called a *skimming price* strategy. (See 'Cost of marketing', page 116.) The great thing about this approach is you build up a strong core of top-of-the-market customers and later leverage for your gains through gradual price reductions to sell to the middle market aspiring to buy top-of-the-range products and services.

One point of warning concerning the *introduction* phase of the PLC – make sure you have the infrastructure in place to guarantee that your customers can actually get hold of your products or services. Poor distribution at the start spells disaster. It gives your competitor the opportunity to jump on the bandwagon powered by all the hype you created. The competitor then offers customers a cheaper priced, alternative. (This is quite commonplace in the world of high fashion marketing where a new range of clothing from a high-end fashion house catering for the rich and famous is copied and adapted for a mass market.)

Launching any product or service takes money. Ideally only invest something that can at least allow you to recoup your costs should the worst happen. Design your marketing communications to be stylish, relevant, cost effective and able to support every stage of your PLC.

Growth

It's a big, bad, dangerous world out there. Your product is no longer as distinctive as when it first entered the market. That's good news for bigger companies who want to muscle in on your success. General statistics suggest that up to 60 per cent of companies fail within the first year of business. Following the recession of 2009, that figure became even more acute.

Yet, it's not all doom and gloom. During the green roots of growth stage, expect profits as well as escalating, if only in a modest sense, sales. Your customers know you so are more likely to get to know you even better. Now is a great opportunity to sell them some complementary products or services from your portfolio. (The sooner you sell to a previously delighted customer, the greater the chances that they will listen to you.) This tactic is perfect for selling over the web. Just before a surfer clicks to buy a product, you can sell them a complementary service that enhances their experience and adds a few more pounds into your profits-pot. It's also a good time to talk to dealers or distributors. You've proved your value. Now consider other opportunities, such as joint promotions, targeted viral marketing and advertising – all of which create niche market demand.

Maturity/saturation

Eventually even your best sellers begin to get tired. Profits slide. Prices fall as you try either to secure or defend your market position. Your customer base is probably as wide as it can go. By all means consider new options but concentrate on maintaining your market share. Offer greater value, encourage existing customers to remain loyal, rather than venture off into pastures green and untested.

Pareto

An Italian economist and political sociologist called Wilfredo Pareto (1848–1923) devised the 80:20 Pareto Rule, also known as 'the law of the trivial many and critical few'. It is based on the idea that, for the majority of business activities, 80 per cent of potential value can be achieved from just 20 per cent effort. However, too many businesses end up using the remaining 80 per cent for relatively little return. This can be even less fruitful than it first appears. Imagine, for example, what would happen if a manufacturer produced goods which were only 80 per cent okay. Marketers simply cannot afford to look at the world in that way.

ABC method

A marketing method called the *ABC method*, classifies products into either fast-moving articles or articles that attract less of a demand. The Pareto Rule assumes that 20 per cent of your products – made up of fast and average moving articles – will take care of 80 per cent of your turnover. The same is true of customers. Reward their loyalty and they will reward you – at the expense of your competitors. Equally, look after your distributors. If you allow them to slip away during your maturity/saturation stage of the PLC, they could end up lost forever.

DECLINE

I mentioned that every product or service coming on to the market, has a beginning, middle and, perhaps, end – at least in its first incarnation. Consistently declining sales are warning bells that consumers are tiring of your product or service. Your market wants to move on – either geographically or tactically. Ultimately, like many businesses you could abandon ship as your titanic venture goes down. However, the end is not always as nigh as soothsayers would have you believe. So don't get out the hymn books to sing, 'Nearer my Lord to thee' – well, not just yet.

Could you streamline your existing portfolio of products or services? How about focusing instead on servicing a smaller market – as long as it is still cost effective. Ask yourself why, despite your strenuous efforts, your plans are going wrong. Don't be afraid to pick up the phone or meet your customers face to face. Ask them what you could do to improve. You'll be amazed how people are willing to help, especially when you are seeking their comments on your company. It's all a matter of adopting a considered approach before jumping to conclusions.

Yet, if at the end of the day, 'the horse refuses to go to water', it's time to move on. Learn from your previous PLC model and get it right next time.

Asking the right PLC questions

When your product or service has come to the end of a marketable life cycle ask:

▶ *From the outset, did you minimize your risks?*
▶ *Is it worth an extra effort to try again?*

- *Can you afford to invest that extra effort?*
- *Can you identify previous mistakes?*
- *Can those mistakes prevent future ones?*
- *Can you think beyond blaming failure on individuals and instead pinpoint where specifics went wrong within the overall marketing structure?*
- *Are you brave enough to admit defeat and bold enough to restructure your plans?*

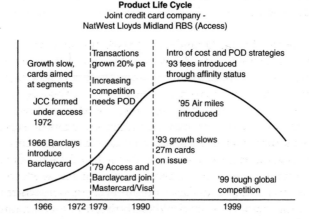

Product Life Cycle
Joint credit card company -
NatWest Lloyds Midland RBS (Access)

Product Life Cycle: Joint credit card company – NatWest Lloyds Midland RBS (Access).

Put it to the test

1 *Detail a PLC for a Hi-Def TV and player set box.*
2 *You market a non-melting chocolate bar. Show how you will stimulate each market segment from innovators to laggards.*

The customer is always right

The early 2000s saw the merger between mass marketing and direct marketing. The sales process became 'through the line'. Companies regarded the economy as a through-the-line business, where product and profit control necessitated looking at the world from a global perspective rather than just a local commodity perspective. Marketing no longer separated traditional channels like television, press, posters and radio from newly emerged web-based opportunities such as on-demand TV via the web or *ambush* or *guerrilla marketing* tactics, such as using unconventional media like 'street tag painting' . Whilst many consumers – especially those still reeling from the recession – wanted cost effectiveness. It was no longer a case of 'pile 'em high and sell 'em cheap' alone, but, 'give 'em what they want, at the right price, spell their name correctly on a shortly worded benefit-packed email and they'll sure remember yours'.

As SEO (Search Engine Optimization) marketing bloomed, Product Life Cycles shrunk. A new breed of specialist service industries was created. Its premise was based on a philosophy as old as the fourteenth century when the Italian politician Niccolo Machiavelli said, 'a prince does well to surround himself with serious advisors'. With this in mind, stringent sole trader 'experts' competed against each other to win contracts for assignments. Small consultancies grew worldwide. By the first decades of the 2000s, around 90 per cent of direct marketing mailings which generated over a million dollars worth of business were written by independent copywriters or within marketing departments, rather than by large multinational advertising agencies.

Overheads were further reduced thanks to breakthroughs in technology ranging from high-speed internet links, to international video conferencing and the World Wide Web. It no longer mattered from where you serviced a contract: the main criteria were – could you deliver – and how soon?

Selling the invisible

Thanks to mass redundancies from the global recession at the start of the twenty-first century, many previously employed marketers had to start marketing their own services as consultants. All service marketing falls under one of four classic categories:

Service attribute	Definition of service
Inseparable	Consumption and production are inseparable. For example: a restaurant prepares a meal (production); a diner eats the meal. In such a case marketing has to reassure the diner that the serving of the meal is as good as the food on the plate.
Intangible	There are few tangible physical aspects of the service. For example, a Financial Services Advisor's service: here tangibility is demonstrated through marketing opportunities such as websites, brochures and even how telephones are answered.
Changeable	Services change according to customer needs. For example, a marketing consultant may offer one kind of solution to a specific client and a different one to another. Here, marketing has to impose a set of guidelines to ensure consistency of delivery – whatever the specific service.
Variable	Services may be in demand for a short period and lay dormant at other times. For example, a turkey farmer may be very busy during the build-up to Christmas, but less hectic during the rest of the year. Here marketing has to help him create opportunities to keep his business active.

At each deliverable stage of a service, marketing has to demonstrate its value to customers.

Stage one
The actual service (concentrating on service features)

Basic service and accompanying features. This stage incorporates marketing design, terms and length of service, styling and so on.

Stage two
The expected service (concentrating on service promises)

This stage deals with reassuring customers that the service features at least the basic features that they would expect. For example, that a bank is regulated.

Stage three
The augmented service (concentrating on support and service)

Here marketing aims to show that a service meets customer needs beyond their expectations. For example, offering support systems such as customer help websites.

Stage four
The potential service (concentrating on service transformations)

Here marketing aims to explain all the future changes which a service may undergo. For example, a psychologist who will also branch out into team-building programmes.

Put it to the test
Discuss a marketing campaign including recommended marketing communication tools, which demonstrates the integrity of marketers.

Did you know?
In the United States imaginative Internet code encryptors have to apply for an export licence to cover the knowledge contained in their brain if travelling to certain countries.

The changing face of the market

During the first decades of the 2000s, crucial shifts in working patterns had huge implications on core market structures.

Technology turned the home into the SOHO – Small Office Home Office. The advent of iPhones, Blackberries and other Wi-Fi enabled pocket devices meant that work would never be more than an arm's length away.

Traditional views of the sexes even changed. Perfume manufacturers marketed products that some twenty years earlier would have been unthinkable. For example, metrosexual men were encouraged to buy sensual deodorants, facial creams and soaps – hitherto the traditional domain of women. Taking the lead from jeans manufacturers of the 1980s, fashion houses designed unisexually rather than targeting men and women separately. Just as the traditional work roles changed so, thanks to communications, travel and technology, markets became internationalized and reaching markets became a 24/7 opportunity to sell, sell, sell.

Did you know?

When Pepsi entered the Chinese market, its slogan, 'Come alive with the Pepsi generation' translated as 'Pepsi brings back your dead ancestors'. Likewise in 1920, Coca-Cola's brand name in Chinese was translated as, 'Bite the wax tadpole'!

OLD-AGE: NEW MARKET

A further development in the dying stages of the twentieth century occurred in the way companies marketed their products or services to the more mature market. In the 1970s and 1980s, marketers portrayed the geriatrics as the over sixties. By 2002, in America, marketers described this key market as aged 55 plus. By 2010 newborns in the UK could expect to live to about 80 (women, in general, five years longer than men). Since 2007, for the first time in British history, there were more people over pension age than children. Every subsequent year thereafter the numbers of elderly people relative to the number of younger working people supporting them continued to grow. This new old-age group wanted the same goods and services sought by much younger consumers, for example cinema tickets, blue-ray players, snack foods. It was the birth of a whole new demographic for marketers.

Akio Morita – one-time Chairman of Sony – coined the phrase 'global localization'. (The Japanese term for adjusting to regional markets is called *dochakuka* – from a Japanese agricultural word for adjusting planting and harvesting for local soil conditions. The English variation is 'glocal'.)

Globalization had a greater impact on markets than first expected. Well-established local national brands became sub-brands of global corporations. At the start of the twenty-first century, out of 25 financial institutions occupying London's famous 'square mile' only six were owned by British companies.

Glocalization led to brand standardization. Even local chocolate brands were renamed under the banner of global identities. One hamburger restaurant or coffee bar began to look the same as any other. The more similar they looked, the more consumers demanded brands to offer individuality.

Did you know?
When the Berlin wall fell, top of the list of products to be imported by former East Germany was the 'All-American' McDonald's.

The euro market

The circulation of 50 billion euro coins and 15 billion notes marked the introduction of the euro as a single cash currency in the 12 countries of the Eurozone. Its launch on 1 January 2002 made it easier to market throughout Euro-land.

The Europe-wide integration of the euro was years in the making. In 1957 The Treaty of Rome declared a common European market as a European objective, with the aim of increasing economic prosperity and contributing to 'an ever closer union among the peoples of Europe'. The Single European Act (1986) and the Treaty on European Union (1992) built on this, introducing Economic and Monetary Union (EMU) and laying the foundations for the single currency.

The third stage of EMU began on 1 January 1999, when the exchange rates of the participating currencies were irretrievably set. Euro area Member States began implementing a common monetary policy, the euro would be introduced as a legal currency and the 11 currencies of the participating Member States became subdivisions of the euro. Greece joined in January 2001, which meant that by the start of the euro's introduction the Member States of the European Union comprised:

- *Austria*
- *Belgium*
- *Finland*
- *France*
- *Germany*
- *Greece*
- *Ireland*
- *Italy*
- *Luxembourg*
- *Portugal*
- *Spain*
- *The Netherlands*

Certain members of the European Union – Denmark, Sweden as well as the United Kingdom, at the time the fourth strongest economy in the world – didn't initially take an official part in the single currency, preferring to see if the biggest economic experiment in history would actually yield good results. This said, recognizing the new opportunity to be perceived as market leaders, many major retailers in those three countries quickly accepted both euros and local currency, especially companies operating businesses at airports and seaports or based in tourist areas. Almost overnight, business-to-business companies started trading in euros. Denmark's currency, the Danish krone, was linked to the euro, although the exchange rate was not fixed.

PARLEZ VOUS EURO?

Upon the euro's introduction, whilst hoping for an economic boost, many Germans felt that all their long-held efforts to establish a relatively strong German Deutschmark would be wasted supporting countries with weaker economies. On the other hand, the people of Belgium were delighted that for once they would have to carry only one currency in their pocket rather than a fistful of multitude denominations.

Local tax changes affected the cost of goods across what was supposed to be a borderless Euro-land. At the time of the euro's full introduction, German value added tax stood at 16 per cent, whereas in The Netherlands it was 19 per cent and Belgium 21 per cent. So, for the first time ever, European consumers could see clearly at first glance how prices varied across borders. The euro's centralization of interest rates resolved some issues whilst exacerbating others. In France, for example, the cost of a cup of coffee crept up from 6 francs to 6.50 francs – as it translated into a nice round euro. Consumers became wary of marketing promises such as an advertised opportunity to buy goods at a bargain price of 'under 200 euros'.

The challenge for marketers was to encourage the 300 million European Union citizens (equivalent to the entire population of the United States of America) to feel that companies were continuing to put value and quality before euros and cents. Marketers working in Euro-land had to instil a sense of pride in consumers and businesses alike for being part of an economy big enough to stand up to the American dollar and strong enough to retain clear identities.

Businesses and suppliers working outside Euro-land also had to come to terms with dealing with one currency throughout several countries. Member States were given economic competitive advantages to secure contracts and the permission to work across borders. This generated greater competition from workers and bigger boosts to local economies.

Today, whilst the feel good factor for member state citizens like Germans visiting Ireland and paying in the same euro currency as at home is important, European marketers have to ensure that the new logo changes on currencies have greater positive impact on local communities than the equivalent of a company updating its corporate letterhead, or merging with a competitor, only to leave a general sense of feeling that more has been lost than gained.

This includes catering to a melting pot of cultures with different languages and backgrounds – but all with aspiration to improve their lives and so build stronger markets.

All marketing has to address universal HUMAN NEEDS, PASSIONS and GOALS. The successful marketer tailors every part of the marketing plan to focus on customers rather than companies alone. The imaginative marketer identifies needs and so offers products and services with the functionality to deliver answers. Such strategy-led marketing requires a blueprint. In the next part of this book you'll start to shape your marketing plan.

The changing challenges to marketers

Then	Next
Well-defined markets	New opportunities
Stick to what you know	Learn more – develop more
Give the customers what they want	Explain what they could have
Throw enough money at something and eventually it will work	Invest less in trying to be everything to everyone. Take longer in becoming something to someone – who will then tell everyone on your behalf
Produce more and more products	Offer better service
Show them the details	Get to the point

Did you know?

Six months prior to the introduction of the euro, a key industry report revealed that, of 1,250 organizations across banking, insurance, healthcare, education and government sectors, one in three organizations didn't have a euro strategy. The total European bill for Information Technology to embrace the euro was estimated to exceed £606 million; more than 200,000 cash dispensers and just under 4 million vending machines throughout Europe needed adjusting.

ESSENTIALS FROM THIS CHAPTER

▶ *Marketing value is delivered through features as well as practical and emotive benefits.*

▶ *Demarketing discourages the consumer from buying or consuming something rather than stimulating him or her to do so. A typical example is when people are asked not to hose the garden during a drought.*

▶ *The Boston Matrix suggested that every service or product can be categorized into quadrants. The vertical axis indicates the growth of a market, while the horizontal indicates market share.*

▶ *A Product Life Cycle is the period between introduction and decline of a product or service life span.*

▶ *Customer diffusion categorizes consumers into:*
  ▷ **Innovators** *who will try out any new product.*
  ▷ **Early adopters** *or opinion leaders who adopt new ideas early but cautiously.*
  ▷ **Late majority** *who are sceptical, buying once everyone else has done so.*
  ▷ **Laggards** *who are suspicious of change and buy only when it becomes the norm to do so.*

▶ *All service marketing falls under one of four classic categories:*

  Inseparability – Intangibility – Changeability – Variability

▶ *Innovative marketing campaigns address: HUMAN NEEDS, PASSIONS and GOALS.*

2

Shaping your marketing plan

In this chapter you will learn about:
- *push and pull strategies and PESTLE analysis*
- *the balanced scorecard*
- *positioning statements*
- *the Ps of marketing*
- *SWOTs and TOWs*
- *marketing objectives and measures*
- *strategic business units and frameworks*
- *the ten-point creative plan*

What made you buy this book? An impulse purchase? Was it the title? Are you what marketers call 'an influencer', like a training director wishing to develop new skills? Were you impressed that it is part of the internationally renowned *Teach Yourself* series – or simply because it seemed to cover most of the marketing topics you need in one easy-to-read bargain guide?

All these considerations – and more – are taken into account when designing a marketing plan. An effective marketing strategy balances and blends elements which generate compelling reasons to invest in a service – or in the case of this book – product.

More often than not, each component of a seamless marketing plan either directly or indirectly influences the other. It's like a giant Russian doll. Alone each segment looks impressive – together they fit as a family.

Push and pull, Porter and PESTs

I once saw a painting of a British army regiment fighting in the Boer War. (No, I am not that old!) War is never straightforward and needs orchestration to handle pushing and being pulled in all directions. In the picture, the enemy didn't attack neatly from the front; the regiment was forced to deal with ambushes from all sides. This is demonstrated in marketing by a classic theory called Porter's Forces.

A well-constructed and considered marketing plan orchestrates the relationship between a company, its customers and competition.

A simple way to understand the marketing landscape for a new product or service is to consider another classic marketing analysis tool: PEST. This considers:

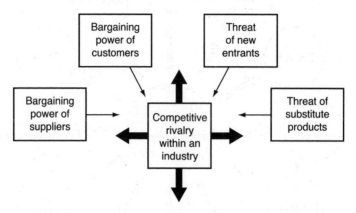

Porter's five forces (Michael E. Porter, Harvard Business School c.1979).

Political environment and factors
For example:

1 *How stable is the political environment?*
2 *Will government policy influence laws that regulate or tax your business?*
3 *What is the government's position on marketing ethics?*

Economic environment and factors
For example:

1 *Interest rates*
2 *The level of inflation*
3 *Employment level per capita*
4 *Long-term prospects for the economy*

Social environment and factors
For example:

1 *What is the dominant religion?*
2 *What are attitudes to foreign products and services?*

3 *Does language impact upon the diffusion of products onto markets?*

Technological factors
For example:

1 *Does technology enable cheaper/better quality products?*
2 *Do the technologies offer more innovative products and services such as online banking?*
3 *How is distribution changed by the Internet. Mobile phones?*

A longer version of analysis also considers **legal and environmental** issues. This is called PESTLE. Variations on PESTLE include:

- **PEST analysis (STEP analysis)** – *Political, Economic, Sociological, Technological*
- **PESTLE/PESTEL analysis** – *Political, Economic, Sociological, Technological, Legal, Environmental*
- **PESTEL analysis** – *Political, Economic, Sociological, Technological, Environmental, Labour related*
- **PESTLIED analysis** – *Political, Economic, Social, Technological, Legal, International, Environmental, Demographic*
- **STEEPLE analysis** – *Social/Demographic, Technological, Economic, Environmental, Political, Legal, Ethical*
- **SLEPT analysis** – *Social, Legal, Economic, Political, Technological*
- **STEPE analysis** – *Social, Technical, Economic, Political, and Ecological*
- **ETPS analysis** – *Economic, Technical, Political and Social – scanning the business environment*

PESTLE CHECKLIST

Use this table to plan your organization's future strategies. These suggestions are examples. Include or add more.

	Observations: How might the factors listed on the left affect your organization?	Impact		Implication and importance	
	H – High M – Medium L – Low U – Unsure	**Timescale** 0–3 months 3–9 months 9–18 months 18+ months	**Type** + Positive – Negative ? Unknown	**Impact** > Increasing < > Unchanged < Decreasing ? Unsure	**Urgency** Critical Important Un-important Unsure

Political – SWOT (see page 80 Trading policies Funding, grants and initiatives Home market lobbying/pressure groups International pressure groups Government policies Elections Inter-country relationships/attitudes Internal political issues	
Economic – SWOT General taxation Market and trade cycles Specific industry factors Disposable income Employment Exchange rates Tariffs Inflation	

Social – SWOT				
Consumer attitudes				
Media views				
Buying access and trends				
Ethnic/religious factors				
Ethical issues				
Lifestyle changes				
Population shifts				
Education				
Diversity				
Immigration/emigration				

Technological – SWOT
Associated technologies
Replacement solutions
Consumer buying
mechanisms
Innovation potential
Intellectual property
issues
Global communications
Research
Energy
Communications
Rate of obsolescence
Internet
Transportation

Legal – SWOT Current legislation Future legislation International legislation Regulatory bodies Environmental regulations Employment law Consumer protection Industry regulations		
Environmental – SWOT Ecological Market values Stakeholder/investor values Global factors EU-based factors		

'PUSH', 'PULL' AND 'PROFILE'

If a website developer wants to encourage customers to 'pull', for example, a useful application from a mobile phone, a 'pull' marketing strategy is needed. Most pull strategies need some kind of advertising to attract a market, like pizza companies offering free deliveries – it could be a combination of PR, word-of-mouth, web banners, viral emails and so on.

On the other hand if a company wants to drive a product or service into the mind and heart of the consumer, it could opt for pro-active telesales or direct marketing activities, in which case, a 'push' strategy is required.

Pull and push incentives may include running prize draws or competitions, distributing special discount vouchers – such as pizza discounts – or even offering free software updates. When shove comes to push, 'push' and 'pull' often feed off each other. A company may use promotions to 'pull' in a prospect. The prospect becomes a customer who needs to be professionally managed using techniques such as customer care services. Alternatively, stocks will need to be kept full. A full warehouse encourages or 'pushes' a sales team to stir up business that, in turn, 'pulls' the whole thing around again.

The power of price incentives should never be underestimated. At the height of the notorious British BSE scandal, supermarkets initially slashed the price of beef products. Despite all the scare mongering in the British press, consumers herded to buy beef. In one television interview, a consumer was asked if she was concerned about contracting the fatal disease. She replied that she was, but just couldn't resist the price reductions. A few years later, during the Foot and Mouth disease outbreak in the UK, similar consumer behaviour was displayed.

Similarly, during the recent global credit crunch, rather than spend a little more money on environmentally sound products, many consumers preferred to opt for cheaper options, which – if such options also happened to be 'green' – all the better. During the height of the recession in the laundry sector, brands such as Unilever, encouraged consumers to be both green and efficient. Unilever marketed a Cleaner Planet Plan. As Vice President of Unilever's Laundry Category, Europe, Seb Munden explained at the time to the press:

When we were creating the Cleaner Planet Plan we discovered some good things. When you align the needs of economy and ecology, the result is a very powerful force. So that's what we're trying to do – helping consumers to save money, while doing the right thing for the planet. We employ a lot of bright graduates who want to do the right thing and we listen to them. Who you are and what you do is as important as your brand values.

Communications to stakeholders such as the community, trade unions and suppliers are part of what marketers call 'profile' strategies.

As the economic recovery entered the marketplace, so environmental products became both more cost effective and efficient.

Ultimately, effective marketing deals with give and take. More pertinently, it's about knowing when to do so and which tool to use, such as advertising, PR, direct marketing, electronic commerce (e-commerce), design and so on. That's why your marketing plan will feature an element of 'push' 'pull' and 'profile' stratagems.

Preparing your plan

Before you get too involved with whether your organization is a 'pusher' or a 'puller', you have to develop a plan to carry out your motives. Think of it like this. Like me, you have probably had to endure participating in meetings about marketing meetings. Unlike a meeting about a meeting, the process of thinking about what you want your plan to achieve often saves time rather than adds to the bureaucratic process.

From the start, your marketing plan must be logically constructed and so eminently readable. After all, it's all well and good producing reams and reams of facts and figures. But it's not very imaginative, and certainly won't communicate in a clear, compelling way what you want people to know.

Put it to the test

You market a vegetarian beef-substitute hamburger. Suggest two ways to communicate your message using (a) mainly a PUSH strategy, (b) mainly a PULL strategy.

EVERY PLAN HAS ITS BLUEPRINT

This is my business

What are your company's strengths and weaknesses? How attractive are your products and services? Are they part of a larger range? Do you specialize? If so, why and how do you differ from competitors? Who would want to buy from your company?

My ambition

- ▶ *Where do you want to be in three months from now?*
- ▶ *How about a year or two?*
- ▶ *What do you want your marketing to accomplish?*
- ▶ *Do you want to increase your market share?*
- ▶ *Do you want to extend your business through more outlets or do you want to confine your activities in a concentrated area?*
- ▶ *How does this fit in with your overall communication objectives?*

Both your business position, and your company ambitions have to take not just your expectations into account, but those of your partners, shareholders, and so on.

Corporate objectives always take into consideration financial issues like turnover, return on investment (ROI), machinery as well as administrative costs. ROI is crucial to all marketers. Knowing your financial objectives helps you to calculate how to achieve corporate expectations through the creation and on-going management of brands, goods and services. This gives you the key to reach financial objectives. When setting out to measure the effectiveness of your marketing (also known as 'marketing metrics') you need to consider what exactly you are measuring in the first place and so how the success or otherwise of your marketing campaign will be judged.

Did you know?

According to Cranfield School of Management, 76 per cent of marketers have growth targets; 69 per cent of marketers have revenue targets; 27 per cent of marketers have operating profit targets; 13 per cent of marketers have economic profit targets.

Key marketing metrics questions

- *What is a healthy 'return'?*
- *What specifically are you measuring?*
- *How effective are specific elements of your marketing communications mix?*

Can you pinpoint a direct correlation between a campaign and tangible results. For example, the number of 'hits' to your website and when as well as where those 'hits' came from?

- **The reality check.** *Are we truly assessing what we set out to measure?*
- **The focal point check.** *Are we evaluating only what we set out to measure?*
- **The relevancy check.** *Is it the right measure?*
- **The uniformity check.** *Will the results always be collected in the same way?*

- ▶ **The ease check.** *Is it easy to find and capture the measurement information?*
- ▶ **The lucidity check.** *Can the results be misinterpreted through being too vague?*
- ▶ **The action check.** *Will the results be acted upon?*
- ▶ **The aptness check.** *Can the information be accessed frequently enough for action?*
- ▶ **The value check.** *Is the method used to measure worth the cost of measuring?*
- ▶ **The stimulus check.** *Is the measure likely to encourage inappropriate behaviours? (For example, people answering surveys just to get a free gift and so making their answers biased.)*

Communication objectives

Again, in terms of your communication objectives, what do you want to accomplish? Perhaps generate pre-launch awareness of a particular service, or secure your market position as being the leading choice of brand? Maybe you want to tell the market that your new orange juice has more oranges than any others. Eventually, all these requirements will form part of your marketing plan.

The traditional balanced scorecard

In management, a system called 'the balanced scorecard' measures, monitors and helps improve both internal as well as external communications. It is a performance measurement system that delivers a 'balanced' view of an organization's accomplishments.

Many marketers have adapted the system as a means of taking a bird's eye view of marketing performance.

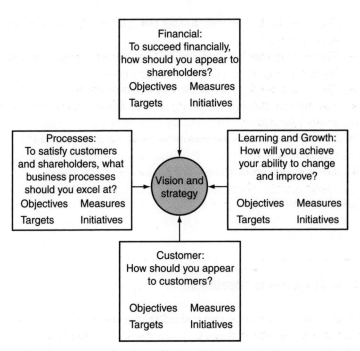

The marketing balanced scorecard.

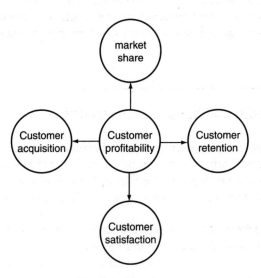

Balanced scorecard – marketing customer perspective.

I once compiled a book called *The Meaning of Life*. It featured answers to what must surely be the biggest question of all: what is the meaning of life? I received answers from people of all backgrounds including movie stars, royalty as well as ordinary people like you and me. The best answers were the simplest. Equally, when it comes to positioning your company, a clear, direct, benefit-led argument is far better than trying to hide under a bushel of superlatives and thorny clichés.

Put it to the test

Imagine you have less than a minute to sell (position) your company to me.

- ▶ *Who is your company aimed at?*
- ▶ *What, specifically do you do?*
- ▶ *How and why are you qualified to do it?*
- ▶ *Why do you do it better than anyone else?*

Or to really get to the point:

For _____

It is _____

Only we can _____

Because _____

When it comes to marketing yourself, you must be convincing rather than 'cute'.

_____

Mission believable – not impossible

An organization's mission statement should not be confused with either a sales positioning platform, corporate or marketing objectives. A mission statement is an inspirational executive summary that explains an organization's purpose and spells out its vision. Both aspects are essential when formulating a marketing plan, but neither can be implemented without first answering the second question of your sales positioning platform: 'Only we can...' this forms the foundation for all your marketing exercises.

A mission statement clarifies rather than confuses your communication objectives. It either confirms key corporate philosophies, or otherwise.

Without careful planning, writing a mission statement can leave you contemplating your navel rather than constructing a viable objective that will inspire your partners, staff, suppliers and customers. Good mission statements get to the point and avoid jargon or platitudes. They should be credible, attainable and logical.

Avoid making your mission statement a business description. They should be inspiring, brief, believable, understandable, verifiable and acceptable to all connected with or working for your organization.

When writing your mission statement, consider the impact of competition on your business and finances as well as legal, industrial, pharmaceutical (if applicable) and other commercial issues affecting future operations. Having said that, never write a mission statement as a predication.

Essentially, the mission statement should address:

1 *Why your organization is here (e.g. to make money, raise money for charity, inform, entertain).*
2 *The commercial advantages of your organization (e.g. 'offer peace of mind' rather than 'sell insurance'; 'provide the tools to succeed' rather than 'manufacture business software').*
3 *What makes your organization so special (see 'USPs', page 183)? For example, is the company better at publishing a particular type of book than its nearest rival? Does the*

mini-cab firm employ local people familiar with the local routes?

4 *Your ambition – every company must have an ambition; at the very least, aim to achieve it.*

Famous brand mission statements

Mission statements can adapt to changing long-term circumstances. So if and when you have achieved all four points (above) it might be time to consider new missions and goals.

The following is a selection of mission statements, along with slogans from some of America's most successful marketing-driven companies. (Source – corporate websites 2009.) If you are not sure what any of the organizations actually do, look them up on the web. You may be surprised by what they say they do and what their mission statement says they want to achieve. In some cases, even more unfocused and confusing are their slogans and mottoes. (Also check out http://manchmission.blogspot.com.)

Avon Products, INC

Slogan/motto

The company for women.

Mission statement

The Global Beauty Leader. We will build a unique portfolio of Beauty and related brands, striving to surpass our competitors in quality, innovation and value, and elevating our image to become the Beauty company most women turn to worldwide.

The Women's Choice for Buying. We will become the destination store for women, offering the convenience of multiple brands and channels, and providing a personal high touch shopping experience that helps create lifelong customer relationships.

The Premier Direct Seller. We will expand our presence in direct selling and lead the reinvention of the channel, offering an entrepreneurial opportunity that delivers superior earnings, recognition, service and support, making it easy and rewarding to be affiliated with Avon and elevating the image of our industry.

The Best Place to Work. We will be known for our leadership edge, through our passion for high standards, our respect for diversity and our commitment to create exceptional opportunities for professional growth so that associates can fulfil their highest potential.

The Largest Women's Foundation. We will be a committed global champion for the health and well-being of women through philanthropic efforts that eliminate breast cancer from the face of the earth, and that empower women to achieve economic independence.

The Most Admired Company. We will deliver superior returns to our shareholders by tirelessly pursuing new growth opportunities while continually improving our profitability, a socially responsible, ethical company that is watched and emulated as a model of success.

Barnes & Noble, Inc

Slogan/motto

If we don't have your book, nobody has...

Mission statement

Our mission is to operate the best specialty retail business in America, regardless of the product we sell. Because the product we sell is books, our aspirations must be consistent with the promise and the ideals of the volumes which line our shelves. To say that our mission exists independent of the product we sell is to demean the importance and the distinction of being booksellers. As booksellers we are determined to be the very best in our business, regardless of the size, pedigree or inclinations of our competitors. We will continue to bring our industry nuances of style and approaches to bookselling which are consistent with our evolving aspirations. Above all, we expect to be a credit to the communities we serve, a valuable resource to our customers, and a place where our dedicated booksellers can grow and prosper. Toward this end we will not only listen to our customers and booksellers but embrace the idea that the Company is at their service.

Chevron

Slogan/motto

Human energy.

Mission statement

At the heart of The Chevron Way is our Vision to be the global energy company most admired for its people, partnership and performance.

Citigroup

Slogan/motto

Knowledge is your greatest asset.

Mission statement

Our goal for Citigroup is to be the most respected global financial services company. Like any other public company, we're obligated to deliver profits and growth to our shareholders. Of equal importance is to deliver those profits and generate growth responsibly.

The Dow Chemical Company

Slogan/motto

Living. Improved Daily.

Mission statement

To constantly improve what is essential to human progress by mastering science and technology.

The Estee Lauder Company

Slogan/motto

Bringing the best to everyone we touch.

Mission statement

The guiding vision of The Estee Lauder Companies is 'Bringing the best to everyone we touch'. By 'The best', we mean the best products, the best people and the best ideas. These three pillars have been the hallmarks of our Company since it was founded by Mrs Estee Lauder in 1946. They remain the foundation upon which we continue to build our success today.

Ford Motor Company

Slogan/motto

Various, including:

Built for the road ahead.
Feel the difference.
Ford has a better idea.

Mission statement

We are a global family with a proud heritage passionately committed to providing personal mobility for people around the world.

Global Gilette

Slogan/motto

Welcome to Everyday Solutions.

Mission statement

We will provide branded products and services of superior quality and value that improve the lives of the world's consumers. As a result, consumers will reward us with leadership sales, profit, and value creation, allowing our people, our shareholders, and the communities in which we live and work to prosper.

Harley-Davidson, Inc

Slogan/motto

Various, including:

Define your world in a whole new way.
The road starts here. It never ends
It's time to ride.
The legend rolls on.
Live to ride. Ride to live

Mission statement

We fulfil dreams through the experience of motorcycling,
by providing to motorcyclists and to the general public an
expanding line of motorcycles and branded products and
services in selected market segments.

Lockheed Martin Corporation

Slogan/motto

We Never Forget Who We Are Working For.

Mission statement

We assist LM companies to obtain product sales financing
that (a) fit their customer's economic profiles, (b) use
financing strategies tailored to each market, and (c) protect
Lockheed Martin Corporation. We utilize our expertise to
develop services that add value at each phase of the LM

business development cycle. We evaluate and implement new strategies in response to changing customer profiles and market conditions.

Lucent Technologies

Slogan/motto

Deliver More Value Over IP.

Mission statement

Philanthropy supports the social responsibility cornerstone of Lucent's mission: To live up to our responsibilities to serve and enhance the communities in which we work and live and the society on which we depend.

Mattel Inc

Slogan/motto

The World's Mattel.

Mission statement

Mattel makes a difference in the global community by effectively serving children in need. Partnering with charitable organizations dedicated to directly serving children, Mattel

(Contd)

creates joy through the Mattel Children's Foundation, product donations, grant making and the work of employee volunteers. We also enrich the lives of Mattel employees by identifying diverse volunteer opportunities and supporting their personal contributions through the matching gifts program.

McKesson Corp

Slogan/motto

Empowering Healthcare.

Mission statement

Our mission is to provide comprehensive pharmacy solutions that improve productivity, profitability and result in superior patient care and satisfaction.

MGM Mirage

Mission statement

MGM MIRAGE (NYSE: MGM), one of the world's leading and most respected hotel and gaming companies, owns and operates 24 properties located in Nevada, Mississippi and Michigan, and has investments in four other properties in Nevada, New Jersey, Illinois and the United Kingdom. MGM MIRAGE has also announced plans to develop Project CityCenter, a multi-billion dollar mixed-use urban development project in the heart of Las Vegas, and has a 50 per cent interest in MGM Grand Macau, a development project in Macau S.A.R. MGM MIRAGE supports responsible gaming and has implemented the American Gaming Association's Code of Conduct for Responsible Gaming at its properties. MGM MIRAGE also has been the recipient of numerous awards and recognitions for its industry-leading Diversity Initiative and its community philanthropy programs. For more information about MGM MIRAGE, please visit the company's website at www.mgmmirage.com.

Microsoft

Slogan/motto

Your potential our passion.

Mission statement

At Microsoft, we work to help people and businesses throughout the world realize their full potential. This is our mission. Everything we do reflects this mission and the values that make it possible.

NIKE Inc

Slogan/motto

Just do it.

Mission statement

To bring inspiration and innovation to every athlete in the world.

The Walt Disney Company

Mission statement

The mission of The Walt Disney Company is to be one of the world's leading producers and providers of entertainment and information. Using our portfolio of brands to differentiate our content, services and consumer products, we seek to develop the most creative, innovative and profitable entertainment experiences and related products in the world.

Put it to the test

On its website (c. 2010) the Coca-Cola company lists not just its mission statement, but values, vision and more. Consider it and then compare to your own mission, values and visions.

COCA-COLA

Our Mission

Our Roadmap starts with our mission, which is enduring. It declares our purpose as a company and serves as the standard against which we weigh our actions and decisions.

To refresh the world ...

To inspire moments of optimism and happiness ...

To create value and make a difference.

Our Vision

Our vision serves as the framework for our Roadmap and guides every aspect of our business by describing what we need to accomplish in order to continue achieving sustainable, quality growth.

People: Be a great place to work where people are inspired to be the best they can be.

Portfolio: Bring to the world a portfolio of quality beverage brands that anticipate and satisfy people's desires and needs.

Partners: Nurture a winning network of customers and suppliers, together we create mutual, enduring value.

Planet: Be a responsible citizen that makes a difference by helping build and support sustainable communities.

Profit: Maximize long-term return to shareowners while being mindful of our overall responsibilities.

Productivity: Be a highly effective, lean and fast-moving organization.

Our Winning Culture

Our Winning Culture defines the attitudes and behaviors that will be required of us to make our 2020 Vision a reality.

(Contd)

Our values serve as a compass for our actions and describe how we behave in the world.

Leadership: The courage to shape a better future

Collaboration: Leverage collective genius

Integrity: Be real

Accountability: If it is to be, it's up to me

Passion: Committed in heart and mind

Diversity: As inclusive as our brands

Quality: What we do, we do well

Focus on the Market

Focus on needs of our consumers, customers and franchise partners.

Get out into the market and listen, observe and learn.

Possess a world view.

Focus on execution in the marketplace every day.

Be insatiably curious.

Work Smart.

Act with urgency.

Remain responsive to change.

Have the courage to change course when needed.

Remain constructively discontent.

Work efficiently

Act Like Owners.

Be accountable for our actions and inactions.

Steward system assets and focus on building value.

Reward our people for taking risks and finding better ways to solve problems.

Learn from our outcomes – what worked and what didn't.

Be the Brand.

Inspire creativity, passion, optimism and fun.

Once you have considered your mission and vision, briefly summarize its essential message. This brand summary must be to the point, yet never diluted. For example, the former British prime minister, Margaret Thatcher famously said, 'The lady's not for turning'. This captured the strength of her determination and the spirit of a political age simultaneously. The original UK lottery slogan, 'It could be you' was the essence of why someone would want to participate in playing the lottery. 'Cool Britannia' (accredited by British Prime Minister, Tony Blair to *Newsweek* magazine) was meant to capture the UK nation's dynamism. Pop songs, too, often feature short titles that encapsulate a spectrum of feelings, hopes and aspirations.

The Five Ps (plus) of marketing

Which combination of marketing communication tools (promotions) will you use to tell the world about your message: advertising; PR; direct marketing; viral marketing?

Draw up your list and consider how each affects the other and then how all deliver a clear message to your chosen audience.

Having decided upon your set of tools, you can begin to develop a plan.

The original marketing mix, named by Jerome McCarthy, was referred to as 'the Four Ps': Product, Price, Place, Promotion.

Then came *People*.

Within the Five Ps, (Four Ps plus People) any company, service or manufacturing based enterprise, may have the following:

Product
- *Guarantees*
- *Brand name*
- *Service support*
- *Warranties*
- *Benefits*

Price
- *Credit terms*
- *Payment terms*
- *Structure*
- *Special deals*
- *Discounts*

Place
- *Types of distributors*
- *Store locations and retail/ office environment*
- *Geographic coverage*
- *Office locations*
- *Online vs. offline*
- *Transportation*

Promotion
- *Direct Mail*
- *Sales promotion*
- *Press advertising*

- *Personal selling*
- *E-shots (email campaigns)*
- *Web banners*
- *Cinema advertising*
- *Radio*
- *Product endorsements*
- *Posters (internal)*
- *Branding*
- *Web 2.0 techniques*

People
- *Location*
- *Experience*
- *Respect*
- *Aptitude*
- *Personality*
- *Care*
- *Industry knowledge*
- *Enthusiasm*
- *Vision*
- *Logic*
- *Professionalism*
- *Innovation*
- *Team players*
- *Understanding*
- *Dynamism*

The extended marketing mix

What makes your service or product desirable?

Is your **Product** peerless? Perhaps you spent years in research? How does the **Price** match up to the competition? Is your **Place** of trade important? For example, do your customers enjoy meeting you at plush offices or do you want to highlight 'value for money' by trading from a 'pile 'em high, sell 'em cheap' warehouse? What about the way in which you tell the world about your product or service, in other words, **Promote** yourself? Maybe you use only email or rely on recommendations from satisfied customers. Are you making full use of your **Physical** presence, such as in-store design or website accessibility? Finally, what's special about the **People** associated with your organization? Are your employees especially trained? Do your customers have distinctive lifestyles or needs? Does your team operate differently from your competitor's employees? For example, do staff treat customers like friends from the moment they meet (such as in an American-style restaurant) or do they adopt a detached 'professional' kind of approach?

Then there is what has become known as the 'seventh P' – **Process** and its cousin, the 'eighth P', **Physical evidence**. **Process** often refers to manufacturing processes including type of packaging and production-line timings – both important, especially when matching your deliverable goods to the market needs. In the UK industry is service led rather than manufacturing based. However, even from a service stance, process still plays an important marketing role.

Physical evidence refers to how you interpret your marketing message through tangibles like web pages, paperwork (such as invoices) leaflets, furnishings and décor, corporate uniforms, business cards and so on.

IMAGINATIVE MARKETING THROWS ARROWS AT TARGETS, NOT TOPPINGS ON PIZZAS

As I explained, marketing is driven by the ultimate consumers. Your job is to win their hearts and minds. That means offering better value, faster service, higher reliability, greater relevance and so total satisfaction. To achieve this, you have to identify the kind of environment which most naturally suits your target audience.

Environments may include economic, social, technological and political. (Also see, 'PESTLE' on page 42.)

Every part of the marketing process aims at directing the ultimate consumer to your company. To satisfy consumers' needs you have to target your total communications mix.

Your communications mix may include a blend of any of the following:

- *Advertising*
- *PR*
- *Direct marketing (Including email campaigns)*
- *Tele-business*
- *E-commerce*
- *Word of mouth*
- *Internal communications*
- *Sales promotions*
- *Exhibitions*
- *Packaging*
- *Networking (Including web-based social networking sites)*

Everything we do – we do it for you

We:
- *develop a product or service*
- *plan our pricing strategy*
- *place and deliver our products professionally*
- *promote our products creatively*

Because you need:
- *something that suits your requirements*
- *a keen cost*
- *an easy way to access us*
- *understandable information to make an informed choice.*

Planet is the biggest P of all. It is concerned with environmental issues. Green marketing, also known as sustainable or environmental marketing, affects all businesses of any size. What used to be considered as too 'left-wing' for many mainstream marketers has become centre-field for all.

From banks offering responsible commercial investments that don't encourage deforestation, to eco-friendly clothing, all marketers are featuring **Planet** as a sales benefit. However, just as with many aspects of marketing, over-use of any feature can lead to consumer fatigue. Many green marketers have been accused of 'greenwashing'. That is using environmental issues as a device, often to hike up costs or save expenses, rather than because an organization is genuinely concerned.

To combat this a close 'cousin' of Planet – 'transparency' – has risen up the marketing ranks of tools. Typically this involves listing full details of ingredients or manufacturing processes on websites, or boosting marketing spend in areas such as social networking blogs, podcasts and customer feedback sites. This shows customers that a brand is 'transparent' and so accessible, thus trustworthy.

The ironical fact is that thanks in part to consumerism – fuelled by marketing – our planet is being over-polluted with marketing paraphernalia such as packaging as well as industrial pollutants needed to manufacture goods. The good news is that the same marketing techniques used to encourage consumerism can be used to educate. It is all a matter of marketers balancing immediate profits with future security.

When the debate about marketing and Planet first came to prominence in the early part of the first decade of the twenty-first century, I was asked to address a large audience of interested parties at the British House of Commons.

Explaining that it was ultimately up to marketers to have the courage to change how marketing is planned, devised and delivered, I concluded my talk in the House with a famous poem by Rabbi Yisrael Salanter (1810–83):

> I wanted to change the world but it was too large of a task for one person – so I tried to change my community.
>
> That was also too hard, so I tried to change my family.
>
> That was also too hard, so I decided to change myself.
>
> And though it was very hard, once I changed myself, I discovered my family changed, the community changed, and the entire world changed.

By changing attitudes towards global warming, marketers can aspire to leave a legacy of good rather than regret.

It is up to you.

Put it to the test

Using the above, list how the Six Ps (plus) of marketing are relevant to your business.

Did you know?

Marketing timing is vital. It took 45 years after the invention of the tin can to invent the modern tin can opener!

The DIY MOT (Marketing Overview Test)

With so many marketing questions demanding answers, where do you start to find them? One way is to conduct an inspection of your company, or, to be more precise, *two audits*. One audit deals with the processes, products, services and people within your organization, the other with the marketplace and external influences.

Internal factors
1 *People – are they experienced? Can sales people reach customers?*
2 *Are you up-to-date (e.g. can your factory machinery cope)?*
3 *Products – are they still relevant?*
4 *Services – can they be supported?*
5 *Financial data – do profit margins look healthy?*
6 *Promotional data – what worked and at what cost?*

External factors
1 *Who wants you?*
2 *Are your competitors offering a better web service?*

Can you match their offer?
1 *Where does your product/service fit in the PLC (e.g. Introduction, Growth, Decline)?*
2 *What/who influences your potential buyers (e.g. social peers)?*
3 *Does government legislation open opportunities or prevent them?*

You can liken the importance of carrying out internal and external audits to getting up in the morning. You get all wrapped up for a winter's day. Yet, when you step outside, it's a heat wave. Audits help to ensure that your clothes: (a) fit; (b) are in good condition; (c) are appropriate for the business climate.

Put it to the test
Who devised the original marketing mix?

SAMPLES OF PART OF AN INTERNAL PROMOTIONAL AUDIT

Promotional analysis

Promotion	Where?	When?	Previous promotions	Results?	Details of new offer
Banner ad	Marketers' website	February	Leaflet	150 hits	10%-off consultancy
Cost?	Target	Testing?	Followed-up?		
500	Marketing Directors	Also, Selling site	e-shot		

Customer analysis

Client	Sector	Demography	Last sale	Value	Cost of enquiry
Acme	Financial	South-east	Copy for leaflet	8,000	200

SAMPLES FROM EXTERNAL AUDIT

Sector analysis

Client	Sector	Demography	Last sale	Value	Cost of enquiry
Acme	Financial	South-east	Copy for leaflet	8,000	200

My sector	Current status	This time last year	Key developments	My share of market	Hot issues
Creative Advertising	Sector under pressure	Buoyant	Copy for social networking sites	2%	Multi-platform marketing

Competitive analysis

No. key competitors	No. cos. in market	Major competitor	Competitive promotional activity	Our response	Results
19	2000	New Face	e-shots	Direct mail and Press	Three new deals

Ignoring competition is like leaving a tea-bag in the cup. The longer it stands idle, the stronger it (the competition) gets. Sometimes you match a competitor's offer and still customers prefer your competitor. This could be down to many external or internal factors, including style of promotional activity, service and brand perception. That means asking more questions.

Put it to the test

Using the above example tables as a template, list a competitive, customer and sector analysis for your business.

UP PERISCOPE

Imagine that you are the captain of a submarine. You are cruising at a depth of 1,400 metres (4,500 feet). Above you, a flotilla of ships sails. Each is a competitor. Before you decide which course to steer in search of new marketing opportunities, you have to plot your position in relation to the other ships.

Let's assume that you market luxury adult ice-cream called, 'Sinful Bites'. Now look at the radar below to gauge your position in the market.

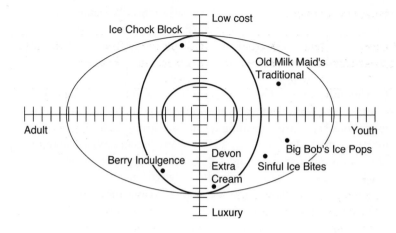

The illustration shows that Sinful Ice Bites is 'hitting' the luxury side of the youth market. You may assume that it was in direct competition with Berry Indulgence or Devon Extra Cream. So this could be good or bad news, depending on how you look at it. It's bad news if you thought your ice-cream had more of an adult appeal, but it's great news when you see that your nearest youth competitor is Big Bob's Ice Pops – nothing to do with your more 'sinful' creative appeal.

SHARING THE CAKE

Measuring market share can be deceptive. Let's say that during one year you sell 120,000 tubs of Sinful Ice Bites out of an overall market consumption of 1,000,000 tubs of ice-cream. So your share of the market is 12 per cent. Okay, so far, we are not talking 'rocket science' here. Now, another consideration: the weather takes a turn for the worse and summer is a wash-out. Total market consumption tumbles to 500,000 tubs. You sell only 30,000, so your market share is just 6 per cent. Should you be confident or wary about the immediate future?

First, you can never be sure of the weather (See 'Watching the detectives', in Chapter 4). Next consider on what you are truly basing your market share. Units sold? Or money received? How about the share of ice-cream eaters (albeit sinful ones!)?

Getting the picture? There's more to this conundrum: How many of those ice-cream 'sinners' were under 21 years old? (Statistically, ice-creams are more appealing to that age group). How many were male? (Statistically less likely.) How many female? What share of ice-creams did married couples buy? (This is a proven growing market that stores ice-cream in the fridge to enjoy whilst watching television.) What about those buying ice-creams more than once, twice or even five times a year?

potential customers ÷ demand = your market

The variables are endless. Yet if you ignore them by selling to every potential buyer who might purchase only one ice-cream, rather than market to fewer, yet more targeted people who'll buy lots of ice-creams, you'll end up short changed. So concentrate on looking at more than one market share measurement. Do so and you can develop campaigns that don't just look good on paper but can't be licked.

SWOT and TOWS

Another classic way to identify your company's market position is the SWOT analysis:

Strengths   *Weaknesses*
Opportunities   *Threats*
SWOT

Strengths relate to either your company's or your competitor's enhanced value to a customer. For instance, a supermarket may offer shorter queues at its checkouts. Or a manufacturer may have a particularly good distribution system. So you can purchase a particular product virtually anywhere in the country.

Weaknesses could include a small marketing budget or an inefficient customer service department.

Opportunities could relate to watching for changes in consumer habits. Or competitors who have become 'uncreative' in their approach and offer.

Threats may arise from a competitor moving on to your territory.

Conduct your SWOT analysis methodically. Consider every aspect of your business, including sales prospects, human resources, service issues, product availability, competitive positioning, and so on.

Keep the SWOT analysis short and to the point – in a bullet-point or table format. Give an outline rationale why a situation looks healthy or poses a problem. There are two compelling reasons for this:

1 *It's a 'snapshot' of your position within the market.*
2 *Often the only overview key indicator, SWOT is vital in your final marketing plan.*

Many marketers adapt SWOT to TOWS – Threats, Opportunities, Weaknesses, Strengths – with the idea of the analysis being on a positive: *strengths*, rather than negative, *threats*. (Also see 'PESTLE', page 42.)

Put it to the test

Visit three competing fashion websites and compile a SWOT analysis of each.

KEEP TACTICS SIMPLE

When developing your marketing plan, assumptions play an essential role. They can include changes in legislation, corporate globalization, political instability, job losses and gains, project losses and gains, too many competitors – the range of assumptions is as wide as you can speculate. As with investment speculation, remember: what goes up, can also go down – so be aware and be market prepared.

Marketing objectives

Setting marketing objectives helps pinpoint commercial goals. By listing objectives you can determine which of your products or services are appropriate for individual markets. You could sell an existing product or service to a new market or approach an existing market with a re-launched product.

Whatever your direction, you have to be sure of your objectives. If you are not, every other part of your marketing plan becomes 'woolly'.

You should be able to seal the **LID** on your objectives:

LIST exact measurements of your objectives (e.g. by costs, returns, share of market, weight, volume, etc.). Seek to **IMPLEMENT** a specific result (e.g. sell 40 per cent more size 6 shoes than you did this time last year). Set a **DEFINITE** deadline for seeing your objectives in action – Remember, it's better to act first than react later.

The Ansoff Matrix

Born in 1918, Igor Ansoff was Professor of Strategic Management at the US International University in San Diego. He had a great reputation as a strategist and a bit of a marketing guru. The eminent professor devised his famous Ansoff Matrix in 1965. If a product or service falls within the top left-hand corner of the matrix, it is probably moving along quite nicely as the company has the experience of what works and what doesn't. At the other extreme, the bottom right-hand box in the matrix represents the biggest risk for a company. This can be one of the most exciting areas for an imaginative marketer to work at. However, great results come only by thorough preparation. Real 'creativity' can be achieved only once lessons have been learnt from developing all, or at least two of the other 'boxes'. Then, in theory, when it comes to venturing into new markets with new products, you can spring your service or product on a pleasantly surprised market without expecting any surprises – pleasant or otherwise.

Market penetration or expansion

Market existing products to existing customers.

Increase revenue perhaps by promotions or repositioning.

Product development

New product marketed to existing customers. You can develop and innovate new offerings to replace current ones for existing customers.

Market development

Market existing product range in a new market. So the product remains the same, but it is marketed to a new audience. Perhaps by exporting, or marketing in a new region.

Diversification

Market completely new products to new customers. Either by related diversification which means remaining in a familiar market or industry. Or unrelated diversification where you have no previous experience.

Ansoff Matrix.

There's a gaping hole in my bucket – gap management

You've probably heard of the term 'filling the gap in a market' or a similar one. Gap analysis generally refers to predicting opportunities for your business not covered by the competition. Using appropriate imaginative marketing, you can make contingency plans to bridge the gap.

The planning gap was another of Ansoff's brilliant concepts. He demonstrated the gap by considering the effect on sales if a company either did nothing about a marketing strategy or if a marketer developed a strategy to 'plug' the 'hole' in the market. Ansoff suggested that by adjusting the gap (called a market penetration strategy) market share and demand for products or services from existing customers could be increased. This would mean giving existing customers more of what they want. Alternatively, a company could concentrate on selling products or services in new markets. This would generate new customers and enhance further sales (a market development strategy).

The more products or services you can offer customers, the wider your potential market. Choosing which direction to take – new products, new services or a combination of both, depends on the width and depth of your market gap. For example, if your chocolate ice-cream is bought by 90 per cent of ice-cream eaters in London, you could try to expand – and so close your market gap in other areas through market development by selling your ice-cream in other cities or diversifying into other flavours.

Below is a possible creative approach for a new line of adult ice-cream flavours.

You went crazy for our Chocolate Crunch.

You went mad for our Marshmallow Munchies.

Just wait till you nibble our Nuts!

Customer buys	Customer hankers for	You offer
Ice-cream with nuts.	Ice-cream with syrup.	Ice-cream with assorted extras.
Lots of ice-cream locally.	Authenticity	Organic – locally sourced – internationally marketed ice-cream brand.

Three ways to plug that gap:

- ▶ *Improve your productivity.*
- ▶ *Increase your sales or share.*
- ▶ *Invest in different areas and resources.*

Productivity improvements may include:

- ▶ *making your sales team more cost-efficient*
- ▶ *streamlining your pricing*
- ▶ *encouraging your factory workers to be more time-efficient, and so on.*

Methods to increase sales or market share may include using promotions to encourage a particular product line or adapting your packaging to make a product more appealing to a certain type of market (e.g. the youth market).

Investing in areas and resources may require you to expand in other countries or develop new products, both of which will require a re-allocation of your capital and perhaps even adaptation of your product or service to suit local tastes.

Did you know?

Before you start, consider the end – here's my strategy.

There are four sides to every box. However, when you are in a marketing corner you can never assume that every square peg fits into your box. Through carefully planned strategies, you can reflect on the dynamics that influence your customer:

- ▶ *Cultural influence*
- ▶ *Social influence*
- ▶ *Personal influence*
- ▶ *Psychological influence*
- ▶ *(The marketing term relating to the behaviour and customs practised by a society is 'Mores'.)*

Strategic Business Units

Some companies set up Strategic Business Units (SBUs). These
independent 'think tanks' are meant to focus minds on long-term
profits rather than short-term tactics. Multinational corporations
such as food conglomerates typically have lots of SBUs. Each
develops a market sector as if it were an independent company.
All report back to a central board.

SBUs for a catering conglomerate may include:

▶ *Fresh meats*
▶ *Dairy produce*
▶ *Beverages*
▶ *Frozen foods*
▶ *Health foods*
▶ *Home delivery via Internet*

In Japan, rather than large teams of strategists, some conglomerates
rely on individuals who have an idiosyncratic approach to thinking.
Such people look at customers, the company and competition as a
whole and then formulate a set of objectives.

The leading Japanese management guru Kenichi Ohmae said
that Japanese strategic thinking is basically creative, intuitive
and rational. According to Ohmae, great strategy is based on the
Strategic Three Cs.

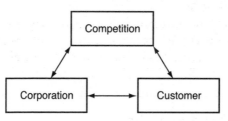

Ohmae's strategic three Cs.

Each corner of the triangle has specific objectives and interests. A strategist must look at ways towards achieving outstanding performance vis-à-vis the competition. Likewise, a strategy has to match the corporation's strengths with the needs of a clearly defined market. Only when this has been achieved can there be a lasting relationship with customers. Ohmae explains:

'In strategic thinking, first one seeks a clear understanding of the particular characteristic of each element of a situation and then makes the fullest possible use of human brain power to restructure the elements in the most advantageous way.'

Did you know?

In the late 1940s, the Japanese travelled, picking up ideas for new technology. The best were adapted for local use. In post-war America, they spotted a system to get workers to collaborate on ideas for new products and services. The Japanese adopted the so-called Quality Circles System. Today, some 12 million Japanese workers belong to Quality Circles (Or 'Kaizen').

How would you prefer your strategy – with or without ice?

There are three main kinds of strategic approach. Depending on your objectives, simply adjust one on its own, or a combination of the three.

1 **Acquisition** *of new customers. Strategies could include e-shots, advertising, banner ads, sales promotion and cross selling with other complementary companies (e.g. If you are a design agency, a print company could share customer data).*
2 **Preservation** *of your existing customer base and renewal of lapsed customers. Strategies could include loyalty programmes, offers to customers to 'come back'. On-going customer contact programmes like sending newsletters or viral marketing campaigns, regular customer care phone calls and personal sales visits.*
3 **Up-grading** *of your service or product. Strategies could include offering passengers a choice of on-demand movies during flights. Modern database technology is powerful enough to let the imaginative marketer recognize a passenger's preferred type of in-flight movie at the point-of-ticket sales. The result – an unsurpassed standard of customer care and so 'repeat' business opportunities.*

Who do I want to do business with?
Where do your prospects live/work? What age group do they fall within? How do they make their purchasing decisions? What/who influences those decisions? Why would they buy from you rather than from your competitor? All these questions and more need to be considered.

(See page 120 for further elaboration.)

Who will help?
What staff do you need? Who will be responsible for what? Can your business be franchised? If so, what training plans will be

needed? Will you need to invest in suppliers like transportation companies, specialist manufacturers or intermediaries? Perhaps your business is seasonal requiring extra staff at peak periods?

What can I afford?
Does your product represent outstanding value for money? Do you want to make it expensive and so attract only a highly discrete market? How best to allocate your budget? What happens if you run out of money? (See 'DIY MOT', page 73, Internal audit', page 77, and 'Cost of marketing' on page 98.)

It is vital to keep your finger on the purse strings of your campaign. From the outset, watch your costs. Seek a return on your investment (ROI). This is looked at in detail on page 101.

When should I start?
How long before you are satisfied with the intricate aspects of the business to be launched? Should you allow extra time for research? Should you launch your service or product in stages – testing its viability on smaller markets, before going nationwide or globally through e-commerce?

How I'll measure success
How will you judge the effectiveness of your marketing plan? Perhaps by increased sales or more specific enquiries? Should you put a timescale on your plan? (Many companies set targets for up to three years.)

How will you assess productivity? Perhaps you set quarterly or annual targets. Maybe you prefer to maintain a dialogue with customers, typically asking via the phone or email questionnaires: 'How are we doing?' or 'Could we do more?' or even 'Could we also be of service to a colleague?'. (Never be afraid to ask what you may think is obvious. Sometimes by overlooking courtesy you may well miss opportunities.) Maybe you can measure success by monitoring how fast rather than how many goods are sold. If you sell food, one method of measuring speed could be to look at 'swipe' figures from electronic point-of-sales (EPS) machines in supermarkets.

If you are in the service industry, you could measure effectiveness through customer feedbacks such as questionnaires. If you are in the delivery business, you could look at efficiencies within your pick-up schedules. The ways to measure are as long or short as you need.

Collecting the information is only half way to measuring the effectiveness of your marketing plan. How do you make heads or tails of all that information? It needs to be methodically recorded, assessed and followed through. If you don't, the entire marketing plan exercise would be worthless.

Typical marketing measures

PROFITS
- ▶ *Product profits*
- ▶ *Regional profits*
- ▶ *Sales-team profits*
- ▶ *Size-of-order profits*
- ▶ *Franchise profits*
- ▶ *Customer-type profits*

CHARGES
- ▶ *Expenses by customer type*
- ▶ *Costs by market sector*
- ▶ *Costs by sales region*
- ▶ *Costs by salesperson*

CUSTOMER CONTENTMENT
Tracking and dealing with complaints has become a powerful management tool.

- ▶ *Number of praises*
- ▶ *Loyalty to the company*
- ▶ *Type of praise*
- ▶ *Number of orders*
- ▶ *Level of praise*
- ▶ *Number of lapsed customers*

Implementing the marketing plan.

- *Number of suggestions*
- *Number of complaints*
- *Type of suggestion*
- *Type of complaint*
- *Repeat purchases*
- *Number of unique website visits*
- *Brand perception*
- *Overall impression of the brand.*

Instant marketing problem-solving frameworks

Albert Einstein said: 'The formulation of a problem is often more essential than the solution'.

When looking at the logistics of the assembly production line (something he invented) Henry Ford turned the question, 'How do we get the people to the work?' on its head by asking, 'How do we get the work to the people?'

Likewise Edward Jenner 'cracked' making a vaccine for smallpox by going beyond the obvious question which everyone asked ('Why do so many people have smallpox?') to, 'Why are milkmaids less prone to contracting smallpox?' Once you understand the fundamental principles behind devising marketing plans, you can easily adapt the formula to suit your specific needs.

The Crux and Nut procedure
This simple framework works well if you want a plan that can be easily updated as time goes by. It forces you to think ahead – and so, hopefully, stay ahead!

- *This is the crux of the problem.*
- *Here are the different questions arising from the problem.*
- *Here are some possible solutions to those questions.*
- *Here is the over-riding solution.*
- *This is what is needed to make that solution work.*

The following three-step framework is based on the thoughts of Helmhotz, a German philosopher.

1 *Allow lots of preparation time to look at a problem from all angles.*
2 *Allow time to let the problem incubate itself whilst you think about something else.*
3 *Open your mind to illuminating ideas which arise from the first two steps.*

Psychologists term the inability to think laterally as functional fixedness or 'fixity'. For example, the only purpose for having a saw is to cut, rather than to use it as a musical instrument. On the other hand, functional reasoning comes when you allow yourself to draw reasonable conclusions based on your knowledge of a subject as a whole.

What kind of a creative marketing thinker are you?

Divergent thinkers:

▶ *Look at detail from multiple perspectives.*
▶ *Lots of possible statements.*
▶ *Produce lots of ideas.*
▶ *Develop criteria for evaluation of options.*
▶ *Evaluate possible actions.*

Convergent thinkers:

▶ *Identify the most important data.*
▶ *Select specific problem statements.*
▶ *Develop 'rich' options.*
▶ *Choose and apply criteria.*
▶ *Formulate a plan for action.*

Put it to the test

Try this simple test to see what kind of a creative marketing thinker you are.

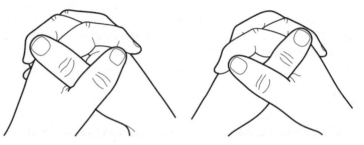

Left thumb on top of right thumb – divergent.   *Right thumb on top of left thumb – convergent.*

The ten-point creative marketing plan

1   *Accept that there is a need to make a new plan. (You'd be amazed at how many marketers don't even get past this stage.)*
2   *Ask what marketing means to your organization and your customers.*
3   *Find out everything about a market from competitors to types of products and services – don't be afraid to ask questions.*

4 *Study the facts coolly and impartially.*
5 *Assess your findings.*
6 *Question whether your findings address both yours and your customers' needs.*
7 *Consider costs in implementing the plan.*
8 *Allow your thoughts to incubate.*
9 *Compare your ideas against your real business capabilities.*
10 *Get your plan on the road.*

Thinking imaginatively about your options requires you to look at the evidence of your plan and then allow such evidence to plant seeds growing in different directions within a structured framework.

Louis Pasteur summarized it as follows:

The greatest derangement of the mind is to believe in something because one wishes it to be so. Imagination is needed to give wings to thought at the beginning of experimental investigation into any given subject. When, however, the time has come to conclude, and to interpret the facts derived from observation, imagination must submit to the factual results of the experiments.

ESSENTIALS FROM THIS CHAPTER

▶ *PESTLE analysis considers the following factors that may affect your marketing campaign:*
  ▷ *Political*
  ▷ *Economic*
  ▷ *Social*
  ▷ *Technical*
  ▷ *Legal*
  ▷ *Environmental*

▶ *Pull and push incentives may include running prize draws or competitions, distributing special discount vouchers – such as pizza discounts – or even offering free software updates.*

▶ *The balanced scorecard, measures, monitors and helps improve both internal as well as external communications. It is a performance measurement system that delivers a 'balanced' view of an organization's accomplishments.*

▶ *The classic marketing positioning statement is:*
  ▷ *FOR: [target audience]*
  ▷ *IT IS: [definitive statement]*
  ▷ *BECAUSE: [summary statement]*

▶ *The original marketing mix, named by Jerome McCarthy, was referred to as 'the Four Ps': Product, Price, Place, Promotion. The extended marketing mix includes: People, Process, Physical Presence (or evidence) and Planet.*

▶ *A classic way to identify your organization's market position is SWOT analysis: Strengths, Weaknesses, Opportunities, Threats.*

▶ *The Ansoff Matrix comprises four boxes: marketing penetration; product development; market development; diversification. If a product or service falls within the top left-hand corner of the matrix (market penetration) it is performing well. At the other extreme, the bottom right-hand box in the matrix represents the biggest risk for a company and so encourages the company to diversify.*

▶ *Strategic Business Units (SBUs) are think tanks that focus minds on long-term profits rather than short-term tactics.*

▶ *Ohmae's Strategic Three Cs = Competition, Corporation, Customer.*

▶ *Divergent thinkers are lateral. Convergent thinkers are focused.*

3

The cost of marketing

In this chapter you will learn about:
- *measuring marketing effectiveness*
- *future brand growth*
- *pricing*
- *legal aspects of marketing*

Price and profit are at the heart of a well-planned marketing strategy. They complement each other in the same way that food complements health; without one being substantial the other can't survive. As such, it is essential that you have a basic grasp of how to make all those facts and figures add up.

Did you know?

John Wanamaker (1838–1922) and Lord Leverhulme are among the many distinguished people attributed to have said: 'Half my money spent on advertising is wasted, but I don't know which half'.

If you were a shareholder in a large organization and the chairperson knew the company was losing half of its money but couldn't tell you where or how, would you still feel confident in that organization?

I knew an advertising agency which believed that every employee should wear the latest fashions and drive a limousine. One day, I asked the agency Chairman about his insistence on spending resources on chrome wheels and sharp jackets for the staff.

When my people turn up for a client meeting, they should arrive feeling good, looking good and ready to address the client's needs. Plus prospective new business contacts like to deal with successful people who look affluent and act assuredly in the way they behave. I suppose clients assume a well-dressed person will diligently work to produce a crafted marketing solution. It goes down to that old belief that success will rub off on them. It's a marketing investment which pays real sales dividends.

Some accountants may question the cost of this exercise. Indeed, many like to see profits now rather than listen to marketing people's promises of dividends through making impressions later.

And perhaps arguably who can blame them?

Traditionally, accountants would suggest that the best way to set a price is to add up how much it costs to deliver a service or product. That calls for assessing the cost of labour, materials and so on. Then, add a reasonable gross profit margin. It's never that easy.

Made-to-measure costs

According to what John Wanamaker and/or Lord Leverhulme said, general advertisers, who produce 'awareness' rather than 'response-led' advertising, can waste 50 per cent of their marketing budget. Direct marketers (including e-marketers) on the other hand, claim a minimum of around one per cent response to a marketing campaign (and they are proud of their response rate). However, even if in the unlikely event that every e-shot or direct mail piece performed equally, direct marketing still mis-spends an incredible 99 per cent of the budget – or does it? (See 'From d-mail to email and online', page 281.)

FROM PRIVATE TO GENERAL

Accountants generally view marketers as tactical experts rather than shrewd strategists. Similarly, when it comes to demonstrating marketing value, some marketers ask themselves how many reactive tasks – often generated by the sales department – are needed to satisfy short-term needs or capture a market share. These tasks may embrace e-campaigns, posters and so on.

Marketing departments are inclined to look at how much money they were allocated in the previous year, allow a percentage for inflation and then submit their costs for the following year. (I once received a call from a client wishing to spend the remainder of his marketing budget in the three weeks leading up to the end of the fiscal year to justify a bigger budget – I of course obliged – needless to say, purely out of selfless reasons.)

To warrant costs, the budget is often broken down as follows:

We need £X

This is how much it's going to cost us to get to that figure.

Here are the margins we'll make trying to get to that figure.

We'll allocate that expenditure against prospects.

That gives £Y for marketing expenditure

Finally we'll split the expenditure amongst different marketing options like advertising, exhibitions and so on.

Financial directors need to calculate how much return the organization is receiving for its investment (return on investment – ROI). This often boils down to the general management belief that sales profits support marketing costs, which is just one reason why, at budget planning times, marketers and financiers can be at such loggerheads. Depending on sales performance in the previous year, the Y cost for marketing can be sanctioned, increased or slashed.

> **Everything that can be counted does not necessarily count; everything that counts cannot necessarily be counted.**
>
> Albert Einstein

Your accountant may ask, 'How many sales and so how much bottom line profit, did the ads generate? What's our ROR (return on resources)?' The key to dealing with accountants is staring at you. The answer is in the word 'accountant'. Your accountant asks you to account for your marketing budget. Rather than make excuses, make yourself accountable. Ensure that your marketing plans make as much financial sense as creative acclaim.

Much of the trouble with assessing the cost of marketing is that you can't always base your pricing on overheads, such as hardware or storage costs. In today's environment, the psychology of how you deliver your product or service and its perceived quality (the anticipated substance and character of your product or service) plays an increasingly important role. In fact, the perceived value of your brand has a direct effect on your financial performance. (See also 'Image is everything', page 189.) But how do you set a value on service? How much can you afford to invest in quality when you need to prioritize on more pressing needs like breaking even? What with the up-hill struggle of just fighting off the competition, who, you may wonder, cares about investing in extra whistles and flashing lights for your basic product or service?

What about building your reputation and brand? It all takes time, and time costs money. This is why you have to divide marketing budgets into distinctive areas.

Did you know?

Employees are one of your most valuable marketing investments. They are your internal customers. Every employee wants to feel that they are 'in-the-loop' in some

(Contd)

way, however modest, about what you are working on in marketing. Where applicable and appropriate, keep them informed, including showing them examples of up and coming campaigns to launch products or services. There are other ways too that you can use marketing to make employees feel part of the team. Some are very subtle but, in practical terms, make huge impressions in terms of an employee's feelings and loyalties. For example, by offering the right combination of benefits from free tea, coffee and biscuits to training programmes, a pension, even the choice of company car, you show you care about their welfare.

Remember just as, and in some cases more, important than paying them high wages is to pay them attention. This is especially true when economic climates are difficult and wages have to be tight. Above all, find time to listen to their ideas and so encourage them to feel part of a team. In return they become more pre-disposed to care about the success of your company.

IMMEDIATE BUSINESS GROWTH MARKETING

Here, the customer investment return is short term and variable. Providing the return continues to exceed your costs, you can continue to invest in growth.

FUTURE BRAND GROWTH MARKETING

The return from this activity is long term and sustained. Branding is accountable. It is much more than making your customers feel 'warm and cuddly' about your company. Without the brand, a company may be compared to a car without a body. It has no image or style. Just as you maintain your car so you need to invest in maintaining your brand. This reinforces your brand value and, like developing a successful car model, allows you to re-shape the brand shell to suit changing needs and trends. In this way a brand can be seen as a financial asset rather than a marketing eccentricity. (See also 'Branding in action', page 205.)

THE RIGHT TIME, PLACE AND COST

One way to value service is to price it by time. Simply divide your own time or that of your employees, into cost chunks per hour. Then calculate the time spent on a specific project.

Whether you arrive at a business meeting in a high-powered car or low-cost bicycle, leaving the right impression by offering value-added benefits, satisfying the needs of your customer is paramount. If the customer demands, you supply. The most valuable asset you can offer your customer must always be your or your team's talent.

Did you know?

For about £100 ($140), one ice-cream manufacturer imaginatively generated millions of pounds worth of advertising and publicity. He simply clothed cows grazing by the side of a motorway with billboards advertising his ice-cream. (An example of a viral marketing campaign – as drivers told drivers who spread the message as far as this very page, and beyond.)

Budgeting for results

Once you accept that it's not what you do with your marketing resources but what your targeted communications do for you, you can budget in a brighter light. Profits aren't generated by corporeal resources like machinery, brochures, direct mail, Internet sites and so on alone. Your definitive source of income is the customer and their expenditure on loyalty is measured in trustworthiness. The rest is just media. Therefore, before you can place a price on a marketing budget, reflect on the value of getting a customer. That needs answers to further pertinent questions:

▶ *What are your existing customers worth?*
▶ *What is a new customer worth?*

- *What is a lapsed customer worth?*
- *Who are they?*
- *Based on the way they responded in the past, why (if applicable) are they currently acting differently?*
- *What have they been worth to you in the past?*
- *What might they be worth to you in the future – NET (inclusive) – after all costs have been provided for?*
- *Can you influence them?*
- *If so, how? Maybe a viral campaign, a poster campaign, a direct sales campaign, a telemarketing campaign ...*
- *How will those activities influence how much customers spend with you?*
- *What's the likely overall return on your marketing resources?*

MORE BUCKS FOR YOUR BOUNCE

Add all that up and you'll arrive at a marketing budget based on spending less time and money doing lateral tasks and more on profitable areas. You'll no longer have to increase your budget periodically. You'll implement imaginative campaigns which make a bigger impact on bottom-line accounts for less marketing spend. Instantly, your marketing is less led by sales, less tactical – much more strategic.

Did you know?

Consider retail-marketing budgets in terms of space. Instead of long-term rent agreements, utilize spaces along shopping mall central walkways. You'll make more per square shopping metre and so will the mall's landlord.

Put it to the test

What is ROR?

SETTING A PRICE ON SOMEONE'S HEAD

Everything about the Wild West is not as clear as it first appears. The famous Pony Express never used ponies – only horses.

The Wild West period itself was a matter of years, not decades. When it came to placing a price on a convict's head, that too, was a hit-and-miss affair. Should a murderer be valued at $1,000? What about two murders? How about a kidnapper? $550 per person, adding another $100 for each ear sent as part of a ransom note?

There is a similar marketing dilemma in identifying how much to spend on either recruiting or maintaining a customer.

FOR A PRICE, I'LL TELL YOU WHAT I'M WORTH

Imagine you are a building contractor. A property developer wants to place an order that will bring your firm £50,000 ($70,000) worth of business. How much of your budget should you invest to seal the deal? Would £1,000 ($1,400) be too little? How about ten per cent of the deal? How about whatever it takes, even if it means making a loss in order to make a bigger profit next time?

Ideally, the more a customer invests, the more of your marketing budget you should reinvest in a customer. Adjust your expenditure according to the percentage you want to make on your money. So, to make the traditional advertising percentage of 17.5 per cent from your greatest possible source of income – your customer – you would spend £8,750 ($12,250).

GETTING A CUT OF THE ACTION

The property developer has confidence in you, so gives you 80 per cent of a project. You have another customer who spends £100,000 ($140,000) on building per year but offers only 5 per cent of the work. Then you have three smaller customers. They offer the odd building job here and there. Each job is worth around £100 ($140). You get a project about once a year. What should you do – develop, maintain or give up their custom?

The answer is to return to the Pareto Rule (see page 26) – concentrate on developing the 20 per cent of customers who generate your greatest income. Then either dispose of the barely non-profitable smaller customers or gradually ease them out, promising that, providing they commit more of their work to your business, you'll offer an even better service than previously.

Alternatively, you may look at other ways to enhance customer value through offering complementary services or products. As a contractor you could offer site and building surveys. An accountant could offer EU tax consultation.

When dealing with customers who spend too little for too much of your time, balance your resources. If you continue to over-invest in trying to serve customers who only have the remote potential to grow, at the expense of those who are ready to flourish, you could end up cutting off your nose to spite your face. The same applies if you ignore the potential to develop other added-value areas which support your core strengths.

Identifying real potential from time-wasting customers again reminds me of the Pareto Rule. Which prospects share the same kind of values, needs and characteristics as your existing profitable customer base? If you don't have them but want to, invest in direct marketing – also see 'The brand egg' on page 200.

Put it to the test
What is the traditional advertising commission percentage?

Balancing service and quality values

Today, with so many products and services vying for increasingly smaller slices of the action, to give you the edge over competitors, tangible quality and practical service must function harmoniously.

Put it to the test
What do direct marketers suggest as a minimum response rate?

Do you believe that if you pay more, more often than not you get a better service or product? Price your product or service too cheaply and people may question its quality. Price too high and people may not even give it a second glance. If you have a top-of-the-range product like a flashy sports car, a high price tag can be perceived as an added indication of luxury. When your product costs the same as your competitors' you have to add extra value through additional features or non-price points including packaging, service and quality. A typical example of this are Pizza producers. Many offer the same price, but not the same delivery times or special toppings.

Balancing your books

You can make more than originally planned. Set an hourly rate for your marketing expertise. This should be higher than the sum total of all your working hours, divided by your targeted income. By doing so, you can allow for discounting, negotiations as well as non-chargeable time.

If, for example, you expect to 'work' 1,600 hours a year (roughly 230 days @ 7 hours per day) and charge a total of £80,000 for that time, the simple sum is:

$$\frac{80,000}{1,600} = £50 \text{ per hour}$$

To allow for discounting as well as any time that is not justifiably chargeable to the client, your 'official' charge-out rate will have to be considerably higher than your anticipated earnings of £50 per hour.

Depending on how much flexibility you can allow for, by charging just £11.50 more per hour – based on a general average rate of tax less any special concessions, you can anticipate an additional £23,000 for actually doing no more work than originally planned!

HOW MUCH IS TOO MUCH?

Making money isn't just about setting high prices. As the late Lesley Crowther, a British television game-show host, used to say, 'It's all about getting the price right'. Many retailers build global empires by offering low prices – at a profit – but selling lots of products en masse. Book publishers often sell relatively cheaply to produce short books for children at higher prices than more substantial adult titles. Part of the marketing strategy behind this could be because adults are happier to spend more on books for children, actively encouraged to read, than on books for themselves. For an imaginative marketer, it's all a matter of balancing production and demand costs against marketing potential.

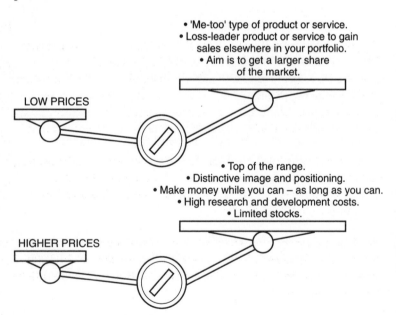

The demand curve.

The relationship between price and volume. The steeper the 'slant' or 'demand curve' the less price sensitive your market – ideal for a niche service or product.

MEETING CHALLENGES BY MANAGING DEMAND

The 'demand slant' or 'demand curve', is a classic way of looking at price scaling. The steeper the slant, the less price-sensitive your market. So if you are in the position whereby you can charge more but sell less to people who are willing to pay a premium, the incline will appear quite vertical. This is a good strategy for businesses offering a niche service or product.

A typical example is a pop band whose fans are prepared at a concert to pay a premium for T-shirts and other merchandise promoting the band. Similarly, the government can continually raise taxes on cigarettes, cashing in on the addiction of smokers and their price insensitivity.

The less price-sensitive your market, the more you can charge
This is an ideal pricing policy for marketing within a highly competitive environment; for example, one toilet-paper manufacturer slightly lowering prices to gain sales from a competitor with an almost identical product. Likewise, this technique is profitably used by supermarkets selling own brand products similar to major brands.

The jump in cost for a price-sensitive product leads to a dramatic fall in sales volume. (If you can secure a firm brand loyalty, changes in price won't affect your sales volume. This ideal price plateau is called Price Haven.)

Products or services for which a small change in price will cause large change in sales volume (penetrated items such as FMCG – Fast Moving Consumer Goods), a change in price will have little effect on sales volume.

If sales increase proportionately more than prices fall, then the demand slant or curve is said to be 'elastic'. (This is typified by

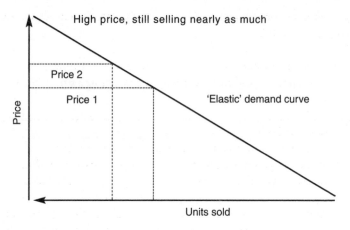

High price, still selling nearly as much

Price 2

Price 1

'Elastic' demand curve

Price

Units sold

Price elasticity of demand.

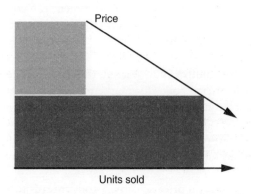

Price

Units sold

my example of the supermarket food versus the brand leader's similar product.) However, if your price is higher than the market demand, the curve or slant is less 'elastic'.

Just because you might slash your prices in half, it doesn't always follow that demand doubles – or even moves at all. When this happens, demand becomes 'less elastic'. If this is the case, there's not really any point in using price incentives like discounts to induce the market. In fact, if you do you'll end up with a double whammy of lower numbers of sales and smaller profits. Whilst if your demand corresponds to your price change, the curve is known as being 'in unity'.

Demand slants or curves tend to be a little wavy at times. However, demand and pricing always even out at a point when supply and demand interact.

Did you know?

Once you are a marketing millionaire, if you count all your money pound by pound, assuming it takes a second to count each pound or dollar, it would take 11 days, 13 hours, 46 minutes and 40 seconds to count all your cash – without stopping. Alternatively, you could invest about £400 ($560) in an electronic money counting machine and gain a good night's sleep.

DISCOUNTS AND CHANNEL DISTRIBUTORS

Distributors are in business to make money and so will want a share of the profits. Those profits have to be shared across all the channels of distribution (e.g. warehouse suppliers, wholesalers, retailers and so on).

It's all a question of 'live and let live'. If you want to get your product or service in front of the consumer, it is vital to keep the entire distribution channel happy. To achieve this, you can opt for carefully planned distributor incentives.

Distributor incentive	Result
Promotional cash discount	Distributors can enjoy cash cuts for quick settlement of bills. Also a share of any specific product promotion.
Quantity discount	Buy more, save more.
Trade discount	Stock more, save more.

Did you know?

One classic discounting scheme actually makes you more money, the more you discount: invite customers to spend at

(Contd)

least the same amount next time they call. Then discount any amount over and above the previous sale. They win. You win. Everyone's happy!

Another variation of discounting is Push Money or Spiffs. Offer salespeople added commission to sell accessories to your product. (For example, lens cleaning cloths to opticians, book sleeves to book shops, mobile phone cases to communication shops.)

When price planning an incentive, bear in mind that marketing costs can be seen in two different lights, namely: the profits you get back in the short-term return for creating incentives; what you can anticipate through developing messages in the long term.

Did you know?

Align your organization with a credit card affinity scheme. In addition to receiving a fee each time a card transaction is made and for each new cardholder who is recruited, you'll gain a new communication channel via leaflets enclosed with credit card statements. (Be wary of card point incentive schemes – with so many being offered, the market is in danger of becoming over-fragmented.)

WHAT GOES UP ALWAYS GOES DOWN?

To discover the percentage increase in unit sales is needed to earn the same gross profit when a price is cut, look in the column headed by your present gross profit and match it to the row that shows the intended price decrease.

For example, if your present gross margin is 30 per cent and you cut your selling price by 10 per cent, find the 10 per cent row in the left-hand column and follow across to the column headed 30 per cent. You find that you need to sell 50 per cent more units to earn the same gross profit as at the previous price.

% cut in price	Current profit margin				
	20%	25%	30%	35%	40%
5%	33.3	25.0	20.0	16.7	14.3
7%	53.8	38.9	30.4	25	21.2
10%	100	66.7	50	40	33.3
12%	150	92.3	66.7	52	42.9
15%	300	150	100	75	60
17%	566.7	212.5	130.8	94.4	79.6
20%		400	200	133.3	100
25%			500	250	166.7

Price planning

The classic demand curve requires an ideal world in which markets act in perfect textbook harmony.

▶ *The demand is huge.*
▶ *Everyone sells the same kind of thing.*
▶ *Everyone is welcome to enter the market.*
▶ *Everyone charges the same.*

The UK rail network used to be nationalized creating a monopoly. After 1997, the last all-British-Rail-owned train shunted out from a station. During the following year, the British railway system was split among a number of companies. If this had not been regulated, one company would have had total control of prices and profits. At one time in the United States, cartels of individual companies used to collaborate to achieve the same effect. Now in that continent as well as in Europe, such practice is heavily penalized.

In economies where only a few suppliers service the market, an **oligopoly** takes place. These suppliers may collude or independently set their market prices. Often, a limited number of suppliers go for high prices at their peril. For example, in the UK, prior to the opening of the Channel Tunnel, there already existed limited travel facilities for the Brits to travel across the channel. Prices were kept reasonably low. If one travel company – say a ferry company – raised its prices, the other enterprising companies would enter the market with 'slashed to the bone' deals. The same is true in the airline business. Although the industry is price controlled by some operators, once an airline raises its prices, in today's free-trade environment, a maverick airline can enter the market offering airline tickets at rock bottom prices. This line of thought is called **Contestable Markets Theory**.

On the other hand, **oligopsony** occurs when there are only a small number of buyers for a particular product or service. (The opposite, 'polyopsony', is when there are lots of buyers who want a specific product or service.)

As the demand curve or slant alters, your plan readjusts. Returning to the Product Life Cycle, you have a number of pricing options available to you at each stage of the PLC. Each can be categorized either into a risky option or a less risky alternative.

Life Cycle stage

INTRODUCTION
The scenario:

Nobody really knows you. Few are innovators.

Take the risk
Whack on a hefty price tag. Innovators don't mind paying for something brand new – after all you need to recoup your investment. Or risk even lower initial profits by undercutting the competition, keeping your prices low until your products or services start paying for themselves and you penetrate deeper into the market (Penetration Policy).

Take it easy
Make an offer, try a low price introductory offer. Capture interest before increasing prices.

GROWTH
The scenario:

People appreciate your prices are reasonable. But watch out – the competitors are on your trail.

Take the risk	**Take it easy**
People are seduced by a low introductory offer. Subtly increase prices.	Keep your prices keen and your competitors at bay. Or opt for a skimming policy in which your price decreases as costs become more manageable.

MATURITY/SATURATION
The scenario:

You've passed the winning post! People adore your company. But just as drink can lead to drowsiness, so familiarity can breed contempt. Your customers might look elsewhere.

Take the risk	**Take it easy**
How long can this last? 'Milk' your product or service for everything it's got before it dies of natural causes.	Use profits to develop other price profit potentials. Offer even greater service to ardent fans of your company – but for a price which makes it worthwhile to you and provides that extra personal touch to the customer.

DECLINE
People are either complacent or fixed in their ways. Like a popular television soap character, you have become part of the furniture. Customers either take to you or leave for alternative enterprises.

Take a risk	**Take it easy**
Why bother with wasting any more money? Look to pastures new and invest elsewhere.	Keep your loyal customers happy. If they are going to leave they will. You might as well maintain a high cost – providing you maintain your commitment.

Pricing tactics – at a glance

Price tactic	Method
Market penetration	Involves setting a low price to gain a high volume of sales.
Market skimming	Involves setting the price at a higher level and positioning the product to 'skim' the top of the market.
Premium costs	Charging more than the current generic market price, using actual or perceived quality as support.
Product line pricing	Stepped according to the difference in cost to produce, their benefits or features etc. This is the way competitors price their equivalents, e.g. toothpastes may vary in price even though they are produced by the same company.
Competitor parity – meeting the market	Prices match the competition. Marketing must be used to differentiate from competitors in areas other than price.
Price challenger	Just below 'meeting the market cost'.
Price aggressor	Low cost gains market share from existing incumbents – but at what price?
Psychological pricing	Set prices at predetermined price points (e.g. £399 or £19.99) in the hope that customers will feel they are paying less than if the price was rounded up.

By the legal book

The currency of imaginative marketing is ingenuity and insight. The currency of the best legal advice is caution. Combine the two. Your currency hedge should be some legal checks to minimize your risks. There are many laws regulating advertising (in the

United Kingdom). They include trade descriptions, consumer credit and loan advertisements, food labelling, estate agents' descriptions, and more. Their enforcement depends on a variety of authorities – trading standards officers, the Office of Fair Trading, and others.

Your first port of call should probably be the British Codes of Advertising and Sales Promotion (the Codes). These are the rules promulgated by the advertising watchdog, the Advertising Standards Authority (ASA). If the ASA receives a complaint about an advertisement and they find that the advertisement breaks the Codes, they will ask the advertiser to withdraw it. If the advertiser refuses, the ASA can generate adverse publicity by making public criticism, deny access to media space (by asking the media to enforce their standard terms which require compliance with the Codes) and ask for sanctions by trade associations. Ultimately, the ASA can ask the Office of Fair Trading to apply for an injunction to prevent the advertisement. However, it rarely comes to that.

Apart from being prosecuted by one of the enforcement authorities, your advertisement could trigger a legal action by a third party for 'trade libel' if a piece of comparative advertising is so pejorative about the products or services of another person's company that the third party can sue for defamation. Compliance with the Codes would normally prevent such a risk because the Codes require comparative advertising to be fairly presented. If in any doubt, speak to a lawyer first rather than have to face the costs of not doing so when it's too late.

Put it to the test
Which is true?

1 *The steeper the demand slant, the less price-sensitive your market.*
2 *The steeper the slant, the more price-sensitive your market.*
3 *The steeper the slant, the more evenly price-sensitive your market.*

ESSENTIALS FROM THIS CHAPTER

▶ *ROR means 'return on resources'.*

▶ *To understand customer values consider:*
  ▷ *What are your existing customers worth?*
  ▷ *What is a new customer worth?*
  ▷ *What is a lapsed customer worth?*
  ▷ *What have they been worth to you in the past?*
  ▷ *What's the likely overall return on your marketing resources?*

▶ *The demand curve shows the relationship between price and volume. The steeper the 'slant' or 'demand curve' the less price sensitive your market – ideal for a niche service or product.*

▶ *Oligopsony occurs when there are only a small number of buyers for a particular product or service. Polyopsony, is when there are lots of buyers who want a specific product or service.*

▶ *Market penetration involves setting a low price to gain a high volume of sales; market skimming involves setting the price at a higher level and positioning the product to 'skim' the top of the market.*

▶ *Premium costs involve charging more than the current generic market price, using actual or perceived quality as support.*

▶ *Product line pricing is stepped according to the difference in cost to produce, their benefits or features etc ...*

▶ *Competitor parity involves meeting the market by matching prices with competitors.*

▶ *Price challenger markets just below 'meeting the market cost';*
price aggressor advertises low costs to gain market share from
existing incumbents.

▶ *Psychological pricing sets prices at predetermined price points*
in the hope that customers will feel they are paying less than if
the price was rounded up.

4

Identifying needs

In this chapter you will learn about:
- *types of research*
- *Maslow's Hierarchy of Needs*
- *Freudian Theory of Motivation*
- *socio-economic grouping*
- *psychographic targeting models*
- *research methodology*
- *the seven stages of research*
- *research and the web*

The *Oxford Dictionary of Business* defines 'marketing research' as: 'The systematic collection and analysis of data to resolve problems concerning marketing, undertaken to reduce the risk of inappropriate marketing activity.'

As you have learned, marketing concerns profitably keeping existing customers happy and, even more importantly, prospective customers. Understanding how to keep people happy includes knowing:

- ▶ *Who they are.*
- ▶ *What they want.*
- ▶ *How they want it.*
- ▶ *Why they want it.*
- ▶ *Where they want it?*
- ▶ *When they want it.*
- ▶ *Which alternative they prefer.*
- ▶ *How you can help.*

Janet Jackson, the international pop star sister of the late Michael Jackson, sports a fetching tattoo featuring a South African saying: 'Walk into your past to deal with your future.' Similarly, the more you know about the background of your prospective target audience, the greater the benefits you can offer and the greater your own rewards.

Today imaginative marketers understand more about customers than ever before.

Types of research application

Companies use research to acquire all kinds of information such as:

▶ *customer contact*
▶ *new product development*
▶ *competitive understanding*
▶ *new market exploration*
▶ *social network new media testing*
▶ *emails*
▶ *direct sales*
▶ *direct marketing*
▶ *events*
▶ *exhibitions*
▶ *sponsorship*
▶ *PR*

Data intelligence

Raw information provides the foundation for knowledge. Knowledge provides the pillars for understanding. Understanding provides the floor for intelligence. Intelligence provides the house for marketers to develop campaigns and teach others how to build their own homes to be eventually filled with potential and promise.

Information for information's sake is useless. You need to interpret the data and so accrue intelligence. Marketing intelligence lets you appreciate human needs which compel prospective customers either to accept or decline the opportunity to react to your imaginative marketing programme.

Ever since a gentleman called Ernest Dichter studied consumer behaviour in the 1940s to 1960s, based on the views and the subconscious of individuals, marketers have developed the intriguing field of motivational research.

Perceptions

People react according to how your product or service looks, costs or is delivered. Imagine you run a kebab shop. Potential customers passing by may notice that your kebabs are dripping congealed lumps of fat. From a PR viewpoint, in terms of their perception of your restaurant such assumptions may be too high to digest. Similarly, if you sell DIY furniture and the instructions appear

Modern interpretation of Maslow's hierarchy of needs.

too complicated, even before reading a word, the confused DIYer would assume that the process is too convoluted.

From the outset, your product or service must appeal to a prospective buyer's psychological needs. In 1970, one of the twentieth century's greatest psychologists died. Abraham Maslow left a legacy which included one of today's most often quoted target market research formulas – Maslow's pyramid.

Maslow argued that there are different sets of motivational factors that influence people. The bottom two tiers are concerned with the physical. The middle section, social and esteem, deals with emotions. Development deals with aesthetic needs. The top tier is about self-fulfilment. As each need intensifies it evolves into a motive to be fulfilled. Your job is to fuel that need so the person acts or is influenced by your marketing message. Once that motive is satisfied, a person steps up to the next level in the pyramid. Compelling motives further escalate towards the pyramid's pinnacle. Imaginative marketers aim to ensure that, through understanding how to balance complex personal emotions with goals, the pyramid's hierarchy is easily fulfilled. Once fulfilled, marketing's job starts afresh, convincing customers that complete fulfilment only comes from more and more consumption of new and updated products and services.

At one time pensions and life assurance were some of the most significant growth areas within the UK marketing sector. At the time of writing the world's population stood at 6,692,037,277. By 2050, the world's population could swell to a staggering 9,300,000,000 (UN figures). During the twenty-first century, people's perceptions of the state caring for their future welfare will be most probably as eroded as actual state benefits. At the time of writing, UK law stopped automatically prosecuting anyone assisting a suicide. According to reports in Oregon, pills were offered to terminally ill patients with only about six months to live. The pills would end the patients' lives as well as ending the welfare burden to the local health sector.

Right now, imaginative marketers are in a powerful position to influence would-be pensioners to buy private pensions and health plans. Looking at the Maslow model, you could adapt your communication messages as follows:

1 **Physiological needs.** *Will a pension pay for food and shelter?*
2 **Safety needs.** *Will a pension protect the family's welfare?*
3 **Social needs.** *Will a pension enable continued membership of a sports or social club?*
4 **Esteem needs.** *Will a pension maintain a lifestyle?*
5 **Exploration.** *Are there competitive pensions on the market?*
6 **Self-fulfilment needs.** *Will a pension free a customer to achieve later what the customer is too busy to achieve currently?*

Pension power will also affect other industries such as fashion retailing. Every seven years, the fashion retail sector redefines 'old' by adding another two years to its previous age limit.

Put it to the test

What do you think are your customers' cognitive costs?

Freudian Theory of Motivation

Sigmund Freud (1856–1939), the renowned psychologist, held an opposing view to that of Maslow. He argued that from a psychosocial view, people didn't consciously realize what motivated them. Instead of systematically addressing needs, Freud suggested, people repressed cravings only to deal with them through dreams, slips of the tongue (Freudian slips) neurotically, phobically, obsessively or psychotically. So, from Freud's perspective, someone who hankers to give up smoking may suck on a plastic cigarette which reminds him/her of suckling at a mother's breasts.

A woman in a television commercial standing beneath a waterfall with her mouth open to the freshness of the stream, overtly representing the 'fresh' taste of a mint, may in fact covertly represent something far more libidinous.

A woman may use a strong detergent to clean her kitchen because, as in Shakespeare's Lady Macbeth character who vainly tries to clean her hands of her crime, she feels 'dirty' about guilt within herself.

> **Out, damnéd spot! out, I say! One: two: why, then 'tis time to do't. Hell is murky!**
>
> (*Macbeth*, Act V, scene 1)

Teenagers may surf in search of blog sites, because deep down they want to break free from the confines of officialdom. On the other hand, they may just want to have a bit of fun – what do you think?

Freud wrote, 'the ego is not master in its own house'. The ego was one-third of a trio of influences: the ego, the super-ego, and the id, or to name them in Freud's words, *das Ich, das Über-Ich* and *das Es* ('the I', 'the over-I' and 'the it'). Explaining the id, Freud said:

> **It is the dark, inaccessible part of our personality, what little we know of it we have learnt from our study of the dreamwork and of the construction of neurotic symptoms, and most of this is of a negative character and can be described only as a contrast to the ego. We approach the id with analogies: we call it a chaos, a cauldron full of seething excitations ... It is filled with energy reaching it from the instincts, but it has no organization, produces no collective will, but only a striving to bring about the satisfaction of the instinctual needs subject to the observance of the pleasure principle.**

Freud classified the id as 'life' (in Classical terms Eros – the libidinal energy of love) and 'death' instincts (Thanatos). Life instincts addressed pleasurable survival such as sex, food and status. Death instincts dealt with unconscious wishes to die or put a stop to everyday struggles. The desire for peace was one interpretation of the Thanatos death instinct. Hollywood escapism and branded utopian worlds also fell under this category.

The external world's social influences on the internal consciousness of consumer affect the ego. As Freud said:

> **The ego represents what may be called reason and common sense, in contrast to the id, which contains the passions ... in its relation to the id it is like a man on horseback, who holds in check the superior strength of the horse; the rider tries with his own strength; the ego uses borrowed forces.**
>
> (Freud, *The Ego and the Id*, 1923)

The ego allows the id to realize, and subsequently release its desires. For some this view still holds in the twenty-first century. For example, many alcoholic or perfume brands continue to be positioned as conduits freeing, often young, consumers to make themselves appear alluring or sophisticated.

In 1981, Al Ries and Jack Trout described how positioning was a marketing communication tool used to reach target customers in a crowded marketplace. They explained that whilst positioning started with a product in a broad market, the real nub of the issue was to specifically position that product in the mind of the customer. Al Ries said of IBM:

> **It's the first company to build the mental position that has the upper hand, not the first company to make the product. IBM didn't invent the computer; Sperry Rand did. But IBM was the first to build the computer position in the prospect's mind.**

During the 1990s, marketers covertly filmed young men chatting-up women in nightclubs. The men proudly clasped the bottles of branded beer with labels pointed outwards. It was argued that this suggested the men were subconsciously saying to the women, 'This brand identifies who I am and what I believe in. Date me; enjoy the brand's advertised values and lifestyle.'

Whilst the ego represents a rational control over the more rampant id, it doesn't guarantee total control. However, when presented in the right light to the id, it offers a degree of acceptable control.

The ego can also be swayed by the excitement of the raw id. At this point the super-ego stands in as a classical 'father figure' making sure that passions don't get out of control. To keep things in check and so maintain a sense of morality, the super-ego hands out sentences of guilt, anxiety and inferiority.

The super-ego instils common sense. Always at odds with the more tolerant ego, it is the aspect of the human psyche that addresses issues such as religion or morality. Serving as an irritant to the defiant id and ego, the super-ego remains the most difficult of soul trading tactics to employ.

Market research techniques seeking personal interpretations learnt from one-to-one interviews, adopt a psychoanalytical approach to pin-pointed motives. This method often spawns Freudian interpretations. On the other hand, a psychological approach towards motivational research asks groups to relate their collective feelings, influenced by their social culture and environment. (Also see, *Soul Traders*, published by Marshall Cavendish, 2009.)

Did you know?

Enterprising imaginative marketers have helped turn the understanding of human motives into a huge industry. It is estimated that in the United States, there are over 415 types of therapy available; from cognitive behavioural therapy to existential psychotherapy. Best of all, many sessions can be 'charged' to heavily marketed private health schemes!

'POWER IS THE GREATEST APHRODISIAC OF ALL' (HENRY KISSINGER)

It is interesting to ponder on how much research into personal drives and motives actually has a serious relevance on a person's public and professional life. For instance, can an individual's clandestine obsessions have any adverse effect on his/her *persona grata* status – and so relevance to a common market? Are that person's public and personal thoughts interrelated – even if subconsciously? If so, are these important factors to consider when trying to understand hidden motives to either accept or reject a marketing proposition?

Two years before the planned completion of his second term presidency, the world gasped when it was alleged that US President Clinton had possibly had affairs with several women. Worse still, they were supposed to have occurred within the precincts of the White House. Prior to previous and similar accusations initially being thrown out of court, later to be accepted, in addition to his own initial denial, the President's wife contested that it was part of a political right-wing conspiracy.

Political as well as social commentators around the world questioned whether a man in his fifties, apparently unable to control his sexual urges was suitable to control the nuclear arms of the most powerful nation on earth. On the other hand, should someone with a tight grasp on foreign affairs be criticized because he had a looser hold on personal ones?

In some European countries and Middle and Far Eastern countries it would be considered odd if a male leader in power never strayed. (Historically, the Emperor of Japan would regularly be supplied with concubines on the premise that a personally fulfilled Emperor would make better policy decisions.)

Assessing personal motives – especially provocative ones – is why all research questions must be asked in context. If not, wrong conclusions can be drawn about the propensity of a target audience towards something, which may in reality, have little or no bearing on a wider, more relevant issue.

Uncovering the hidden persuaders

In 1957, Vance Packard published his groundbreaking book, *The Hidden Persuaders*. In it, Packard brought to the public's attention the manipulative practices of big brands looking to win the hearts and mind of consumers. He implied (but never actually said) that advertising was full of subliminal messages.

Advertising agencies paid psychoanalysts to run focus groups (then called, 'panel reaction' and 'group interviews'). Through free-association techniques consumers were encouraged to openly discuss feelings about products and services. Reported attitudes were then neatly compartmentalized into 'product', 'features' and 'empathy'.

Through such groups it became apparent that housewives wanted more than just convenience. They demanded to reclaim their skills as individuals. So products became marketed as statements of individualism. Even cake mix manufacturers began to include instructions for housewives to add an egg to mixtures for the perfect finish. Not because the ingredients were incomplete without the egg, but because the act of cracking an egg made the housewife feel that she had made an essential personalized contribution to the entire baking process.

From this point on marketers sold products, services, commodities, even celebrities and politicians – based not just on what each could actually do – but how they emotionally connected with consumers, businesses and voters.

Thinking deeper

Ever since experiments took place in California during the late 1960s and early 1970s, neurologists believe each side of the human brain specializes in certain regions of consciousness housed within a pleated casing, some 2.5 mm (0.1 inches) thick, called the cerebral cortex.

Each of the two hemispheres has lots of cavities called ventricles. Prior to modern scientific understanding, people thought that these ventricles cupped the human spirit. Both hemispheres are connected by an intricate collection of nerve fibres called the Corpus Callosum. The left side of the brain deals with practical issues and controls the right side of the body. The right side of the brain deals with creative and symbolic issues as well as controlling the left side of the body. Marketing researchers developed this into an area called braintyping.

Strategic marketers have often cited that a typical 'left-brain' thinking person is thought to be good at understanding order and structure. (This side is particularly apt at language skills.) Ideally, at our most imaginative, we make best use of both spheres.

Did you know?

Even taking your marketing brilliance into account, the difference between your DNA and that of a chimpanzee is less than one per cent.

The typical 'right-brain' thinking person is meant to be creative and emotionally led. Some business consultants believe that certain business managers don't exercise enough mentally. They may worry too much about tactics rather than allow themselves freedom of self-expression. The extent of the problem is such that the manager becomes stressed. Marketers, as well as neurologists, further assert that most people are influenced by one side or the other. Yet, unless mentally impeded, nobody thinks just linearly with either! So people don't look at marketing campaigns wearing either just their 'creative' or 'logical' thinking cap.

The imaginative marketer connects right and left brain potential.

Tactical, disconnected thinking can lead to 'half-baked' ideas.

Through visualizing an ambition and detailing a supporting plan you can aim for an achievable marketing goal.

INSPIRATION IN A FLASH

Each side of the brain comprises subsystems of some 10,000 million-brain cells (or neurons). Neurons allow messages – including marketing messages – to enter and leave the brain and the nervous system, once your marketing communication has been 'registered' by your customer, a dendrite which is like a star burst at the end of the neuron, converts it into an electric signal transmitted all the way down through the nervous system.

At the centre of the brain sits a cluster of cells called, the amygdala. These amplify people's instinct to either 'fight' (confront an issue), 'fly' (turn away from an issue) or 'freeze' (become overwhelmed by an issue).

While the amygdala helps give someone a 'gut-feeling' that they should pay attention to a piece of marketing, another part of the brain called, the posterior cingulate cortex, helps give people a sense of value. So, for example, if sending an e-shot, make sure that it comes from a known email address, especially if that email address is respected by the recipient. (The greater the respect, the higher the assumed value of your email's contents.)

Because both right and left sectors of the brain are capable, to a degree, of thinking both laterally as well as lucidly, based on the way you present your company, a consumer may or may not act on a hunch to buy. So as you can see, it's all about getting the marketing communications chemistry right – in more senses than one.

> ## Did you know?
> Although it has become a visual cliché, the imaginative marketer really can light up a bulb with every new idea: the brain runs at a power rating of 10 watts per minute and radiates 20 per cent of body heat.

DON'T ASK 'WHY?' QUESTION 'WHY NOT?'

Before you can discover why people may want to deal with you, cast a net wider across the psychographic as well as demographic nature of your prospective audience. Traditionally, marketers categorized their audience in terms of social standing. This is particularly true in the United Kingdom where the entire social structure is based on pecking order in terms of power, money and heritage.

Socio-economic grouping

Socio-economic grouping or 'social grading' classifies social status according to interests, social background and occupation. Each piece of data reflects the job of the head of the household. In the past, however, socio-economic classification tended to grade people by their income.

Social grade	Social status	Occupation of the head of household
A	Upper middle class	Higher managerial
B	Middle class managerial	Professional/Intermediate
C1	Lower middle class	Clerical
C2	Skilled working class	Skilled manual worker
D	Working class	Unskilled manual worker

Social grade	Social status	Occupation of the head of household
E	Lowest level	State pensioner, widow, casual worker, people, dependent on social security

(Originally devised 1921)

In the United States, there is no such universal system to grade people by social status. Instead, American marketers rely on lifestyle data and neighbourhood or geodemographics data such as those often used in UK direct marketing. (See also 'VALS', page 134.)

EUROPEAN VALUES IN A TEA CUP

European classification is harder to pinpoint. However, at one point the European Society for Opinion and Marketing Research (ESOMAR) attempted to harmonize social-grade classifications. Their marketing classification index covered: Austria, Belgium, Denmark, Finland, France, Germany, Greece, Ireland, Italy, Luxembourg, the Netherlands, Portugal, Spain, Sweden and the United Kingdom. ESOMAR grades were based on Terminal Education Age (TEA) as well as the job and the primary household income earner. If the main income earner was unemployed, their occupation was replaced by the general economic status of the household.

Put it to the test
True or false? A left-brain thinker is good at understanding creative issues.

Psychographic targeting models

Have you noticed those stickers at the back of cars – 'Surfers do it standing up', 'Marketing reps do it on commission', 'Match-makers do it with singles', 'Advertisers use the new improved method', 'Direct marketers do it with a money back guarantee'…?

Well, imaginative marketers have many lifestyle-oriented methods of classifying people at their disposal.

Psychographic or psychometric classification targets consumers by attitudes and other intellectual characteristics such as hobbies, interests, political views, family values and career goals, which has led to various acronyms and classifications of typical consumers. Many market research companies have adapted this kind of classification. Typically, such adaptations have included matching intellectual characteristics against age, sex, shopping types, management types, car owner types ... the list is endless.

For example, you could categorize consumers by celebrity fans:

Type	Possible characteristic
Brad Pitt – sophisticated	Experimental, owner-occupier, web-savvy.
Cameron Diaz – aspirational	Believer, house proud, sharing, middle-class.
Robert Pattinson – doer	Working class, social realist.
Angelina Jolie – mover	Affluent, cultural, sophisticated.
Paris Hilton – non-conformist	Sociable, acts on personal agenda.

It really doesn't matter what you call your group. The key thing is to understand your target audience – more than superficially.

Did you know?

A common method to classify a product or service is to liken it to a food or colour. It helps to identify social attributes and character.

Another way to 'name-tag' groups of people into marketing consumer types is the Values and Lifestyles approach (VALS™). This classification, originally devised in 1978 by Arnold Mitchell of SRI International (formerly Standford Research Institute), tracks people as they progress from being altogether apathetic to socially perceptive and virtuously vivacious.

Innovators

Innovators are successful with high self-esteem. As change leaders, they relish new ideas and technologies. Innovators are very active consumers, and their purchases reflect cultivated tastes for upscale, niche products and services.

Image is essential for Innovators, not as evidence of status or power but as an expression of their taste, independence, and personality. Innovators are among the established and emerging leaders in business and government, yet they continue to seek challenges. They enjoy variety and the finer things in life.

Thinkers

Thinkers are mature, satisfied, comfortable and thoughtful. Highly educated, they are well-informed and ready to broaden their knowledge. Thinkers have a moderate respect for the *status quo* and institutions of authority. Good incomes allow them many choices. Thinkers are, practical and want durability, functionality and good value for money.

Believers

Believers are conservative, conventional types with established moral codes: family, religion, community and the nation. They follow established routines, organized in large part around home, family, community and social or religious organizations to which they belong. They choose familiar products and established brands.

Experiencers

Experiencers are young, enthusiastic, and impulsive consumers. They are equally quick to become enthused as they are to lose interest. They seek variety and excitement, savouring the new, and the risky. Experiencers like 'cool' fashion brands, entertainment, and socializing.

Strivers

Strivers are hip and fun loving. Motivated by success, Strivers crave the opinions and approval of others. Money defines accomplishment for Strivers, however most don't actually have as much as they would like. They emulate the wealthy by buying stylish products. Many have a job rather than career. Most won't progress too far.

For Strivers shopping is both a social activity as well as the opportunity to demonstrate to peers their ability to buy. They are as impulsive as their credit cards will allow.

Makers

Makers are very 'hands-on', typically, building a house, raising children, fixing a car or investing in DIY. They live within a traditional context of family, practical work and physical recreation and have little interest in what lies outside that context.

Makers are suspicious of new ideas and large institutions such as big business. However, while respectful of governmental authority they resent government intrusion. They are unmoved by material possessions other than those with a practical or functional purpose. Preferring value to luxury, they buy basic products.

Survivors

Survivors are relatively poor. They feel that the world is changing too quickly. So they focus on meeting needs rather than fulfilling fast moving changing desires. Survivors are cautious consumers. They represent a very modest market for most products and services. They are loyal to favorite brands, especially if they can purchase them at a discount.

(Based and developed on the original Value-Added Lifestyles typology. See www.sric-bi.com.)

Put it to the test

Detail a psychometric classification chart for well-known politicians.

Sisters are doing it for themselves

In my experience, women make the best creative marketers. By the 2000s, men's concerns over their disappearing traditional roles climaxed in their reconsideration of the Men's Movement (launched in the United States in the 1980s). For these unpolitically correct, chest-thumping men, the term WIFE was no more than an acronym for Washing, Ironing, Feeding, Etc. Clearly the movement was unfocused. More importantly, for a few marketers this represented the first seeds of change in politically correct stereotyping of the sexes. Liberation was promised through a rising backlash against women's escalating assertiveness. Although never spoken of in public, this ideal covertly tugged at the sociological heartstrings of males who believed in the law of natural discrimination which postulated that those women who 'could', 'did'; those who 'couldn't' became feminists.

The majority of European countries' populations have more women than men. As we progress into the twenty-first century, this population contrast between the sexes will become even more acute, thereby providing the imaginative marketer with a tremendous market potential.

Marketing target acronyms

Invariably when it comes to research, imaginative marketers develop acronyms even further. Below are a few popular psychographic terms including acronyms, that may help identify your target audience.

Young/ dynamic	Married/ Partner/ Divorced	Established	Retired
Bank-buster Early adopter who wants to change bank-charge burdened society.	**Hoho** Happy, optimistic home owner.	**Woopies** Well-off (over 55). Pre-retirement (aka **Grey Panthers**).	**Wrinklies** People in their twenties during the sixties.

(Contd)

Young/ dynamic	Married/ Partner/ Divorced	Established	Retired
Buppies Black upwardly mobile professionals.	**Dinkies** Dual income, no kids, married couple.	**Glams** Greying, leisured, affluent, middle-aged.	**Silver Market** People aged 60+.
Road Warriors Well-travelled executives – usually salespersons.	**Empty Nesters** Couple, no kids.	**Markas** Middle-aged re-nester, kids away.	**Internots** Web-2.0 phobes.
Crusty Lifestyle – rough clothes, matted hair.	**Managing Mums** Guilt-ridden mothers.	**Jolies** Jet-setting, 49–59, free of financial worries.	**Dippies** Dual income pensioners.
Yuppies Young upwardly mobile professionals.	**Minks** Multiple income, no kids.	**Whannies** We have a nanny.	**Farte** Fearful of ageing or retiring too early.
Y-people Y-person – Yuppie.	**Puppies** Previous young upwardly mobile professionals.	**Holiday Junkies** 'Hooked' on holidays.	**Guppies** Breed guppy fish. (Also 'green' yuppie.)
Netizen Member of web community.	**Islington Person** Social left-winger.	**Methuselah Market** Rich, five years pre-retirement.	**Suppie** Senior urban professional

Young/ dynamic	Married/ Partner/ Divorced	Established	Retired
Bimboy Male bimbo.	**Foodie** Hobby is food.	**Fluffy** Feminine, loving, understanding – faithfully yours – typified by the anti-feminist wives of the early 2000s.	**Rappie** Retired affluent professionals.
Grumpies Grim, ruthless, upwardly mobile professionals.			
Sinbad Single income, no boyfriend and absolutely desperate.	**TIK** Two incomes with kids.	**Power Bimbo** Killer Bimbo Careerist, previous Airhead.	**Opal** Older people with active lifestyles.
Mouse Potato Hooked all day to the Internet.	**TINS** Two incomes no sex.	**Lombard** Lots of money but a real dickhead.	

(Contd)

Young/ dynamic	Married/ Partner/ Divorced	Established	Retired
Media Clam Selectively chooses marketing messages or type of preferred media (Such as internet TV on demand as opposed to regular TV broadcasting).	**Muppie** Middle-aged urban professional.	**Zuppie** Zestful, upscale person in their prime.	
Recessionata Consumer who turns away from premium brands to cost-cutting alternatives.	**Yappie** Young affluent parents.	**Tinkie** Two incomes, nanny and kids.	
Twitrover Someone who feels an increased sense of bravery when Twittering, as opposed to in person.	**Orchid** One recent child, heavily in debt.	**Current Boomers 45–55** Baby boomers who resist 'growing old'.	
Skippy School kid with purchasing power.	**Oink** One income no kids.	**Sandwich Generation** Cares for ageing parents and children.	

Young/ dynamic	Married/ Partner/ Divorced	Established	Retired
Yeppies Young, experimenting, perfection seekers.	**NILOB** No income, living off benefits.	**Baby Boomer** Originally people who grew up after the 1960s baby boom. Also refers to people born at historic periods of population increase.	
	Sindi Single, independent and divorced.	**Baby Busters** Born just after original Baby Boomers generation so, in the 1990s, had less need of housing and goods.	
	Sitcom Single income, two kids, outrageous mortgage.	**Guppie** Gay urban professional.	

Put it to the test

Draw up a list of six potential new titles for magazines aimed at the over-65 age group and identify the different characteristics of each title.

Sex in marketing

In the 1980s, feminism 'invented' the New Man who changed
nappies in the morning and cried over soppy films at night (whilst
bottle-feeding the baby). From the beginning of the 2000s on,
marketers encouraged women to become sexual predators. Take,
for example, the famous Wonderbra advertising campaign created
by advertising agency TBWA. Rather than irritate the women's
movement, the ads became icons symbolizing a new, more
confident, more controlling woman.

There are certain creative keys when using sex in marketing:

- ▶ *sophisticated humour*
- ▶ *used as 'the finishing touches' to an already powerful message,
  rather than the central message*
- ▶ *intelligent delivery*
- ▶ *must be supported by great products or services which at least
  go towards fulfilling consumer expectations.*

Just as the ancient Greeks warned against having everything in
moderation and nothing in excess, eventually there will be rumblings
of serious trouble when attempting marketing to women – or for
that matter men – using sexual imagery. The more the public sees
overtly sexual images, the more immune they will become to the
message. (Remember, to the imaginative marketer the message,
rather than just the medium, is 'King'.) Above all, the message must
have a tangible and relevant meaning.

To avoid this communication impasse, creative marketers can
either make sex more explicit – and so increase the initial titillation
but compound the overall effect, or return to Victorian values.

As this would all occur within the twenty-first century, it could mean reverting to ideals more than 100 years after they were originally spoken of by the Edwardian suffrage movement.

It's really EC–PC

With all this background to consider, you can appreciate why your own contemporary marketing plans and campaigns need to be more than simply Politically Correct. They also need to be Emotionally Correct. In other words, you need to target human motives, social sentiments and personal emotions rather than just civic and class stereotypes.

Did you know?

It is said that one of Coca-Cola's advertising agencies once sent a letter to US magazines offering guidance on the appropriate placing for Coca-Cola ads. A list of inappropriate editorial adjacent to advertising included:

▶ *sex-related issues*
▶ *negative diet information (e.g. bulimia, anorexia, quick weight loss)*
▶ *political issues*
▶ *drugs (prescription or illegal)*
▶ *articles containing vulgar language*
▶ *religion.*

Offering ideals

Returning to more general research issues, have you noticed how pop music programmes are watched mostly by people who aren't old enough to get into a 12a certificate film, let alone a rave? That is because marketing campaigns featuring specific lifestyles often target the lifestyle (including age group/social group, business type and so on) one level social or age group lower than depicted within the marketing collateral. This gives an appropriate audience something to aspire to.

On the other hand, in the fashion business, women aspire to have slimmer waistlines. This is greatly influenced by advertisements showing slender-waisted models. The irony, however, is that the majority of UK women wear size 16 (USA – 14, Europe – 44). It is why, at the end of fashion sales, there are invariably more smaller sizes left over.

Finding your 'little list' (customer sources)

Commercial marketing lists are widely available from specialist agencies and suppliers called list brokers. You can purchase such lists to include all kinds of targeting information. Be sure that your list is 'clean'. This means it has been updated within the previous three months or even earlier.

Typical targeting lists are broken down by the following mailing segment profiles:

- ▶ *Age and sex*
- ▶ *Marital status*
- ▶ *Education*
- ▶ *Mortgage status*
- ▶ *Job title*
- ▶ *Housing*
- ▶ *Household type and relationships*
- ▶ *Type of magazines read*
- ▶ *Employment characteristics*
- ▶ *Size of company*
- ▶ *Race and ethnicity*
- ▶ *Place of birth and citizenship*
- ▶ *Types of entertainment enjoyed*
- ▶ *Journey to work*
- ▶ *Standard Industry Classification codes (SIC).*

Your best list source, however, is the one hidden in boxes or within computer systems somewhere in your office.

Coupons or email questionnaires should make discreet enquiries of your customers – without over-burdening them with questions. Similarly, you should emphasize that answers should be legible and consistent in order to not over-burden the person deciphering the coupon. List not less than three simple (tick box option) questions which may be useful in future marketing exercises. For example:

> ▶ *How many computers do you have in your office*
> *1–3* ☐ *4 or over* ☐
> ▶ *How many other credit cards do you have? 1–2* ☐
> ▶ *Which cards? VISA* ☐ *MASTERCARD* ☐ *AMERICAN EXPRESS*
> ☐ *OTHER* ☐
> ▶ *Have you purchased any IT equipment with your credit card in*
> *the last month? Yes* ☐ *No* ☐
> ▶ *What was the value of the purchase* _____ *(Please*
> *complete)*

... Plus, whatever else is applicable to your type of business.

Yet another source of information gathering – with permission – is email data when people sign on for web-generated news and other useful information.

Sources for Research

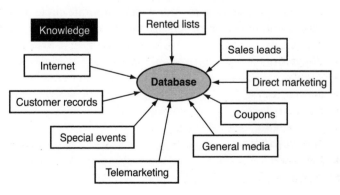

Research methodology

There are many ways to find out about your internal as well as
external markets. Whichever you choose, aim to be at least on
a knowledge level equal to your competitors. This closes the
knowledge gap about your market and so attracts customers
towards your business rather than theirs.

In addition to asking your customers for views, a great source of
collecting information is your sales force. Every day your sales
team meets and talks to people – prospects who may already be
buying from your competitors. The trouble with staff research is
that findings may be biased. Recognize that your top sales person
will naturally consider how his/her answers will be interpreted in
terms of loyalty to the company. Likewise, key managers must be
awarded a 'Licence to Drill' suspects for information.

ENTERPRISE INFORMATION SOURCES

It's surprising how much publicly available information you can
acquire simply by listening to your wider corporate circle of
contacts. Useful information squealers include:

- *distributors*
- *suppliers*
- *agents*
- *plant workers*
- *tele-workers*
- *administrators*
- *van drivers*
- *receptionists*

You'll also need:

- *a 'safe house' to store all your information*
- *a way to access the information – either manually or electronically (via a data-warehouse, or perhaps barcode reader if, for instance, you are researching stock-related issues)*
- *an 'A-Team' of senior managers to interpret the information, guide prospectors towards the right direction to collect more data and ensure that findings are acted upon.*

In addition to watching your competitors, keep an eye and ear open for what's happening in the market generally. For example, developments in IT may affect the way you service customers in the future. Keep reading, listening and talking to people who thoughtlessly could give you the one snippet of information that could make or break your planned long-term success. As Eleanor Roosevelt put it: 'If we are to live together, we have to talk.'

The seven stages of research

1 *Consider your objectives. Except in the case of exploratory research, restrict yourself to questions which are directly connected to the objectives.*

2 *Which research best reveals the answers you need? (Be prepared for conditional conclusions. In other words what you should do if the results veer towards a certain direction necessitating further questions.)*

3 *Make sure that either you and/or your researcher are fully briefed as to the kind and depth of information sought.*

4 *Let your researcher know the complete purpose of the research, including the commercial implications of possible findings.*

5 *Compare findings against previous research studies. (If those interviewed are already conversant with your company, they will give biased answers. Likewise, if your respondents currently deal with your competitors, based on the kind of questions asked and more importantly, the approach and style of those questions, you may actually deter them from giving you business.)*

6 *Interpret your findings qualitatively rather than purely mathematically.*

7 *Act upon your research.*

Once you have completed each of the seven stages of the research process, plan periodic reviews by exploring changes in the market.

Put it to the test
List your information sources – including the less obvious ones.

FINGLE'S LAW OF INFORMATION

The information we have is not what we want.

The information we want is not what we need.

The information we need is not available.

Research and the web

The first Google index in 1998 already had 26 million pages, and by 2000 the Google index reached the one billion mark. By 2009 Google systems processing links on the web to find new content discovered 1 trillion (1,000,000,000,000) unique URLs on the web at once! Today the new content continues to expand. Clearly the web is a vast pool of knowledge. However, just because something is published on the web, it doesn't automatically follow that it is factual. Anyone can publish anything as long as it is not overtly pornographic or covertly violent. This said, if you defame someone on the web, wherever the information is viewed it is subject to that country's laws.

The Internet can be used to collect data, however, only with permission from surfers. Being impersonal it immediately does away with a researcher's personal influence on a group. Your website should contain a page which enables people to tell you a bit about themselves.

FOUR PRACTICAL WAYS TO ASK A QUESTION VIA THE WEB

1 **One question at a time.** *By revealing only each question in line, you can eliminate problems of respondents being influenced by the following question.*
2 **Multiple-choice full screen.** *In this instance, you reveal all the questions but offer a choice of answers which are selected by dragging down boxes on the screen.*
3 **Specific full screen.** *As with '2', here you reveal all the questions simultaneously. However, you offer the option for the respondent to complete the answers in full. If you take this route, make sure that outside the United States you let people download the questions, quit the Internet and then re-log on with the answers at a later stage. This saves people expensive 'up-link' (connection) time on the web.*
4 **Email.** *Send up to ten specific questions and ask the respondent to email you back the reply. This is the most uncontrolled of the four methods. (As well as impractical, both from a legal and usage point of view.)*

General computer-based research is known as Computerized Personal Interviewing (CAPI).

Often the respondent types in answers for himself/herself via laptops. Again, the trouble with this method is it raises the spectre of bias. A surfer may be happy to type directly on a laptop, thereby lean his/her answers accordingly. On the other hand, a person who is not so PC literate will tend to offer answers more grudgingly.

Insurance companies invariably use Fact-Led research techniques – often using laptops. Although complying with industry regulations, these Fact-Led research industry requirements may annoy respondents. The point of this line of questioning is to ascertain that the best advice is given. For example, a Financial Advisor may have to ask repetitive questions such as name, address and current portfolio.

Many research companies are set up as nationwide panels of correspondents. They regularly complete e-forms about anything from shopping habits to preferred pets. This can be extended further through e-conferencing whereby you can interview panellists via a modem Internet camera link to a network computing device. (Particularly useful if your correspondents are widespread.)

All your web information, along with all the other sources, can then be stored in a central electronic data-warehouse which you can cross-reference and 'mine' as you prefer.

Desktop research

There is still a vast source of research available in printed form. So-called 'secondary research' includes a wide pool of information. From trade magazines to national newspapers and CD-ROM directories of companies by industry type, research is consistently being undertaken and reported upon. Business libraries are an excellent source for research. In the UK, members of the Chartered Institute of Marketing, Institute of Direct Marketing and Institute of Directors have access to books, articles and directories covering everything from industry surveys to association listings.

Research, especially statistics, can be likened to witnesses at a trial. Interpreted in a given light, they'll testify for both sides. As with database list buying, make sure the research is relatively fresh. International research can be carried out through record offices, embassies and cultural centres. Key international data includes political yearbooks and forecasts, European Union reports, trade surveys and studies, international marketing statistics, United Nations publications and quango international think-tank studies.

Finally, there is commercial research which can either be purchased as a bespoke document tailored for your needs or via on-going research reports covering industries, buyers, viewers, listeners, and so on.

All desktop and related research should be interpreted with the perspective of what other research indicates as pure 'gut feel'.

Trend research

Desktop research often uncovers tendencies within industries and social sectors. Superficially, trends may appear, at best, to be mildly relevant to your business and, at worst, just a source of tittle-tattle amusement. However, such trends can provide more than just small-talk around a dinner table. For example, in France, home of culinary cuisine, office workers have steadily abandoned their traditional lunch-time meals at restaurants. Instead, due to pressure of work, they eat at their desks. 'So what?' You may ask. 'We are all busier these days.' Well, if you work within the catering industry or even a related industry, this trend may have more significance than you, or more significantly, your competitor initially notices.

For example, if office workers are having their lunch at their desks, does that mean they are eating more sandwiches or cooking meals with an office microwave oven? If it is the latter, a supermarket chain could start to provide special office lunch micro-meals. A microwave manufacturer may want to develop a personal microwave oven. A book publisher may consider producing the office microwave cookbook or an e-book. A Tupperware company may want to look at the possibility of producing re-useable eating trays which keep the office desk tidy; a fitness company may want to develop a portable exercise machine that can be used at lunch-times in the office and then packed away into a drawer. (In the UK, the average lunch hour is now 32 minutes. According to a Diet Coke survey, men have longer breaks than women – 42 minutes compared to 31.)

As you can see, for the imaginative marketer, the possibilities are endless. All you have to do is open your mind and recognize a marketing potential.

> ## Did you know?
> French fast food is so 'fast' that around half of the McDonald's chain of restaurants in France feature drive-through facilities.

> ## Put it to the test
> List three methods to pose a question via the web and discuss the merits of each one.

Primary research

A quantitative project can be either carefully shaped or completely unstructured. Planned surveys require predetermined questions which are usually answered through preset multiple-choice options. In the case of mailed surveys, there are several important factors to consider.

STEPS FOR MAILED (INCLUDING EMAIL OR WEB-BASED) QUESTIONNAIRES

1 *All research should be unambiguous and unpatronizing. So, explain what's the purpose of the questionnaire. Reassure respondents that answers are confidential. If you intend to use the answers for other divisions within your company, offer the option declining to share data with other related services. (If any division is a separate company, normally, under the Data Protection Act you are prohibited in the UK from sharing data with other companies or businesses.)*

2 *If specifically requested at the end of the research session, you may offer respondents a sales brochure about the business on whose behalf the research is being conducted. Likewise, you could consider rewarding answers with a free gift. Covert, 'pushy' selling via research isn't just illegal but, from a marketing point of view, stupid. You'll probably alienate more potential customers than recruiting prospects. Overt selling*

disguised as research is called sugging (a cross between selling and mugging).

3 Make your first question particularly easy to answer. (You don't want to scare people off!)

4 Complete a sample question to show how to answer the rest of the questionnaire.

5 Occasionally, there may be an argument to plan your questions so that they first refer to a concept and gradually build up to a specific product or service that caters for a need. (Once again be wary of sugging.)

6 Ask one question at a time (e.g. Do you have a pet? not, Do you have a dog/cat/fish?).

7 Try, whenever possible, to avoid open-ended questions (e.g. Could the future be rosy?).

8 Always use simple words rather than complicated ones (e.g. use paperwork not collateral).

9 Whenever possible, avoid leading questions (e.g. Do you catch the train because it is more comfortable than the bus?).

10 Don't ask people about subjects of which they obviously have no in-depth knowledge.

11 Don't intimidate your respondent (e.g. Are you the type of person generally considered by peers as being rather ill informed? (This is a particularly bad line of questioning. In addition to being intimidating, it is impertinent and irrelevant as the people who should be questioned are the peers – any other answer would be subjective.)

12 Always offer a choice of answers to specific questions, including a not applicable option, e.g.
Are you married? ☐   Single ☐
Divorced ☐   Separated ☐
Living with a partner ☐   None of the above ☐

13 Be aware of the influence of semantics. Don't use language which reflects your personal views (e.g. in politics, we use Labour, not left-winger or socialist).

14 Include a Don't know option. If the respondent really doesn't have an opinion on a specific question, the person may think it is too difficult to answer and so give up on your entire questionnaire. (See 'Posing a general research question', page 158.)

15 *There are no 'right' answers. Always explain to your respondent that your questionnaire is not an intelligence test. The only thing being assessed is your product or service.*

16 *Confine your questions to the answers you need, no more. (Don't over-tax your respondent.)*

17 *Don't cram in any one question the probability of getting a variety of answers e.g. rather than,* How many magazines do you subscribe to? *ask about each of the magazine categories by sector, one at a time and then:*

    In a month do you buy one □, *two* □, *three* □, *marketing magazines?*

    Which titles do you read?

    Marketing Herald □   *Marketing News* □
    Marketing Times □

18 *If you have to be familiar, do so tactfully. Instead of asking,* How much do you earn in marketing?', *try:*

    Is your annual income between:

    £15,000–£25,000 □   £25,000–£35,000 □
    £36,000–£45,000 □   Over £45,000 □

    If you can't avoid confidential questions, explain why you need to ask and clarify e.g. don't ask, Do you offer your employees tax-free concessions? *Instead ask:*

    To establish how we can provide a discreet, totally professional tax advice service, please answer the following:

    Do you offer your employees financial benefits over and above their salaries?

    Yes □   *No* □

    If 'YES', have you sought professional advice that shows some benefits could be 'tax-free'?

    Yes □   *No* □   *Not yet* □

    If applicable, would you be interested in discovering more about 'tax-free' benefits?

    Yes □   *No* □

    Which type of tax advice service do you value most: [This would be a direct-approach survey question as distinct from questions relating to personal impressions about subjects and behavioural attitudes.]

☐ *Highly professional*
☐ *One in which you complete forms and an advisor just
   checks your work*
☐ *One-to-one – very personal*
☐ *Standard, 'form-guided'*
☐ *An online 24-hour service*
*In your opinion, what kind of business people are best placed
to consult tax advisers? (This typifies an indirect-approach
survey question.)*

Shrewd ☐   *Honest* ☐
Crafty ☐   *Forward thinking* ☐

19 *In the case of direct mail, always include a pre-paid envelope
for the respondent to return his or her answers confidentially.
In the case of direct and indirect surveys via the Internet,
always include a confidentiality clause before and after
your questions, plus the option in named cases for people
to confirm that they wish to participate. For example, in
anonymous cases:*

*This survey is totally anonymous. Survey answers are never
written to disk. Plus, of course, we have no idea of your real
identity. So please answer honestly.*

Did you know?

More than 70 million Americans yearly respond to surveys.

Observational research

If quantity rather than profundity is required from your survey,
you need to conduct observational research. This measures how
many times people perform tasks rather than why they choose to
do so.

For example, you can add a visitor counter to your Internet
site which records the number of visits or 'hits' you've had.
Television companies use a similar method to record the

popularity of programmes or commercials. A nationwide group socially representative of the population has its television viewing electronically measured.

Some UK supermarket specialist researchers even equip panels of shoppers with laser-light guided hats. These record which products are most looked at on the shelf and subsequently purchased. Supermarkets can also use electronic scanning equipment at the point of purchase to record the number of products and types sold. Through combining this with data collected from loyalty cards, the imaginative marketer can also research who are purchasing the products and when. The most basic type of observational research – but still effective if the project isn't too large – is simply to watch, write down and then analyse the information in a report.

Quantitative research

This quantifies by measuring in numeric terms and statistical analysis the consumers' behaviour and response to your marketing campaign. It works best with large samples of people who are representative of your proposed target market. Usually, a carefully planned questionnaire is developed which sorts rationalized data into categories and sectors. So, for example, you could calculate how many women per thousand buy a particular type of bra.

If, as can sometimes occur in questionnaire surveys by post or the web, you fail to get sufficient response from your research, which occasionally happens in any type of questionnaire survey, you should either follow up with a telephone call or polite emails.

Did you know?

Over 75 per cent of UK women wear ill-fitting bras, according to a recent survey. Each woman owned 2.6 bras and ideally would have wished for size 34C. The most popular bra size in the UK is 34B.

Qualitative research

Whereas quantitative research tends to deal with big samples (the bigger the more accurate your results), qualitative research cannot be measured or expressed in numeric terms. So, it is useful to explore 'intangibles' such as feelings and emotions as well as opinions. Therefore, qualitative research restricts itself to small groups or individuals and investigates why people think or behave in a particular way.

Jamie Dow is one of the UK's original leading independent consumer market research consultants. As a facilitator Jamie lead consumers through a prepared list of topics in a 'depth interview' or group discussion. This encouraged people to think laterally, ask and, more importantly, answer questions representing the group's views on a product or service. As the session progressed, so the line of open-ended – as opposed to closed – questioning becomes more focused. In the USA, group discussions are actually called Focus Groups.

Often, sessions are videoed for future discussion within the marketing department. If you intend to hold such a session personally, you may not want the groups to know what product or service is being researched. If they did, answers could be biased.

Such sessions should be held in a relaxing environment which frees the participants' minds and thereby loosens their preconceptions and inhibitions. This kind of approach also works well with general brainstorming sessions. (See 'Brainstorming', page 171.)

Put it to the test

Summarize the difference between qualitative and quantitative research.

Posing a general research question

Just over halfway through your multiple-choice questionnaire, reverse the order of emphasis within your selection of possible answers. This stops respondents becoming indifferent to the style of questioning.

Other forms of research

Syndicated research occurs when you share a general questionnaire with other marketers. You can sponsor as many specific questions as you wish and negotiate to have exclusive rights to the answers.

MYSTERY SHOPPER RESEARCH

As the name suggests, here you ask a representative to visit your distributor/retailer to gauge effectiveness. Of course, your agent may have to buy something, so allow for this when budgeting.

CONCEPTUAL RESEARCH

Marketing can be an expensive business. So it pays to test the acceptability of a new campaign or concept before spending vast sums of money promoting it within your marketplace. From testing the viability of the design of a chocolate bar wrapper to the layout of an advertisement, conceptual research is vital. Media such as television are where conceptual research comes into its own. Because of the budgets it often involves, television companies measure the 'reach' (viewership) of commercials via representative members of the public.

?	Method
How appealing do you find it?	Multiple-choice. The beauty of this approach is that you have total control over the questions plus, of course, the survey is relatively easy to turn into a statistical report. However, you can't measure spontaneous observations. (Make sure you graduate the possible answers from one extreme to the other.)
What does this suggest?	Show your respondent a picture or object and ask him/her to 'tick-off' boxes measuring response. (This is often used in conceptual research – interpretation of ink blobs is called Rorschach testing.)
How do you feel?	Respondents have to measure their feelings on a numerical or alphabetical scale.
With or without?	When you offer an alternative answer – YES or NO – the type of question is called dichotomous. Even if the answer is seemingly YES or NO, still always offer alternatives, NOT SURE or DON'T KNOW.

(Contd)

?	Method
Who will win?	This encourages people to predict events or issues. If you follow this route make sure that you have provided enough background on the subject either through:

▶ *relating the leading question to the subject at hand;*
▶ *confirming that your respondents are suitable.*

I'll keep it under my hat.	This conceals the sort of answers you are after. This ensures totally unbiased replies. Make sure you don't influence answers through the style of question.
I'll give you a clue.	This hints at the kind of answers you want. Typically it asks one of the following:

▶ *How do you think ...?*
▶ *Where do you believe ...?*
▶ *How would you assess ...?*

You have to write down the answers to this type of question. So, unless you are a fast writer, or record the conversation, this questioning best helps to determine the sort of subjects to be covered in more specific interviews.

?	Method
What's the first thing that comes in your head?	Paradigmatic and syntagmatic associations are provocative, free-association psychology-led types of questions. Paradigmatic association is any response to a word stimulus by some semantic link, for example table to chair or boy to girl. In syntagmatic association, responses are much looser, like cloud to white. Adults tend to be paradigmatic.

Television and web-promo commercials can be especially expensive to produce – let alone broadcast. If you are considering this kind of advertising activity, test the power of your creative approach by:

▶ *presenting your idea for television graphically on a story-board of key 'frames' from the commercial;*
▶ *depicting your television commercial through producing a simple animation of your proposed commercial;*
▶ *scripting your commercial and get people to read it among a group.*

SIMULATED VARIABLE RESEARCH

This discovers the specific variables that compel consumers to do something (or not). It works only when you are testing specific elements of products or services, whilst ensuring that all other variables don't fluctuate. For example:

▶ *You could experimentally test the effects of changing the prices on two identical products at identical shop branches. This would tell you whether the increased price would lead to lower sales.*
▶ *You could test whether a telephone service is more accessible if a freephone number if offered as opposed to a standard telephone line.*

MOOD MUSIC RESEARCH

A 'classical' example of research in the UK carried out by Leicester University Music Research Group concluded that music affects our choice of food. Depending on the type of music played, diners at a restaurant were either more or less likely to enjoy their meal.

They played three kinds of music followed by the absence of music.

1 *Classical music – Vivaldi and Elgar*
2 *Brit Pop music – Oasis*
3 *Easy listening music – James Last.*

When classical music was played, diners found the food was quite 'sophisticated'. If the music was not conducive to the setting, diners thought they were not getting value for money: they felt the meal was somehow camouflaged.

The more traditionally classical the music, the more diners were prepared to pay. For an average meal when there was no music in the background, diners were prepared to pay £14.30 ($20.00) compared with:

Easy listening	£14.51 ($20.30)
Pop	£16.61 ($23.25)
Classic background music	£17.33 ($24.25)

The lower the 'scale', the greater the dissatisfaction about the meal.

Put it to the test

Test the effectiveness of music on your customers by playing different background tracks and comparing general attitudes towards customer service. Which track worked best and why?

Telephone research

Telephone research can be 'tricky'. Your main problem is time and intrusion. People, generally, have too little time for exercises such as telephone research. However, telephone research is excellent if you want a prompt reaction to something which is about to occur or had recently occurred. This is why so many Opinion Pollsters use the telephone as a rich route towards information.

Another good reason to use the telephone as a research tool is to speak to existing or probable customers. They already know about your organization or your industry sector. So you don't have to waste valuable phone time explaining background details. You could, for example, ask their views about a new service which you plan to introduce. Would it enhance their lives? Add credibility? Save time? Offer flexibility? and so on...

The kind of voice that people hear will also influence their decision to give a few moments of their time to answer questions. Also important is the time of day that you pose your questions, for example:

> **Morning** *They may be less busy (if at home).*
> **Lunch-time** *They may want a break from answering phones – never mind questions!*
> **Close of day** *They may just want to go home.*
> **Evening** *They may prefer to watch television, surf the web or chat with their friends than speak to you. How late should you call? Certainly no later than 9 p.m., unless invited to do so.*

Whenever you call, make sure you ask whether or not it is convenient to speak, and if needed, offer a convenient time to call them back.

DON'T UTTER A WORD UNTIL YOU'RE UTTERLY COMPLIANT (TELE-MARKETING AND THE LAW)

You also have to consider legal obligations. For example, it is recommended that you tell people the name of your organization, even ensure that it is printed in a generally available telephone or web directory. You should explain the purpose of your call and if the person's number was recommended, who provided it. In the UK you can't interview minors, nor can you call ex-directory numbers. Likewise, people who have specifically asked you not to call again should be struck off your list.

If you want to conduct sophisticated, 'high-tech' telephone research, using computerized phone calling, make sure that your local legislation permits it. In the UK such automated research has lots of legislative impediments. In most markets, strict data protection rules apply to storing and gaining telephone and contact name details.

Telephone tips

- ▶ Don't shout at people!
- ▶ Don't talk down to people.
- ▶ Explain all relevant aspects of the product or service.
- ▶ Allow the person to answer questions without interruption.
- ▶ Prepare your questions.
- ▶ Consider using a computerized telephone scripting programme to assist with calls.
- ▶ Don't whisper.
- ▶ Explain the purpose of your questions.
- ▶ Don't speak to someone in the office whilst asking questions over the phone.
- ▶ Don't offer too many alternative answers to a question.
- ▶ Be prepared to be questioned.
- ▶ Consider using a specialist telephone marketing company.
- ▶ Speak expressively.

- ▶ *Explain who you are and who you work for.*
- ▶ *Don't intimidate the person.*
- ▶ *Judge whether the person is getting fed up with your questions by the tone of his/her voice.*
- ▶ *Be ready to know to whom to refer a call in the case of unanticipated questions.*
- ▶ *Log calls. Note types of callers most receptive to questions and their future availability.*

Put it to the test

Devise a short telephone script to sell a business-to-business answering service. Test it on a colleague and then re-plan it.

One-to-one street interviews

Ask questions to potential consumers about your product or service, perhaps offer samples of, say, your latest chocolate bar, sandwich, drink, magazine and so on, then ask for the consumers' opinion.

More formal street interviews can be harder to conduct. People tend to shy away from interviewers who request 'just a few moments of your time'. At least with trial-and-ask street interviews, interviewees, after examining and trying out a product then answering pertinent questions, can anticipate a reward for their efforts. Irrespective of whether you conduct trial-and-ask interviews or sample interviews, make sure that your research is targeted, simple to understand and manageable. Above all, remember that by posing the right questions and thinking about the consequences of answers, you can find a wealth of untapped opportunities.

Empirical research

Empirical research helps to confirm, or otherwise, theories
by identifying current or historical trends, views and general
insights and then testing and comparing conjecture against
facts.

As you have seen, research is a great way to help prepare future
developments. But, generally speaking, you can't rely on it as an
oracle or soothsayer of all knowledge. So what if your product or
service really needs predictive research to succeed? For example,
say you manufacture swimwear. Surely it would be useful to know
whether or not to anticipate an increased demand for your goods,
six months prior to summer? You'd have ample time to schedule
production, distribution, packaging, promotions and so forth.

Growth-predictive industries include political forecasts. What
occurs within a market's local economy is influenced by national
and international trends. This is why typically political predictions
are based on measuring swings within the economy. The more
extreme the swing, the greater the chances of political change.

GET YOURSELF A THINK TANK

Think tanks are more commonly used by governments and
lobbyists. However, their findings often uncover invaluable
research material to assist specific long-term marketing projects.
Such research can be particularly useful for charities seeking new
communication messages such as the impending danger of drought,

famine and so on. They can also help to identify major possible industry and community needs which may offer new, profitable marketing opportunities.

Some sources for global think tanks include:

▶ *BT Research Laboratories (UK). This is a marvellous centre for predictive research (also known as Futurology). It is acknowledged as Europe's leading telecommunications research and development facility in technology. The Overseas Development Institute is an independent, non-governmental centre for the study of development and humanitarian issues. It provides a forum for discussion of the problems facing developing countries.*
▶ *The Arlington Institute (USA) is a policy and research institute which identifies broad-based, emerging national and global trends and events. It was founded by John L. Petersen a futurist and strategic planner specializing in the area of national and global security.*
▶ *SRI International describes their think-tank facility as a medium which invents the future through technology innovations. (SRI was responsible for inventing the PC mouse.)*

Other eminent think tanks:

▶ *The Confederation of British Industry www.cbi.org.uk*
▶ *Library of Congress www.lcweb.loc.gov*
▶ *Foreign and Commonwealth Office Library www.fco.gov.uk*
▶ *International Planned Parenthood Federation www.ippf.org*
▶ *International Monetary Fund www.imf.org*
▶ *European Parliament www.europarl.eu*
▶ *ASLIB Directory of Information Sources in the UK www.aslib.co.uk*
▶ *All UK government links to official organizations and sites www.open.gov.uk*
▶ *Charities Information Bureau (UK) www.give.org*

- *Central Office of Information* <u>*www.coi.gov.uk*</u>
- *Royal Institute of International Affairs (UK)* <u>*www.riia.org*</u>
- *Department for International Development (UK)*
- *Marketing Coaching and Creative Strategies*
  <u>*www.brandforensics.co.uk*</u>

To discover more about central information sources and think tanks, you should approach either a business library, specialist lobby group (for example dealing with old age), trade associations or try accessing the web.

As with all research, think-tank research must be interpreted in the context of your overall objectives and other pieces of research. If you ever get into a situation when you are overwhelmed by the amount of research available for a specific project and are not sure which is best for your needs, use your intuition.

For example, if you intend to open a new restaurant but can afford to research only one market, opt for the one your 'gut-feeling' tells you is most appropriate. Finally, ensure that your main avenue of research reflects the feelings and thoughts of potential end-users of your product or service. After all, it's what they think that really counts.

ESSENTIALS FROM THIS CHAPTER

▶ *Marketing research is the systematic collection and analysis of data to resolve problems concerning marketing, undertaken to reduce the risk of inappropriate marketing activity.*

▶ *Maslow argued that there are different sets of motivational factors that influence people. The bottom two tiers are concerned with the physical. The middle sections are concerned with social and esteem factors, and also deals with emotions, development and aesthetic needs. The top tier is about self-fulfilment. As each need intensifies it evolves into a motive to be fulfilled.*

▶ *Al Ries and Jack Trout described how positioning was a marketing communication tool used to reach target customers in a crowded marketplace. They explained that whilst positioning started with a product in a broad market, the nub of the issue was to specifically position that product in the mind of the customer.*

▶ *Vance Packard's book,* The Hidden Persuaders, *brought to the public's attention the manipulative practices of big brands looking to win the hearts and mind of consumers.*

▶ *Socio-economic grouping or 'social grading' classifies social status according to interests, social background and occupation.*

▶ *Psychographic or psychometric classification targets consumers by attitudes and other intellectual characteristics such as hobbies, interests, political views, family values and career goals.*

▶ *Marketing plans and campaigns need to be more than simply politically correct. They also need to be emotionally correct.*

▶ *Commercial marketing lists are widely available from specialist agencies and suppliers called list brokers.*

- ▶ *Coupons or email questionnaires should make discreet enquiries of your customers – without over-burdening them with questions.*

- ▶ *Research methods at your disposal include:*
  - ▷ *Observational research – measures how many times people perform tasks rather than why they choose to do so.*
  - ▷ *Trend research – uncovers tendencies within industries and sectors.*
  - ▷ *Quantitative research – quantifies by measuring in numeric terms and analyses statistically the consumers' behaviour and response to your marketing campaign.*
  - ▷ *Qualitative research – explores 'intangibles' such as feelings and emotions as well as opinions.*
  - ▷ *Syndicated research – shares a general questionnaire with other marketers.*
  - ▷ *Mystery shopper research – sends a convert person to premises in order to assess effectiveness.*
  - ▷ *Conceptual research – tests campaigns before launching them.*
  - ▷ *Empirical research – helps to confirm, or otherwise, theories by identifying current or historical trends, views and general insights and then testing and comparing conjecture against facts.*

5

....

Brainstorming

In this chapter you will learn about:
- *some of the greatest imaginative thinkers*
- *brainstorming*
- *conceptual charting*
- *cultivating ideas*

Over the centuries, humans have pondered over the question, 'What precisely is an idea?' In my book *Improve Your Copywriting* (see 'Taking it further', p. 339), I explain how the Greek philosopher Plato (427–347 BCE) argued that the senses (touch, taste, sight, smell, hearing) form the basis for reality. Ideas come about through either direct or indirect connection of one set of facts with another. So, according to him, to get an idea you need to have had some sort of experience through the senses of something connected to the idea. Once you have thought of that idea, even if it doesn't exist, for you, it is real.

Put it to the test

Picture a mouse in your mind. Now picture an elephant. The mouse squashes the elephant. Try to imagine that scenario. What if I told you that the mouse is driving a steamroller ... or that both the mouse and elephant are cartoons. Or the mouse is gigantic and the elephant is tiny? If any of these suggestions help you to picture this image, then such images for you are real.

Five steps towards imaginative marketing

1 **Brainstorming.**
2 **Analyse** *every part of a problem in detail.*
3 **Get inspired** *by the world around you – a form of synectics.*
4 **Gut feeling** *– go with a hunch, think 'upside' down, rather than just logically.*
5 **Bench marking** *– study another organization – even not directly competitive to yours and pick out the best aspects of its service/process.*

The four doors towards creativity

For many years I have taught marketers about a metaphorical 'House of Creativity'. The house has four rooms. Each represents an inspirational approach towards answering a creative brief.

The **Room of Great Works** contains outstanding examples of design from a variety of sources.

The **Room of Reason** contains hard facts and figures relating to the project in hand.

The **Room of Precedent** contains previous examples of work either by the company and/or competitors.

Once you have entered every other room, the empty **Room of the Unknown** offers infinite space to be as imaginative as you wish.

Cogito ergo sum ('I think therefore I am')

Réné Déscartes (1596–1650), regarded by some as the 'father of modern-day philosophy', argued that true knowledge comes from pure human reasoning alone. Therefore, you don't even need to have prior sensory experience – even related to the subject in hand, to have an original idea.

FROM SIMPLE THOUGHTS COME COMPLEX IDEAS

John Locke (1635–1704) suggested that ideas are based solely on experience. According to Locke, a newly born baby is rather like a blank sheet of paper. As the child develops so the sheet is filled with information acquired through experience.

The adult, according to Locke, experiences two kinds of ideas:

▶ *Ideas of sensation (seeing, hearing, smell, sight, taste) which he called simple ideas;*
▶ *Ideas of reflection (deliberation, construction ...) which he defined as complex ideas.*

He said that simple ideas are based on experience whilst complex ideas combine those experiences to create abstract concepts.

Aristotle's influence on imaginative marketing is immense. He devised a classic process of deductive logic. He perfected the 'syllogism' – a logic argument structure comprising two major premises, followed by a conclusion.

The major premise states, 'All Xs are Ys, no Xs are Ys, or some Xs are Ys'. The minor premise highlights a more specific relationship, and the conclusion is predetermined by the form of these premises.

For example, 'All marketers are ambitious. I am a marketer, so I am ambitious.'

The late Sir Isiah Berlin argued that ideas could not be divorced from people and their psychological and cultural milieu. In his book *Two Concepts of Liberty*, Sir Isiah wrote:

When ideas are neglected by those who ought to attend to them – that is to say, those who have been trained to think

critically about ideas – they often acquire an unchecked momentum and an irresistible power over multitudes of men.

I market fresh strawberries	Kids enjoy the snow	Why not market strawberry ice-cream?
Simple ideas	**Simple ideas**	**Complex (abstract ideas)**

Today, it is generally regarded that an idea is an episode created in the mind and based on real experience or known facts.

Put it to the test

Which is true?

1 *You don't need any specific experience about something to be imaginative.*
2 *Ideas come only from experience.*

Now answer why each one is true or otherwise.

Still stuck? Throw a dinner party

Have you ever planned an imaginary dinner party with your favourite guests like movie stars or singers? Now imagine that you invited your all-time favourite thinkers to help solve a marketing dilemma. Imagine how each would contribute to the situation. Write down their ideas – you'll be amazed by the results.

Powerful marketing ideas can be likened to arrays of stars, revolving in an ever-expanding galaxy of creative potential. An imaginative marketer finds ways to connect and spin seemingly different constellations into an elegant Milky Way, abundant with innovative thoughts.

Once those thoughts are correlated, through the use of communication tools (the marketing mix) in essence you transplant those ideas into the minds of your target audience(s).

Eureka! Examples of idea fusion

Johann Guttenberg (c. 1400–66) fused the mechanics of a wine press with a coin punch and invented the printing press.

Isaac Newton (1642–1727) fused the movement of waves with falling apples and discovered gravity.

Percy Shaw of Halifax, England, fused the effects of light reflecting on a cat's eye and poor visibility caused by fog and invented the Cat's-eye road studs.

Put it to the test

Through combining unrelated objects, what new object could you invent (however far fetched or fantastic) and which media would you choose to promote it?

Take an idea shower

Brainstorming generates long lists of potential marketing opportunities. The more intensive the brainstorm (also known as a 'thought' or 'idea shower'), the greater your potential source of ideas.

The most effective brainstorming sessions comprise people who, in addition to the core development team, may have no direct experience of a particular product/service or the company developing it.

All brainstorming sessions start quite laterally and narrow in definition as they progress.

Just as it is best not to exclusively include immediate team members in your brainstorm, so it is essential to have an independent facilitator acting as a thought-shower chairperson and encouraging free thought, without also bringing the added burden of any political agenda.

As discussed in my book *Improve your Copywriting* [Teach Yourself] (see 'Taking it further', page 339) brainstorming is best conducted outside normal working premises. Since the first edition of that book was published, my company, Gabay Ltd has developed a particularly effective mode of brainstorming, designed for the twenty-first century, called Virtual Brainstorming™. Here, led by a trained market researcher with psychological marketing skills, brainstormers who make up a synectics-led Focus Group (originally developed in Harvard) are invited to 'step into' a surreal world appropriate to the subject being brainstormed. Then they are led through a highly structured method of rationalizing their thoughts.

Being a chimerical environment, a Virtual Brainstorming™ session can be conducted anywhere your imagination can conceive, from a jungle to the top of a mountain, provided the location enhances imaginative thought and group dynamics energy.

I HAVE NO IDEA WHAT YOU ARE TALKING ABOUT

In my travels I get to hear lots of excuses why brainstormed ideas may be impractical for a company. Most are just excuses.

Ten ways to kill your marketing idea

1 *It's too expensive.*
2 *It will never work – although I can't say why.*
3 *Not my responsibility.*
4 *We're too busy.*
5 *The public won't buy it.*
6 *We have to put profits before people.*
7 *If we still like the idea in a couple of months, we'll look at it again.*
8 *The Managing Director's husband will never approve.*
9 *It sounds just a little too innovative for us.*
10 *Let's form a committee?*

Guidelines for effective brainstorming

Just as there are ways to smother a refreshing breath of an idea at birth, so there are guidelines which encourage ideas to flourish.

1 *No brainstormer can judge another brainstormer's suggestions.*
2 *Every brainstormer is equal.*
3 *The more off-the-wall an idea is the better.*

4 *All ideas can be combined and positively enhanced.*

5 *Brainstormers should make fun their priority and in doing so, break down work-barriers.*

6 *Don't attempt to solve problems step by step. Try more lateral methods.*

7 *Consider every alternative.*

8 *Don't stunt the growth of an idea by brainstorming in a dull or restrictive environment. (A good case for Virtual Brainstorming™.)*

9 *Encourage brainstormers to get to know each other, and so speak more openly.*

10 *Ask your brainstormers to 'leave' their job titles and status by the door before entering the brainstorming environment.*

11 *Restrict your troops of brainstormers to no more than 14 people per group.*

12 *Brainstorm sessions should generate a long list of ideas; however good or bad they appear.*

13 *Include every idea in the final list. To censor ideas is to prejudge them.*

14 *Brainstormers cannot ask leading or intimidating questions, for example 'Surely you agreed that when it comes to actual experience of the subject, you should leave the thinking to professionals – like me?'*

15 *Whether a marketing idea sounds good or odd, be curious to develop it further.*

16 *Once you have all agreed on the most accurate and informed creative options, let the final analysis take pure 'gut-feeling' or intuition into account.*

Did you know?

Imaginative marketers really do let their hearts rule their heads: the heart produces at least twice the amount of electricity as the brain.

ARE YOU LONESOME TONIGHT?

What if you don't have anyone to brainstorm with? Excluding the possibilities that you are anti-social, have bad breath and so on, I still suggest that you find someone with whom you can thrash out your ideas.

If your enterprise is modest, you could ask friends and family or even consider holding an interactive brainstorming session over the web (especially if conducted via webcams and so letting you keep the all-important eye contact going).

If on the other hand you intend to brainstorm in groups, remember that ideas should compete against each other rather than allowing personalities to take up the gauntlet. Also, all brainstorm groups should include leaders, followers and neutral-minded people. Don't allow one to dominate another.

DESIGN A BETTER ROUTE TOWARDS MARKETING IDEAS

Now that you have produced reams of fascinating ideas and research, how do you intend to make head and tail of it all? One highly imaginative method to help interpret your ideas is to become an architect of ideas.

Conceptual charts turn idle doodles on a piece of paper into insightful marketing. (N.B: Spider diagrams are web-shaped hexagonal shapes which help categorize your ideas into clusters.)

Like an architectural blueprint of individual towns, the way you arrange and connect the thoughts in your chart may be quite different from mine. Conceptual charts let you transfer those 'thinking' routes on to paper. They segment your ideas into distinctive areas (like the shopping mall, local school, church and so on). All these places similar to 'B' roads, emanate and divide from a central need or goal which can be compared to the town square or piazza.

Conceptual charts help you to deal with lots of complex projects simultaneously. Now, of course, one could list each idea as it comes. But although nice and neat, it's too restricting and instantly

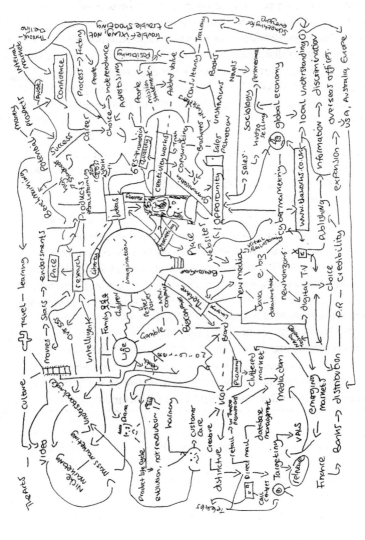

A ten-minute conceptual chart based on the word 'imagination'.

censors which ideas should go under which list. There is literally no space on the chart for an idea to bloom.

Incredibly, up to 95 per cent of your time can be wasted trying to recollect words that have no real bearing on your memory. When those words are commercially significant you need to be able to distinguish between propositions that can all too easily become 'muffled' by linking words and sentences separating them. Making logical connections with the potential to lead to brilliant new marketing concepts can become difficult.

Similar to doodles on a scrap of paper, complete your chart as you 'dream up' possible routes. (As discussed in 'Thinking deeper', page 130, the mind doesn't think vertically – it imagines laterally.)

'Roads' from the centre of your conceptual chart can be drawn in colour (like in a geographic map denoting 'A' roads from highways): one colour per specific subject, per route. The roads may be sign posted like street indicators at intersections with simple pictures summarizing a concept. The more ideas you have the more roads you build until you design a bustling city, brimming with potential.

Put it to the test

Based on the conceptual chart above, re-read this chapter and then writing the name of your marketing project at the centre, let your mind wander as you paint your map.

ESSENTIALS FROM THIS CHAPTER

▶ *Brainstorming generates long lists of potential marketing opportunities. The more intensive the brainstorm (also known as a 'thought' or 'idea shower'), the greater your potential source of ideas.*

▶ *The five brainstorming steps:*
   ▷ *Brainstorm*
   ▷ *Analyse*
   ▷ *Get inspired*
   ▷ *Gut feeling*
   ▷ *Benchmark*

▶ *The House of Creativity has the following rooms:*
   ▷ *The* **Room of Great Works** *contains outstanding examples of design from a variety of sources.*
   ▷ *The* **Room of Reason** *contains hard facts and figures relating to the project in hand.*
   ▷ *The* **Room of Precedent** *contains previous examples of work either by the company and/or competitors.*
   ▷ *The* **Room of the Unknown** *offers infinite space to be as imaginative as you wish.*

▶ *Conceptual charts let you transfer those 'thinking' routes on to paper. They segment your ideas into distinctive areas.*

6

....

Under the microscope – focusing on your business

In this chapter you will learn about:
- **the Emotional Sales Point (ESP)**
- **the Point of Difference (POD)**

From USPs to PODs and ESPs

Throughout this book, you have learnt about the importance of establishing a Unique Selling Proposition or Selling Point (USP). Ironically, most USPs are fallacies. Whilst there is always one main underlying benefit there is rarely just one supporting selling point about a product or service. For the imaginative marketer, every product or service contains a wealth of selling propositions. The real challenge is to narrow those USPs to the most appropriate for each marketing message.

To deal with this, rather than promoting your USP, consider marketing your POD and ESP.

A POD (Point of Difference) is really a set of three distinctive benefits that set your product or service apart from the competition. For example, a pen may feature the following PODs:

Rubber grip

Application: provides a firm grip.

Advantage: you can write comfortably and longer.

Metal barrel

Application: strong and sturdy.

Advantage: your pen won't break from everyday falls and mishaps.

Spring-clip

Application: you can clip it on your pocket.

Advantage: your pen is always at hand.

Put your PODs together and you arrive at a short **benefits statement,** which, when written with a specific audience in mind, helps you develop your main underlining marketing message.

For example:

> This extra comfortable pen is sturdy and, thanks to its spring-clip, always at hand: perfect for the busy student dashing between lessons.

Every marketing company is in pursuit of the elusive underlining POD. The best is compelling and motivating. The Body Shop, for example, clearly identified the opportunity for a pro-animal welfare, environmentally sensitive range of body-care products. This POD was not only distinctive in its time, but highly relevant and ethically compelling.

PODs or USPs are often short-lived. Before you know it, competition moves in to address the gap (see 'The Ansoff Matrix', page 82). The challenge for imaginative marketers is to own that gap and, through positioning, ensure that the brand, product or service best meets consumer needs.

Positioning as a marketing technique doesn't occupy a piece of paper, rather it occupies the minds of consumers. Go ahead and make unsubstantiated statements or promises about your brand and you can be pretty sure that your consumers will subconsciously say to themselves, 'go on, prove it'. Consumer intelligence, through market research, helps provide the competitive edge as can a commitment to update a product, its packaging and advertising to address the changing needs of consumers. Once you have conducted that research you can revisit and expand the positioning statement (see page 54, and 'Brand extension' on page 193).

For _____
It is _____
Only we can _____
Because _____

Which now becomes:

For *[target end user]*

Who wants/needs *[persuasive reason to buy or discover more]*

The *[product/service name]* is a *[product/service category]*

That delivers *[key benefit – based on your main underlining marketing message]*

Unlike *[main competitor]*

The *[product/service name]* offers *[list your three PODs]*.

Did you know?

Every marketing message needs conviction – without it, there is no substance. Follow the AIDCA rule: Attention leads to Interest. Interest leads to Desire for a product or service. Desire leads to Convincing the audience that what they want, they really can afford. Conviction leads to Action to buy.

Getting into the mindset of PODs

Most important of all, your brand should feature an ESP – Emotional Sales Point. This powerful approach tackles one of the most fundamental of all marketing strategies – namely, appealing to the fact that people often think with their heads but act with their hearts. In fact, without an ESP, your brand marketing remains lifeless.

ESPs support your brand vision. They convey how your product or service will make a consumer feel about not only your specific service or item, but your overall brand image.

Through appropriate language, ESPs influence a consumer's perception of your marketing proposition and so beliefs regarding the meaning of your marketing message.

ESPs loosely remind me of something which psychologists call Rational Emotive Behaviour Therapy (REBT). REBT states that sometimes people don't just become upset by unfortunate events, but base feelings on their views of truth through their understanding about their role in the world and its relationship to them.

With REBT, people are taught to adapt those views by learning the A-B-C-model of psychological disturbance and change, which states that it normally is not just an A (adversity or activating event) that contributes to disturbed emotional and behavioural Cs (consequences), but also what people B (believe) about the A (adversity).

ESPs pivot around a consumer's beliefs. The *activating* event is the set of circumstances that leads them to your product or service. The *belief* is what they infer from your marketing message. The *consequences* are what they do and feel about their actions, based on their beliefs of what such actions say to them not just about what they think about your organization but their perceived sense of worth, value and self-esteem through buying your product or service.

Related to this is something called **cognitive dissonance**. This is when, despite what others may say, consumers justify purchases, often by dwelling on the value of a well-established brand or wishing to be aligned with organizations offering a particular innovative or ethical or price sensitive or premium based vision and social caché, over that of a lesser known or more common brand product or service.

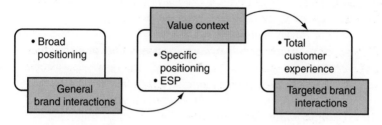

Put it to the test

List the three-level PODs of your car, then list the ESPs for these target audiences.

1   *A busy housewife with kids*
2   *A student*
3   *A harassed marketer.*

ESSENTIALS FROM THIS CHAPTER

▶ *Rather than promoting your USP, consider marketing your POD and ESP.*

▶ *Positioning as a marketing technique doesn't occupy a piece of paper, rather it occupies the minds of consumers.*

▶ *The expanding positioning statement is:*
  ▷ *For [target end user]*
  ▷ *Who wants/needs [persuasive reason to buy or discover more]*
  ▷ *The [product/service name] is a [product/service category]*
  ▷ *That delivers [key benefit – based on your main underlining marketing message]*
  ▷ *Unlike [main competitor]*
  ▷ *The [product/service name] offers [list your three PODs].*

▶ *ESPs convey how your product or service will make a consumer feel about not only your specific service or item, but overall brand image.*

7

....

Image is everything

In this chapter you will learn about:
- *brand types*
- *brand touch points*
- *measuring brands*
- *the Brand Egg*
- *brand presentation*

Does your surname instil a sense of pride? How about individual members of your family? Brothers, sisters, uncles, aunts and so on? When you think about their character and how they represent the family, how do you feel?

Those principles are akin to brand values. Feelings fire up emotions, beliefs and attitudes identifying you with an individual's personality. Such intimacy is essential in marketing. Simply by knowing that a product or service originates from a specific 'brand' name, a consumer has a hunch as to whether or not it is likely to be the sort of thing worth acquiring or investigating further. In other words, it has a good name.

Just as your immediate family unit is probably linked to a parent couple, so many businesses are linked to a parent brand name which may embrace, inspire and drive a group of divisional organizations.

Types of brands

Family brands
These feature trusted company names such as Cadbury, Lever, Heinz, etc. The good name of the family has a 'halo' effect throughout each individual brand – such as Cadbury Dairy Milk or Cadbury Milk Tray. Also known as manufacturer brands, thanks to their consistent brand marketing they act as 'hooks' to draw consumers to retail outlets like supermarkets.

Individual brands
These feature specific brand names (e.g. Rice Krispies, Cheerios, Persil etc.) The great thing about individual brands is that they offer a marketer the chance to build up individual product or service reputations, rather than be dependent on the value of a family brand name. Keep in mind that individual products and services may come and go (through the natural course of their Product Life Cycle), the family master brand, however, goes on ...

Own-label brands
Middlemen or dealers may also put their names to a brand – often referred to as private brands or wholesaler's brands. For instance, a major retailer may include its name on labels (also known as own-label brands), for example Better Buys Baked Beans, Corner Shop Cola etc. When groups of retailers market own labels, the brand is sometimes referred to as a distributor's brand. As Simon Lowden, former Marketing Manager at Pepsi Cola UK told me:

'There will always be a role for cheap brands in a repertoire in terms of branded colas in the UK, people don't tend to be brand loyal, they generally drink by habit and repertoire.'

During the recession of 2009, consumer research amongst a sample of 9,931 UK adults found that one million Britons switched to supermarket own-label brands. Almost three out of four (73 per cent) thrifty Brits opted for supermarket own labels, a figure that tripled from just 25 per cent in 2008.

Much of this increase was attributed to supermarkets increasing their own brand products in a bid to stop consumers switching to cheaper retail chains. Their marketing tactic worked, securing repeat visits from existing customers as well as slowing down the rapid growth of overseas competitors who had entered the British High Street market.

However, it is important that you don't always associate own-label brands with consumers who simply want to save a few pennies on products. For example, it is commonly known that in certain cases, dieters may purchase own-label brands as opposed to mainstream brands. Some may argue that this is simply because psychologically they want to feel deprived of enjoying 'the best'.

Own brands shouldn't be confused with cases in which a retailer not directly associated with a major brand sells it at a discounted price (such as a supermarket selling branded jeans cheaply). In such instances supermarkets are usually allowed to advertise the branded goods as long as the advertisement doesn't seriously damage the reputation of the trade mark.

White-label brands

In this case, the brand owner doesn't actually handle any production process. Instead an outside supplier conducts it. (Richard Branson's Virgin Cola is one such example.)

Just because consumers go for a lesser-known cola, it doesn't necessarily follow that they also opt for other lesser-known brands as well. As you've seen in the section on research, human intellect is far more complicated.

Generic brands

These brands carry no identifiable branding label. For the most part they are very unpopular with the general market consumers. However, they do have a role to play in certain industries and sectors where the content at the right price is worth more than the label on the packaging.

Corporate (umbrella) brands

Many major corporations adopt a single name brand strategy.
This helps with global branding: one name – one trusted source,
throughout the world. Having just one brand name to promote
saves costs and unifies messages. However, if something goes wrong
in one country, thanks to the Internet, the effects can often be 'felt'
throughout every other country where that brand is promoted.

Online brands

In the early days of the dot.com boom, these were rapidly
developed through the Internet. Because the Internet is highly
scalable, both small and international companies compete
equally over the web, which history has shown can lead to small
trader 'bangs' going 'boom' and big corporation 'booms' going
bust. Therefore, making your brand distinctive becomes even
more important. This requires consistent promotion through all
supporting media as well as the web, especially as traditional
webvertising opportunities like banner ads are becoming
increasingly unsuccessful. (See 'Marketing objectives for websites',
page 291.)

Brand extensions

Brands deliver a sense of purpose and value. Interpreting and
conveying those values comes in part through the combination
of a brand's name, terms of business, logo, delivery, packaging
and design. Once consumers are convinced of a brand's sense of
purpose and value and want to continue to be aligned with them,
many brands start to offer variations of products and services
carrying the original brand name. The problem with this is that, in
terms of consistency of value, too many variations (extensions) can
become difficult to manage. Equally consumers can begin to feel
overwhelmed by only being given what appears to be one brand
choice. Worst still, confused by what a brand still means. In turn,
all this may devaluate the brand as it becomes too readily available
and so looses a sense of individuality.

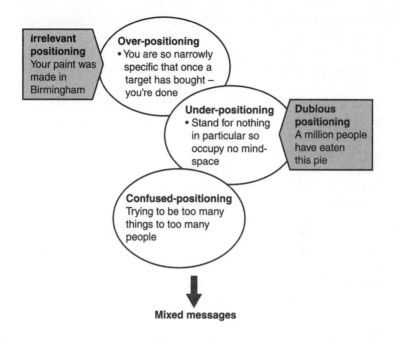

irrelevant positioning
Your paint was made in Birmingham

Over-positioning
- You are so narrowly specific that once a target has bought – you're done

Under-positioning
- Stand for nothing in particular so occupy no mind-space

Dubious positioning
A million people have eaten this pie

Confused-positioning
Trying to be too many things to too many people

Mixed messages

Brand extending, when planned well and implemented professionally can still pay dividends. Chris Holt, the former Head of Design Management at British Airways, takes up the brand extension story:

> Profit is often down to yield. In airlines the bigger yield comes from the front end of the aeroplane. The contribution to the bottom line is much less per passenger in World Traveller cabins at the back than premium ones at the front. So you have to ask yourself how else can we attract more profitable customers whilst keeping them satisfied?
> Part of our marketing strategy was to stretch the brand into an experience beyond just the aircraft seat. After all, the customer encounter of the company isn't just about sitting in an aeroplane, but either side of that. Stretching the brand is about enhancing the travel experience. Whether it's insurance, medical services, ground

transportation, hotels, holidays, theatre tickets, shopping and airport lounges, tailor-made packages for business travellers ... it all counts. As long as the brand extension is directly related to core it is worth exploring.

The beauty of extending international brand values adapting to the needs of localized consumers is that a local division of a conglomerate can nurture poignant, provincial values whilst also gaining international esteem. Moreover, a big international brand name can help local divisions in their regional negotiations to manufacture or produce goods and services. The downside is that without the right kind of brand management, your imaginative creative campaigns may become stifled by restrictions imposed by a head office in another country. This kind of decentralization is typical in a global market. The result is that you spend more time trying to appease HQ marketing departments whilst less time actually getting on with the business of promoting and unifying your brand values and positioning.

A really great brand doesn't initially have to be measured purely in terms of its international standing. It may not be practicable. Brand values relate to how customers distinguish you, your awareness within the market and customer credibility/reliability. Whether yours may not be the final choice, but the most prestigious and so the first name that comes to mind (mind share). This last aspect is the foundation for your long-term branding success, for if you can turn a satisfied customer into a willing advocate for your brand, your acquired values will spread far and wide and as fast as the speed of a customer's recommendation online, in person and by phone. (See also 'Integrated solution providers', page 286.)

Did you know?

A US baby-food manufacturer featured a baby on its African food labels. Sales were low. They didn't realize that in Africa, labels were meant to depict a product's contents.

Many imaginative marketers take advantage from competitive global branding simply through defending their own locally produced products against mega-sized international brand names. In India, for example, Mohun's Corn Flakes re-launched and improved their corn flakes market with notable success in a direct challenge to Kellogg's. Likewise, a locally marketed North Indian fast-food chain enjoyed a 20 per cent increase in sales the year Pizza Hut, McDonald's and Domino's Pizza entered the Indian market.

Brands – bigger and better

With so much at stake, marketing a brand name and so explaining its set of perceived values can be of equal, if not greater, importance as marketing a specific material product or service. In fact, it is safe to say that in marketing terms values may be equal, but nothing is bigger or better than your brand.

The opportunities to communicate your brand values are endless. So called, 'brand touch points' give you the chance to explain and extol your brand every time you 'touch' your consumer.

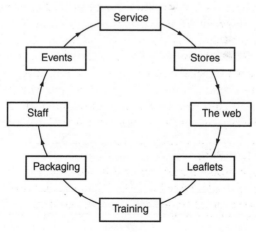

Typical brand touch points.

Brands are as difficult to measure as reputations. What may be austere to one audience may appear as responsible to another. Price can help position a brand as being either cheap and cheerful or only for the select few.

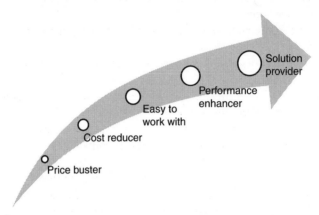

One thing is certain; all brand reputations must be consistent and understood.

Measuring brands

Traditionally people assessed brands like this:

Today considerations include:

- **Intangible earnings** *such as the extra amount people are prepared to pay for a product or service coming from a reputable source.*
- **Leadership** *such as demonstrating innovative design or tackling environmental issues.*
- **Clarity of positioning** *such as how a consistent message remains clear, brief and useful.*
- **Product delivery** *such as how quickly an order is processed and delivered via the web.*
- **Business performance** *such as how financially successful a business becomes and remains within its sector.*

Brand marketing is much more intricate than simply identifying a commercial name or putting a logo on a piece of packaging. It's a bit like an impressive magic trick in that it's not just what you see that fills you with awe but what you can't see. But imagine and associate with the entire experience. Based on the power and conviction of a mission statement, (see 'Mission statement', page 56) brand marketing touches every facet of the marketing mix. It can be recognized and so measured in the congruity of an overall marketing communication plan from the shape of packaging to the design of a website, the style of an advertisement, its design, packaging, targeting and copywriting.

___

Forget brand promise – think 'Brand-Action'

From airlines to corner shops, if your brand promises an ideal, pursue it rather than pay it lip-service. If not you'll alienate the very target audience your brand is trying to attract. People identify with brands on distinctive levels (rather like Maslow's Pyramid – see page 122.)

LEVEL ONE – MY BRAND IS IRRESISTIBLE

I once visited a church in Bethlehem, Israel. Each of its many stained-glass windows featured a picture of Christ as interpreted by individual countries. There were Afro-deities, Asian deities, Western deities ... Looking around I saw that specific portrayals of Christ had particular effects on visitors. One spurred a tourist to identify Christ with very 'mortal' attributes. Another had tears running down her face as she obviously felt Christ's 'divinity'.

Brands, too, should provoke people to recognize evocative, instinctively exceptional qualities that they would want others to recognize admirably in them.

LEVEL TWO – MY BRAND ACHIEVES ALL THIS ...

At an early stage, people want to know how well an individual, family or umbrella brand of products/services performs. How is the foundation brand supported and who developed it? This is often expressed by encapsulating a brand's benefit in a single practical statement. This statement may not be especially distinctive from that of a competitor. However, it is emphatically distinguishable within a broad marketplace.

Examples:

- ▶ *'Apple computers are stylish, fast and efficient.'*
- ▶ *'British Telecom[BT] lets people communicate.'*
- ▶ *'Dell Computers are tailored to your needs.'*

LEVEL THREE – MY BRAND IS DIFFERENT

If taken out of context, this level is the hardest to communicate. However, once it has the support of the other two, it becomes immensely potent and socially, if not secularly, politically and culturally enlightening. These levels of brand marketing are typically interpreted through music, depiction of group values (such as professional, ideological, family, ethnic, sexual or religious) as well as with emotive photography and illustration.

REBEL-REBEL

With all the 'legs' of your brand standing firmly, your brand attracts customer loyalty as consumers return time and time again to become clients. Brand loyalty relies on a core set of strengths and values that never change. These often include quality, people, service, distribution and customer care.

This said, if your brand is to be perceived as being 'trendy', after a while of continuous exposure it can, if not handled properly, start to be regarded as part of the establishment rather than something continuously and refreshingly alive. Which is why drawing on the brand's core strengths and beliefs, it's values adapt to market needs. This would typically apply to fashion and music businesses.

Functional value	Reflecting the utility a consumer perceives from a brand's functional capability, e.g. BMW engineering.
Social value	Representing the utility a consumer perceives through the brand being associated with a particular social group, e.g. drinks market.
Emotional value	The utility a consumer perceives from the brand's ability to evoke particular feelings, e.g. Chanel perfume.
Epistemic value	The utility a consumer perceives when trying a new brand mainly to satisfy their curiosity, e.g. trying out a new chocolate bar.
Conditional value	Reflects the perceived utility from a brand in a specific situation, e.g. ice-cream at home (functional) vs. ice-cream at a cinema (part of the experience).

It could also apply to David and Goliath companies (David initially representing the 'new kid' on the block – such as Richard Branson,

Bill Gates, etc., whilst 'Goliath' is the aged corporate giant) or even political parties promising a lot but delivering a little. Even if your brand is not meant to be valued in those terms, you should still be wary that consumers as a whole are increasingly sophisticated. Therefore, your brand has to be consistently relevant for a target audience.

Brands which fall in this category include rebel brands promoted as anti-establishment.

Put it to the test
What is the difference between an own-label and a family brand?

The brand egg

You may like to think of brands in terms of an egg. The yolk represents the brand's core strengths, whilst the white represents its supporting values and the shell the external, thereby 'first sight', contemporary perceptions.

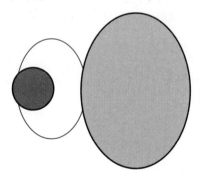

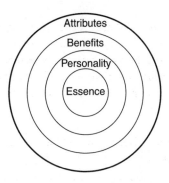

The extended brand egg.

Here the 'yolk' is the essence, the core values of the brand. Next comes the 'white' in the form of the brand personality, for example, 'professional' or 'useful'. The benefits summarize the essence and personality. The attributes are the outward manifestations of a brand (the 'shell') such as website design or leaflet design – all reflecting the brand as a whole.

Other variations on the brand egg include the brand triangle in which the base forms the foundation of the brand, the middle is divided into segments supporting the basic values and the tip, like an aerial, transmits the most accessible values and features to a target audience.

A further variation is the brand volcano. Here each level of a brand's heritage solidifies over time so re-enforcing and enriching its heritage and value.

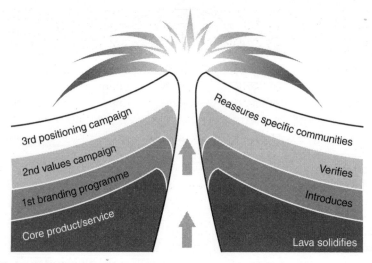

The brand positioning volcano.

Every person has a personality that brings the individual to life. That personality is unique to that person. Think of this person's total self as a 'brand', you would take into consideration his personality and the way he presents himself. This value has an invisible inheritance, being whatever spiritual or emotional aspects that make up the 'brand'. Likewise, a major brand enjoys a singular personality enhanced by the additional features making up the brand 'shell'. Your personal 'shell' includes your voice, hairstyle, choice of clothes and personality. The added features – the equivalent of how you wear your hair, your style of shirt, spectacles, tie and so forth – help people determine how the outer shell reflects the inner man.

A corporation of any kind and size is a bit like that. You have the spiritual and emotional relationship with the brand. Then there are the specific products or services and the way in which they are packaged and presented.

Brand extent	Brand magnitude	Brand sway	Brand affinity	Brand sensitivity
Development into new pastures as well as brand stretching into related product/ service areas without compromising the core potency of a brand's original set of values.	Supremacy in terms of esteem rather than purely apportion within a market sector.	The relative significance of personal association the brand attracts from various segments of the market, including the internal market (employees and share-holders).	The allegiance and admiration the brand attracts from existing as well as potential customers.	The level of emotions evoked by the brand.

Did you know?

Brand management, as a marketing system, was introduced by Proctor and Gamble in the 1930s.

ESSENTIALS FROM THIS CHAPTER

▶ *Brand values fire-up emotions, beliefs and attitudes.*

▶ *Types of brand are:*
   ▷ **Family brands** – *feature trusted company names.*
   ▷ **Individual brands** – *feature specific brand names.*
   ▷ **Own-label brands** – *middlemen or dealers may also put their names to a brand – often referred to as private brands or wholesaler's brands.*
   ▷ **White-label brand owners** – *do not handle any production process. Instead an outside supplier conducts it.*
   ▷ **Generic brands** – *carry no identifiable branding label.*
   ▷ **Corporate (umbrella) brands** – *adopt a single name brand strategy.*

▶ *Brand touch points give you the chance to explain and extol your brand every time you 'touch' your consumer.*

▶ *Brand valuation can take into account:*
   ▷ **Intangible earnings** – *such as the extra amount people are prepared to pay for a product or service coming from a reputable source.*
   ▷ **Leadership** – *such as demonstrating innovative design or tackling environmental issues.*
   ▷ **Clarity of positioning** – *such as how a consistent message remains clear, brief and useful.*
   ▷ **Product delivery** – *such as how quickly an order is processed and delivered via the web.*
   ▷ **Business performance** – *such as how financially successful a business becomes and remains within its sector.*

▶ *In the 'brand egg': the yolk represents the brand's core strengths, while the white represents its supporting values and the shell the external, thereby 'first sight', contemporary perceptions.*

8

Branding in action

In this chapter you will learn about:
- *the stories behind two brands distilling national pride*
- *brand terms*

What do the late Diana, Princess of Wales, Nike shoes, British Airways, Pepsi Cola and an eighteenth-century French prisoner all have in common? From a marketing perspective they all possess a powerful feature – their perceived worth.

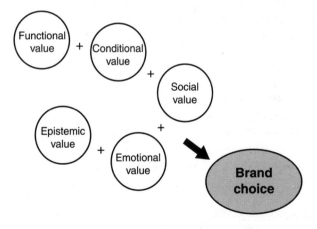

Nike, in contrast to its fame, hardly owns any tangible assets like manufacturing equipment. Yet its brand is one of the most valued across the globe and is strongly associated with an individual's potential to win. (The company's slogan is 'Just Do It'.)

British Airways is internationally recognized as a global ambassador for the UK.

Pepsi Cola is a globally respected brand which aligns itself with popular music and therefore youth culture. This creates a target market affinity.

The youth market drinks more cola than any other section of the market. They drink more carbonated drinks per head. (In traditional demographic terms: from the age of 11 through to about 19/20.)

Successful advertising like Levi's might and Nike appeals to a broad age range of people. Dad may wear an own-label tracksuit and want to get the Sunday morning papers. Yet you still have a six-year-old kid demanding expensive Nike trainers for his birthday because they are the trainers to wear. Once you get the youth mind-set, you capture a high ground.

Revolutionizing perceptions

What of that French prisoner? Imagine it is the 1790s. The French aristocracy have kept a group of peasants chained in underground dungeons. The prisoners see only shadows. After a while, those shadows shape their perception of the world. Then, a prisoner escapes and steps out into the colourful daylight. He sees the world has texture and shade providing new meaning to him. The prisoner returns to liberate the others. His eyes remain dazzled by natural light. Upon seeing his bewildered expression, the other prisoners mistake his ranting about a new outlook on life for lunacy. So it is that, in marketing, perceptions have to be shaped through a realistic communications plan in a way that is as clear as daylight even for those who see nothing but shadows.

Diana – a legacy of hope

Years after her death Diana, Princess of Wales' name is still perceived as having a humane quality. As a universally adapted icon it is so powerful and, from a branding perspective, valuable that marketers fall over one another to capitalize upon its prestige.

Within the first six months of her tragic death in August 1997, Diana memorabilia had netted over £100 million ($146 million) worth of business for companies. To protect her image and name, the Princess of Wales Memorial Fund was created and the official 'Diana' logo registered. Businesses featuring the logo could thereby add a sense of solemnity and authenticity to their product. The logo featured three important attractive marketing devices:

- ▶ *Diana's personal signature.*
- ▶ *Diana's personal favourite colour – purple.*
- ▶ *'Official' support through the caption: 'Princess of Wales Memorial Fund'.*

Just as people felt they 'knew' Diana in life, so, through the combination of the three powerful marketing logo devices, it was intended that they would be drawn closer to her in memory.

Diana's good name and memory became in danger of being devalued by the market. For example, tacky T-shirts were sold with a legend that read: 'Born a princess, died a saint, now an angel.' Mintel research, reported in the trade magazine *Marketing Week*, revealed that most people (60 per cent out of a total of 1,492 adults questioned) felt that companies were 'cynically cashing in on public sympathy through cause-related marketing'. Only weeks after her death, beads were torn from her dresses and sold as earrings at £1,000 a pair. (It is interesting to note that years later, following the tragic events in New York on '9/11', the sales of T-shirts showing the devastated 'ground zero' of the World Trade Center and the slogan 'lest we forget' were considered by many US citizens as 'touching' rather than 'tacky' – a clear example of how market perceptions change according to local perceptions.)

Outstanding brand names become enduring cultural icons which are emulated the world over. In Diana's case her 'brand' paraphernalia included the West African Togo Republic selling special edition stamps for the equivalent of two months' salary in that country. Tourist shops sold everything from Diana mugs and spoons, to Diana medals and plates, and so on. Even the Internet drew capital from the rogue Diana industry through a site featuring a computer game based on Diana's fatal road accident with players 'driving' a Mercedes at high speed while being chased by paparazzi on motorbikes.

Which is why any good name worth valuing is also worth protecting. Too many 'extensions' of a brand can actually do more harm than good. You must ask yourself whether it is better to plaster a brand name everywhere, from watches to soap, or protect a valued name, allowing it to be used only in context.

Just prior to Diana's death, Prime Minister Tony Blair adapted a slogan first heard in 1967 in a song by the Bonzo Dog Doo Dah Band. The slogan reappeared in the mid-1990s as a registered trade mark for one of Ben & Jerry's™ ice-creams (vanilla with strawberries and chocolate-covered shortbread). Third time round the slogan was meant to rebrand Great Britain as über trendy: 'Cool Britannia'.

Government spin-doctors ensured that the Prime Minister and his colleagues were seen with rock stars and celebrities including the newly formed, in 1994, Spice Girls. Like all branding exercises,

'Cool Britannia' needed substance. Things started going wrong when in a Brits™ pop music ceremony, former Cabinet minister, John Prescott, had a glass of water thrown over his head by a member of the pop group – Chumbawamba. The point being that it wasn't enough to talk about being 'cool' – it had to be demonstrated. (On the night of the awards, rather than pay lip-service towards being 'cool' for the benefit of a well-healed audience, the pop group The Verve preferred to play a free concert for the homeless.)

Flying high and proud?

Chris Holt, formerly from British Airways, told me the classic tale of how and why the airline once developed what turned out to be a distinctive corporate branding plan riddled with controversy.

> **British Airways' branding has always meant to be visual manifestation of the company's personality. It's based on what we referred to as the Masterbrand Repositioning Programme. The project was primarily aimed at defining and, if necessary, repositioning the masterbrand of British Airways.**
> **BA carried out research amongst design professionals in the UK as well as customers around the world. BA set about the task of carrying out a visual audit and visual update in key global places to see to what extent our identity was fit for its present as well as future purpose. Initially, BA approached 50 design consultancies, then whittled them down to four. The brief was considerably detailed and quite extensive. They all had the same period of time to respond as well as the same sort of funding. One consultancy at the time, Interbrand Newell and Sorrell, aimed to interpret the airline as being both global and caring in a way appreciated internationally by local communities. This was fundamental to our Masterbrand Repositioning Programme.**
> **Global as well as caring can appear paradoxical in that**

**often the larger the corporation the more impersonal
it can seem to potential customers. British Airways
operates on a global stage. BA was born, bred and based
in Britain, yet dealt with a diverse and rich community of
people from all over the world.
Over the centuries, Britain has been an adventurous
nation. Particularly in the areas of exploration and
world trade. Similarly, instead of being a British airline
with global operations, British Airways had become a
world airline whose headquarters is in Britain, serving a
community of world citizens.**

The identity was meant to capture the spirit of a business
passionately committed to serving customers and linking diverse
communities of the world. The tails on most of the aircraft
(excluding Concorde – the flagship) carried versions of specially
commissioned works of arts and crafts from communities around
the world. The concept was based on the principle that since
mankind could make images in the sand, walls or caves, he has
created likenesses representing the lifestyle in the community.
In other words, British Airways was engaged in the business of
bringing people together from all over the world.

Simon Jones, at the time Managing Director of Interbrand Newell
and Sorrell, took up the story:

**British Airways' concept of world citizenship
was visualized through a series of world images
commissioned from international artists from different
communities. The images are incorporated deeply
throughout the airline's brand communications. In this
way, rather than being a superficial embodiment of
world citizenship within a global community, the brand
philosophy enriched every aspect of design from ticketing
to signage, check-in desks, baggage labels, in-flight food
presentation ... in fact, each instance that the public came
into contact with the brand.**

British Airways unveiled its new corporate image on 10 June 1997. Its previous identity, designed by Landor Associates, dated back to 1984. It featured a harder-edged speedwing. The new colours fortified their reputation for safety, security and professionalism – all epitomized in the airline's British roots. Back to Chris Holt:

Brand design should reflect both a company's style and personality. It shouldn't be a substitute for it, rather a mirror image. From a branding perspective, there's no point saying one thing in your visual identity and through your advertising, PR and communication if your reality isn't matched.

In other globalization terms relating to the brand, we discovered that more people are living longer with more disposable income. They travel further for leisure as well as for business purposes. Competition was tougher equally at the expensive, medium and cheaper end of the market. It was vital that British Airways was perceived as being both Global and Caring and thus the first choice airline all around the world.

By really understanding our customers' requirements, we make our airline appealing. On Japanese routes, we are sensitive to cultural needs, speak Japanese, offer superb Japanese food, provide interesting Japanese in-flight magazines and in-flight entertainment that is not simply subtitled.

Clearly, for British Airways, design played a vital role in their universal branding. It still plays a central role within your own marketing communications mix.

ESSENTIALS FOR THIS CHAPTER

BRAND TERM DEFINITIONS

Brand Name, term and/or design which identifies the products or services of one or a group of providers, and differentiates them from those of competitors.

Brand attributes The functional and emotional associations appointed to a brand by everyone it comes in contact with.

Brand audit: Brand assessment to gauge the strength of the brand, uncover its sources of equity and suggest ways to improve and leverage that value.

Brand awareness An evaluation of marketing communications effectiveness as the proportion of target customers with prior knowledge of the brand. It is measured by two distinct measures; brand recognition and brand recall.

Brand champion Internal and external advocates who spread the brand vision, brand values and cultivate the brand in an organization.

Brand culture A sturdy brand culture is the reflection of management behaviour and everyday working practices of the organization which owns the brand.

Brand equity Brand equity is measured across different aspects including: brand awareness, brand loyalty, perceived quality, brand associations etc.

Brand equity strategy The plan and objectives needed to build and maintain a strong brand equity across a company's portfolio of different brands.

Brand essence A brand essence comprises pert phrases that capture the core spirit and values of a brand.

Branding excellence An indicator of brand strength as well as measure of an organization's brand leadership capabilities. A strong brand is epitomized by a meaningful brand promise and admired brand delivery.

Brand expansion The introduction of a brand to a wider group of customers, geographic areas or sectors.

Brand extension The application of a brand beyond its initial range of products, or outside of its category.

Brand guidelines The internal regulations designed to instruct, validate and inspire all involved in building and maintaining stalwart brands.

Brand identity The distinctive set of practical and intellectual associations the brand aspires to generate or maintain.

Brand image The characteristic associations within the minds of target customers that embody what the brand currently stands for and implies as well as what it promises to consistently deliver for customers.

Brand loyalty The affinity a brand creates with its public, measured by considerations such as repeat purchase behaviour and price sensitivity.

Brand management The process of managing an organization's brand or portfolio of brands to maintain, increase and justify long-term brand equity and subsequent financial value.

Brand mapping A research technique to identify, visualize and assess the core positioning of a brand compared to competing brands.

Brand personality The perceived brand image or identity expressed in terms of human characteristics and traits.

Brand positioning The highly focused (through clear and consistent messages) mental space which a brand occupies in the mind of the target audience.

Brand positioning statement A guiding set of directions explaining a company's marketing communications strategies, programmes and tactics, which set it apart from the competition. This asserts its meaning in the mind of everyone concerned with the brand.

Brand power The dominance held by a brand within its product or service sector and category.

Brand recall The customers' ability to recall a brand when given the product category but no mention of the brand name (also referred to as spontaneous or unaided awareness).

Brand recognition The customers' ability to confirm prior knowledge of a brand when shown or asked unequivocally about the brand (also referred to as aided or prompted awareness).

Brand relevance The alignment of a brand, its attributes, identity and personality against the desires and needs of a target audience.

Brand revitalization A brand revitalization strategy recaptures lost sources of brand equity by establishing new sources of brand equity for the brand or the brand portfolio.

Brand slogan/brand tagline A relevant and memorable phrase capturing the spirit and meaning of a brand.

Brand strategy The long-term plans devised to create enduring brand equity.

Brand tribe A formal or informal group of consumers who are passionate, concerned and loyal to a brand or a portfolio of brands.

Brand value The financial return derived from loyal target audiences willing to pay a premium for the brand or prepared to continue to invest in a brand, despite competitive marketing to encourage them otherwise.

Brand value proposition The rationale (actual and intangible attributes) for choosing one brand choice against another.

9

Roots of some of the world's greatest classic brands

In this chapter you'll learn about the origins of some of the world's best-known and loved brands.

(All trademarks gratefully acknowledged)			
Brand name	**Year of origin**	**Place and origin – other details**	**Founder(s)**
Abbey	1944	Merger between the National Abbey Road Building Society (established 1894) and the National Building Society. (Now part of the Santander Group.)	
Adidas	1920s	Named after founder of sportswear company. (Umbro are the distributors – see below.) In 1997 company acquired French sports company Salomon SA. Now called Adidas–Salomon.	Adolf (Adi) Dassler

Brand name	Year of origin	Place and origin – other details	Founder(s)
Andrex	1945 Changed to Andrex in 1954	Manufactured in St Andrews Road, Walthamstow, London – named after a church. X = excellent or refers to texture.	Merger between Bowater and Scott Paper Company
Aspirin	1899	Derived from Greek by C. Witthauer (scientist) – full name *Aceylirte Spirsäure* (acetylated spiraeic acid + suffix 'in').	Bayer
Babycham	1949	From 'baby chamois'.	Francis Showering (of Showering brothers)
Bic	Bic Crystal, introduced to UK in 1958	Named after Marcel Bich.	The Bich Brothers, inventors of the disposable pen
Birds Eye	1915	Legend has it that the name referred to ancestral court nobleman named Bird's Eye by a queen after he shot a hawk through the eye with an arrow. Latterly and more commonly accredited to Bob Birdseye, New York based fur trader who originated frozen food process.	Clarence (Bob) Birdseye.

(Contd)

Brand name	Year of origin	Place and origin – other details	Founder(s)
Bisto	1910	Possible variation on anagram for Browns, Seasons, Thickens, in One.	Created by RHM Foods
Bovril	First sales 1886–7	Latin 'mix' of 'Bos', short for *bovis* ('ox') and *vril* (from Lord Lytton's novel *The Coming Race*). Bovril AKA Johnston's Fluid Beef. (N.B: 1930s brothels were also known as Bovrils.)	John Lawson Johnston
Brook Bond	1869	Named after tea merchant, Arthur Brook	Alas, no 'secret' Mr Bond.
C&A Modes	1841	Dutch company, initially called Canda (still used) Clemens then Cyamodes, then C&A.	Founded by Clemens and August Brenninkmeyer.
Cadbury	1824 First factory 1831	Birmingham	John Cadbury – highly respected Quaker
Chase Manhattan	1955	Merger between Banks of Manhattan and Chase National Bank of the City of New York.	'Chase' named after US lawyer and statesman Salmon Portland Chase.
Coca-Cola	1886	Named by the druggist, Dr John S. Pemberton's bookkeeper – Frank Robinson. Based on cola nut and coca leaves. Coca-Cola	Created by Dr Pemberton as a brain tonic. First produced in a three-legged pot in his back. (Initially following

Brand name	Year of origin	Place and origin – other details	Founder(s)
		trademark was registered in 1893. John Pemberton sold Coca-Cola in 1888 for $2,300.	his first advertisement only 13 drinks a day for eight months were sold.)
Dr Martens	1947 – first air-cushioned soles produced. UK production started 1960.	Following a skiing accident (1945) Dr Maertens developed an air-cushioned sole to help to relieve discomfort.	Orthopaedic surgeon Dr Klaus Maertens and Herbert Flunk – engineer.
Disprin	Registered 1944	Cross between 'dissolvable' and 'aspirin'.	Registered by Roy Vickers of Liverpool
El Al	1948	Established by Israel's David Remez first minister of transport. Taken from Hebrew phrase in Hosea 11,7. 'Through them to the most High.'	David Remez
Esso	Origins 1888. Named assumed 1973	Abbreviation of Standard Oil company of New Jersey, set up in 1888. (*Esso* in Italian means 'It'. *Essence* in French means – petrol.)	Now owned in the UK by Exxon. Originally, set up by Rockefeller.
Fanta	World War II	From Fantasie (developed by Coca-Cola during World War II)	Coca-Cola

(Contd)

Brand name	Year of origin	Place and origin – other details	Founder(s)
Frisbee	1957	From baking tins thrown as a game at Frisbie Bakery, Connecticut.	Fred Morriso
Gillette	Original idea 1895. Production 1903	Dull shaving blades needed expert sharpening, a new method was needed. Razor perfected by William E. Nickerson. (Could this be where the phrase 'nick yourself shaving' derives?)	Idea adapted and improved by then Gillette Safety Razor Company.
Golden Wonder	1947	Probably inspired by a variety of potato – although it was unsuitable for making chips.	William Alexander
Gossard	1901. First office 1921. First factory 1926.	Undergarments originally inspired by figure of Sarah Bernhardt, actress.	Henry Williamson Gossard
Heinz	1876 (F&J Heinz Company.) 'F' referred to cousin Frederick) HJ Heinz Company founded in 1888	Named after Henry Heinz (born 1844). Slogan '57 varieties' inspired by advert on New York railway which read: '21 Styles of Shoes'. Heinz had over 60 products but liked the number, 57.	HJ Heinz Henry and his brother, John.
Hoover	1908	Vacuum cleaner built by J. Murray Spangler. Marketed by William Hoover. (First Hoovers sold for $70.)	William Hoover. (British vacuum cleaner invented by H. Cecil Booth.)

Brand name	Year of origin	Place and origin – other details	Founder(s)
Hovis	1890 (first in shops)	S Fitton & Son of Macclesfield held a competition to name their bread. A student, Herbert Grimes won. Name was based on hominis vis – Latin for 'the strength of a man/ quantity of men'.	Original flour process was invented by Richard Smith. (Smith's Patent Germ Flour).
Imperial Leather	1938	Based on a perfume with the scent of leather (1780s). The perfume was called Eau de Cologne Imperial Leather Russe.	Mr Cusson of Cussons, Sons and Co.
Jaguar	1935	Originally appeared as SS Jaguar (Swallow Sidecar Co. owned by William Lyons). Mr Lyons felt a Jaguar mirrored his car's design and performance. SS was dropped because of the resemblance to the SS Nazi party. (In 2008 Ford sold Jaguar and Land Rover to Indian company Tata.)	William Lyons
Jell-O	First patented in 1845. Mass produced in 1897	Mary Wait, wife of cough medicine manufacturer, John, invented the term for her spouse's gelatine desert.	Pearl and Mary Wait

(Contd)

Brand name	Year of origin	Place and origin – other details	Founder(s)
Johnson & Johnson	1885	Inspired by the surgeon Sir Joseph Lister who identified airborne germs. Robert, brother of James Wood Johnson decided to manufacture prepared sterile surgical dressing. In 1890 in addition to gauze dressings, they sent a tin of Italian talc to a doctor's patient who complained of a skin rash. This was the start of their famous powdered product.	Robert and James Wood Johnson
Kellogg's	1866 – idea 1906 – full production	Wife of Seventh Day Adventist Church minister Dr John Harvey Kellogg suggested a diet to aid 'right living' should be based on foods of vegetable and nut origin. William manufactured a toasted flake of maize to replace a heavy breakfast meal (1876). Battle Creek Toasted Corn Flake Company (1906) was founded. To distinguish his brand, William added his signature to each pack.	William Keith and Dr John Harvey Kellogg
Kodak	1888	George Eastman wanted to simplify photography.	George Eastman

Brand name	Year of origin	Place and origin – other details	Founder(s)
		He developed a camera for the general public. He wrote 'I knew a trade name must be short, vigorous, incapable of being misspelled... The letter 'K' had been a favourite with me... It became a question of trying out a great number of combinations of letters that made words starting and ending with 'K'... Kodak was the result.'	
Lego	Introduced as 'familiar brick' in 1950s. Previously general wooden toys, 1930s.	Ole Kirk Christiansen, a carpenter, made wooden toys. After World War II, his son, Gotfred, recognized marketable value from a connectable brick. The rest is history. *Leg godt* in Danish means 'play well'.	Ole Kirk Christiansen
Lucozade	1930s	From 'glucose' and 'ade'– as in cherryade, lemonade. The drink was originally developed by a chemist for his jaundiced daughter. To make it taste sweeter he added orange and lemon oils.	William H. Hunter

(Contd)

Brand name	Year of origin	Place and origin – other details	Founder(s)
Marmite	1920	From French name for stew pot (similar to the shape of the jar). *Oxford Dictionary of Modern English c.* 1930s –'An extract from fresh brewers' yeast, rich in vitamin B complex. Used for culinary purposes, e.g. making soups, etc., and also medicinally.'	Justus Liebig
Mars	*c.* 1921 Milky Way bar in USA – MARS outside USA.	Franklin C. Mars sold candy from 1902. His son Forrest E. Mars emigrated to the UK in 1932 and introduced the MARS recipe to the English. Originally made by hand, Mars bars sold for 2d each. Milky Way followed in 1935 and then Malteesers.	Franklin C. Mars/ Forrest E. Mars
Max Factor	1909	The family business, Max Factor & Co. was formed in 1909, although earlier, Max Fax Snr, a Polish make-up artist opened a perfume, make-up and hair goods concession at the St Louis World's Fair. Son Max created the first make-up for the film industry and then in 1916 broadened his market to the general public.	Max Factor (Jr)

Brand name	Year of origin	Place and origin – other details	Founder(s)
Nabisco	1898 Registered 1901	National Biscuit Company (Acronym)	
Nescafé	1938	A combination of the Nestlé manufacturer's name – Nestlé– and the French word for coffee *café*.	Named after Henri Nestlé in Vevey, Switzerland.
Ovaltine	1904	Originally called Ovolmaltine (from the Latin *ovum* for 'egg' plus 'malt' and the suffix '-ine'.	Swiss chemist, Dr George Wander
Oxo	1899	From 'ox' plus the suffix '-o'. The product was a refinement of Liebig's (see Marmite) 'Extract of Meat'.	
Pepsi Cola	1898	Originally marketed as an elixir to relieve dyspepsia.	Caleb D. Bradham Ronchetti
Persil	1907 Germany 1909 UK	French = 'parsley'. A sprig of parsley was featured as a trade mark by a Frenchman who added bleach to soap. Also: PERborate and SILicate – two ingredients originally included in the product.	Ronchetti
Pretty Polly	1920	Hibbert and Buckland (manufacturers of PP) acquired the name from a wholesaler who	

(Contd)

Brand name	Year of origin	Place and origin – other details	Founder(s)
		originally took the name from a horse called Pretty Polly which had won him a fortune. His daughter told him that the name brought success.	
Quaker Oats	1877	Two versions – you choose! **1** The founder of an American Milling company wanted a name for his product. He chose Quaker from a dictionary as the religious order shared many qualities of oatmeal – strength, honesty, purity, manliness. **2** The founder's partner, William Heston, was inspired by a picture of William Penn, an English Quaker.	Henry D. Seymour William Heston
Racal	1951	Combination of names of partners who founded the company.	Sir Raymond Brown G. Calder Cunningham
Revlon	1932	From the founder of the company who added an 'L', in honour of one of his partners, Charles Lachman.	Charles Revson (One of their products is called, 'Charlie')
Ribena	1930s	Latin botanical name for blackcurrants is *Ribesnigrum*.	H.W. Carter and Co.

Brand name	Year of origin	Place and origin – other details	Founder(s)
Sellotape	1937	Based on a trade name, 'Cellophane' which is the film used in Sellotape.	
Shell	1897... but its roots...	Marcus Samuel had a curio shop in London's East End. His children used to stick sea shells to empty lunch boxes. Each box was named after a resort. He sold the boxes and then offered customers imported, elaborate shell boxes. His shop was known as the Shell Shop. By 1830 he had nurtured an international business in oriental curios. He found a demand for barrelled kerosene at which stage (1897) the international business became Shell Transport and Trading Co. led by his son.	Marcus Samuel
Typhoo	1863	A Birmingham grocer dreamt up the name for his tea because it sounded oriental 'Typhoon' and Tea or Tips made it alliterative.	John Sumner
Toyota	1930s	A Japanese inventor gave his son, who was building a motor car, a	Sakichi Toyoda/ Kiichiro Toyoda

(Contd)

Brand name	Year of origin	Place and origin – other details	Founder(s)
		patent for an automatic loom designed for a Lancashire weaving company (1929). Being superstitious the family changed the penultimate letter to T since the original TOYODA required ten Japanese letters, TOYOTA only eight which is a lucky number in Japan.	
Umbro	1920s	After BROthers Harold and Wallace HUMphreys (Umbro distributes Adidas, see above).	H. Humphreys W. Humphreys
Unilever	1930	From a merger of Margarine Unie, Margarine Union and Lever Brothers.	William Heskith and then Viscount Leverhulme and James Darcy Lever founded the English firm, Lever Brothers
Vauxhall	1903	First car produced in Vauxhall South London where, in 1857, a Scottish engineer founded the Vauxhall Ironworks.	
Virgin	1970	Name typified the Indie Culture of the 1970s. Plus it entered a relatively 'virgin field' type of approach to business. Richard Branson's first business	Richard Branson

Brand name	Year of origin	Place and origin – other details	Founder(s)
		venture was in 1968 when he published the Student Magazine. Virgin Mail order started to operate from 1970 and the first Virgin record shop opened in 1971. Virgin Music Publishing started in 1973. (It is thought that Virgin Records may have alternatively been planned to be called 'Slipped Disc'.)	
Walls	1922	Named after founder Thomas Wall whose clerk first suggested the concept of ice-cream in 1913. Wall's brother Fred came up with the idea to sell ice-creams from a tricycle ridden around the streets of West London. 'Stop me and buy one' became one of the twentieth century's most enduring phrases.	
Wimpy	1954	After the cartoon character Wimpy (featured in Popeye) who adored hamburgers. In 1977, the business was acquired by United Biscuits. In 1989,	

(Contd)

Brand name	Year of origin	Place and origin – other details	Founder(s)
		it was sold to Grand Metropolitan (Diageo). Grand Metropolitan had acquired Burger King the previous year and they began to convert the 'counter service' restaurants to Burger King restaurants. In 1990, the remaining 'table service' restaurants were purchased by a management buy-out backed by 3i. A second management buy-out occurred in 2002.	
Xerox	Process invented 1937 Xeroxgraphy – popular use 1948	From Greek for 'dry' as xeroxgraphy doesn't use any liquids.	Chester Charlton
Yale	Originally patented 1844 Improved and patented 1861–5	After maker – Yale	Linus Yale

Did you know?

The famous 'Marlboro man' was invented in the 1960s. Originally, the company was British with a shop in Bond Street, London. The name, 'Marlborough' had an aristocratic connotation. In the beginning, the cigarette – then with a red tip, was aimed at women.

ESSENTIALS FROM THIS CHAPTER

▶ *Some of the greatest brand names in the world had humble beginnings.*

▶ *To become a lasting brand, it pays to remember that the actual word 'brand' originated in the Old Norse brandr, meaning 'to burn'. Consider also the Old English word firebrand, which was a piece of burning wood or torch. To cause wood to burn, not scold, so that people hold it high as a burning torch, requires combining the humble elements of where a brand started with marketing 'spark'. Only then does a brand offer an enduring beacon that lights the path ahead.*

10

....

Going on face values (marketing design)

In this chapter you will learn about:
- *types of marketing design*
- *the definition of marketing design*
- *design's role in marketing communications*
- *semiotics and design*
- *logo design*
- *web page layouts*
- *how to brief design agencies*
- *the nine printing sins*

Great design includes everything from the mechanisms of a product or service to corporate literature, packaging and even online brand experiences (e-experiences). When carefully implemented, design can also enhance an existing portfolio or fortify your prevailing brand.

Although you can't hold it, you can dream it and through imaginative marketing, you can realize it. It is a matter of understanding what a product or service does and how to convey those features as well as practical and emotive benefits to consumers.

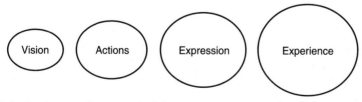

Design steps: from concept to consumer experience.

90% of new product developments which use a professional design consultant make profits and the average pay back period is just 15 months.

Design Council

Design is the shop window, building fixtures and corporate philosophy of your business all rolled into one. Packaging design outwardly declares your brand, product and service values at the Point of Purchase (POP). Long after your sale has been achieved, packaging on a shelf – like a smartly bound book – continues to speak volumes about your brand and its potentials.

Chartered Institute of Marketing definition of design

Planning, decision making and the management of activities which determine the function and characteristics of a finished product or service.

Where does design fit in marketing?

Carefully branded packaging has become an essential marketing tool. In the 1960s when consumers traditionally had more time to linger at supermarket shelves, they would examine each package carefully before making a purchase – so the packaging didn't have to work as hard as it does today.

With less time on everyone's hands, packaging has to convey in milliseconds your brand's total concept. This requires the appropriate use of shape, size, colour, texture and style. These Perceivable Branding Properties (PBPs) unify to make an immediate comforting brand impact which reaches deeply into the subconscious (see also 'Thinking deeper' page 130).

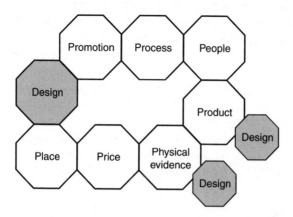

Although humble, one of the first impressions you get of a company is its business card. It tells you about the kind of company and the person's status. In designing the business card it is important to provide a clear understanding of that status. In this way, rather than just being seen as a façade, the values of identity are adopted throughout the company and communicated to current and prospective clientele.

Your business card is just the first step to communicating through design – your company's approach, outlook, values and much more. In highlighting your brand's visually communicated features, even the most modest design modifications help distinguish your brand from your competitors' (D&B – Different & Better).

The House of Marketing – better built by design

In marketing, there are supporting girders of design procedures.

Fashion design. As part of the wider sales promotions' in-store theatre – from the shape of a package to free-gift promotion, wider fashion design embraces clothing, textiles, furniture and car bodies. In the case of clothing, brands may battle for sponsorship space on sporting garments. In catering, again as part of promotional theatre, restaurants often have employees literally wear designs to reflect more than just service on a plate, but with a smile.

Design organization. Rather than being the sole custodian for your design – and concealing its values from the market, aim to be a design champion. (Marketers refer to taking responsibility for a brand as brand stewardship.) If not, what starts as a marketing design masterpiece can end up as a colour-by-numbers exercise with each department arguing over who gets to paint which section. Just as the girders provide support to your overall marketing design structure, so areas of design expertise construct walls embellished with colour and shade.

Graphic design includes corporate identity, television and video titling and form as well as packaging and styling – including brochures, magazines and web design.

Interior design provides visual as well as tactile substance to exhibition stands, events, shops, offices and buildings including special marketing-led structures. (Gillian Thomas, former Director of the Children's Gallery of The Science Museum, in London, is accredited to have said 'By altering the graphic content of an exhibit you could double the number of people who visited it').

During the 1980s, architecture was big, bold and brash, especially commissioned by conglomerates who proudly displayed their wealth peacock-like. Today, successful companies still build big, but not necessarily bold. Many design vast interior open spaces – especially at entrances and receptions. This mimicry of the great outdoors often extends to planting trees indoors (presumably driving a marketing message of openness and confidence to both employees and customers). It is also further indicative of working in a networked age where people can move seating arrangements around different parts of the company – quiet areas, busy areas and so on – all helping to stimulate imaginative thinking.

THE BARBERSHOP POLE SYNDROME

For smaller outlets such as confectioners, hairdressers, restaurants, dry cleaners ... it pays to extend a corporate identity programme to the shop front. Your presence on the high street isn't merely acknowledged, but made exceptional. For example, traditionally, men's hairdressers featured barbershop columns with revolving red spirals outside their establishments. On the upside, the public recognized the service provided. However, this drawing together of barbers into one hair-crops of 'me toos' didn't add any real personality or value to the individual proprietor.

By becoming distinctive you gain the edge over competitive retailers. Then, given a choice based on your total image, the shopper visits your store first. (Designers call this, 'taking ownership' of your identity.)

Product design works hand in glove with the marketing process. The more time invested in perfecting the design of your product, the less is the marketing budget needed to convince the public that they need it.

Branches of semiotics

Chris Holt, formerly from British Airways earlier noted, 'mankind has long created images in the sand, walls or caves'. Today those images have become icons which instantly communicate a brand's value. In many instances, if we want to get more information about something, rather than read about it we'll get the general picture on television then detail from newspapers, radio and of course the web.

Conveying your organization's sense of purpose in design relies on something called, 'semiotics'.

Semiotics rationalizes design into a 'signifier' (the *form* that the sign takes) and the 'signified' (the *concept* it represents). The 'sign' is the whole that results from the association of the signifier with the signified. The relationship between the signifier and the signified is referred to as 'signification'.

Branches of semiotics include:

- **Semantics:** *the relationship of signs to what they represent.*
- **Syntactics (or syntax):** *the formal or structural relations between signs.*
- **Pragmatics:** *the relation of signs to interpreters.*

Company logos combine appropriate image, colours, typeface and size in a visually arresting statement. As products become more alike and competitive, so design makes those products individually attractive.

Your logo mirrors your marketing values. As your company slowly evolves, so your logo may alter slightly over the years until you reach a period of major political or social change – often around ten years. Then it's time to refine the logo dramatically.

All logos need to carry the desired corporate image to the consumer in the shortest possible time. To achieve this consider your logo:

- *font*
- *colours*
- *symbol*

Successful logos look good on huge billboards, websites, gold-embossed door plates, mugs and t-shirts ... Consider the media over which the logo will appear in your design.

Logo characters

Character	Company	Year created
Uncle Sam	Government war bonds	1838
Michelin Man	Michelin tyres	1898
Jolly Green Giant	Green Giant Vegetables	1928
Leo the Lion	MGM Pictures	1928
Mickey Mouse	Walt Disney Co	1928
Tony the Tiger	Kellogg's Frosted Flakes	1951
Columbia Goddess	Columbia Pictures Corp	1961
Ronald McDonald	McDonald's Restaurants	1963
Exxon Tiger	Exxon Oil Company	1964
Pillsbury Doughboy	Assorted Pillsbury Foods	1969
Jeeves	Ask Jeeves	1996

Seven kinds of logos

I have divided marketing logos into seven distinctive categories:

1 *Light-hearted logos reflecting a fresh, youthful approach to business.*
2 *Plain and simple. Just a typeface logo or style of type on a coloured background (usually shaded with the typeface 'reversed out'). It doesn't commit the company to one image or another but conveys efficiency and professionalism.*
3 *Illustrations representing the kind of service the company provides, e.g. a company that fits double glazing could use a picture of a window; a fast-food restaurant serving hamburgers could use a picture of a burger.*

4 *Key letters from a company or a combination of a merged organization. This 'back to basics' approach works if your company doesn't dare take risks with perceptions (many financial institutions opt for this approach).*

5 *Abstract shapes, which appear to be hand finished (giving a personal touch). Examples include abstract designs – often featured by 'trendy' organizations.*

6 *Logos featuring a founder's signature.*

7 *Differentiation. These logos are different. Even the fonts are designed in a custom manner – it could be a completely new font created or tweaking provided to an existing font.*

Your logo type should have its own personality. Once the shape, texture and applications of that imagery have been finalized, you should nurture and keep a logo faithful to your corporate values. Aggressively diluting your image, like irrationally over-stretching your brand name, can lead to confusion and, ultimately, disaster. Family brands, too, have to share some degree of fidelity with the core brand design.

As with the example of Nike, simple, dynamic logos are not simply seen, but taken to consumers' hearts. Usually, to arrive at a final logo, you have to consider scores of choices – often within focus group settings.

Logos are not just painting the face of a company simply for the sake of it – that's too cosmetic. It's making visible by design, the strategy and aspirations of a company. In this way, what is being perceived on the inside of an organization is in line with an external audience's perception.

If you accept that people tend to judge books initially by their jacket rather than take time to glance through their contents, you'll also appreciate why it is important that your logo should be seen as more than just another official mark.

When you design a logo, you are reflecting the personality of an organization. You are peering into the very spirit of an organization and sharing those virtues with a target audience. In this way, an identity is embraced and warmly appreciated as an accessible, relevant icon rather than an inaccessible, aloof corporate figure head.

| Shape | Colour | Content |

Cognition of logos.

Just your type

Every company is absorbed in paperwork. The structuring of forms is another medium of making design responsible to your overall value-added objectives. Organized forms don't merely feature a company badge on every page. (Originally, in the United States, branding was practised by cowboys who 'branded' herds as if badging them.) The style forms should also reflect the company's philosophy towards ideals such as simplicity and professionalism.

Typefaces (collectively known as fonts) provide a further clue to your style and type of company. From **bold** to *italic* to CAPITALS and Upper and lower caps, the form of your typeface hints at the character of your business. The important thing to keep in mind when choosing a typeface is that the style and format of the type on a page or even Internet site, must never obscure your overall message.

There are literally hundreds of thousands of type designs. You can even search the web for typeface based on your handwriting. That said, most organizations stick to either Arial, Helvetica, Times Roman or Garamond.

Kerning reduces the space between letters. This technique is often used by publishers to accommodate words on a page. Professional typographers adjust lettering, so enabling words to create an even pattern.

For example, if you type the word L APTOP, you sometimes get an awkward shape. However, add kerning and, as if by magic, you arrive at a more comfortable and so balanced word – LAPTOP.

Leading originally referred to the lead used to separate lines of text by printing houses. Leaded type is therefore set with leads between the lines. This is because correct leading makes body copy more legible.

Paint me a vision (the use of colour in logos)

Colour doesn't simply make you look different but it makes you and, more importantly, those with whom you come into contact, feel different.

Traditionally, the more 'professional' the company, the more non-partisan the colours. During the 1990s, businesses heavily featured grey or steel colours. Today, companies tend to opt for either vibrant colours like blue on yellow, or more pastel backgrounds, reflecting a gentler yet quietly confident image. It is vital that, when thinking about a colour for inclusion within your identity, that, like corporate designs in general, you don't simply mix and match elements from other companies. Your design must be as individual as your company. The idea is to convey your values rather than hijack someone else's.

Logo colour types

Below are suggested colour types for logos (based on a selection of typical logo types).

Type of product/service	Typical colour
Confident, cool, sincere and fresh Creative, solution provider (One of the most popular options. Works well with complementary colours, especially yellow.)	Light blue
Fresh produce, environmental goods, get-up-and-go products – like invigorating bath oils. (In the Middle East, green often equates to religious symbolism.)	Green
Communication – harmony, design, sales, television/entertainment providers	Yellow
Community or sensual	Peach/pink/apricot
Fast food, Internet gaming, investments	Purple/maroon
Active, such as sporting, discos, clubs	Red
Educational, executive professions	Royal or dark blue
Religious, welfare	Mauve/dark red
Essential, highly practical business services	Brown
Higher market financial services	Gold
Personal, tailor-made services	Silver
One-off services or discreet products	Pale grey/white
'No-nonsense' services – law enforcement, or any authoritative figure. Works well contrasted against vivid, colours such as orange.	Black

Online logos

Get to know your online colours of logos. When adding a colour to your site with HTML, you can often simply type in the name of the colour. But more often than not and to ensure total colour accuracy, you'll need to use what's called the 'hex code', which is something that the browser will be able to understand.

If you plan to animate your logo on the web, do so cautiously. Animation for its own sake will never convey the total 'feel' for your company. Go through the same design auditing process as on printed material – ensuring your values are reflected in every detail of your website's layout.

When designing for the web, remember that surfers are impatient. This is especially true for social networking sites. In fact it only takes around 50 milliseconds for surfers to decide to click on or click out of your site. In that short time, assessing your site they consider:

Fresh
Is it emotive? Is the online brand innovative? Brave...

Adaptive
Does it respond to the surfers' needs – is it data-savvy and updated?

Relevant
Is it useful and targeted?

Transformative
Does it raise expectations – does it do more than just what it says on the label?

Social
Is it a SNS experience? Is it newsy and/or democratic, communal and sharing?

Immersive

Is it multi-sensory – can the surfer lose track of time by becoming totally engaged with the site?

Authentic

Does it seem genuine? Does it feel transparent? Is it consistent and humane?

> ## The 3 Cs of homepage design
>
> **C**onsistency – feature a consistent layout, design (font types, borders etc), tone and navigation.
>
> **C**olours – colours can make or break consistency, highlighting, your tone, and design. Remember your audience.
>
> **C**ontent – don't have too much that it takes too long to load; the first few seconds will make or break a viewer's visit.

Web scanning

Rather than formerly read sites, surfers scan them from the centre to left and then this pattern:

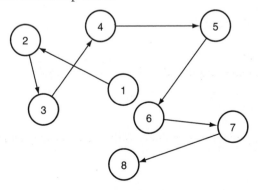

'F' reading (skimming)

Assuming your surfer scans and is still interested in your message, they next 'skim' your site – looking for content, both visual and textual, that clarifies they are on the right page. Such skimming is done in an 'F' shape motion of their eyes. This evolved from Jakob Nielsen's eye-tracking study of 2006 and you can see an illustration of this on a number of websites including www.useit.com and www.searchenginejournal.com. Nielsen has been referred to as 'the King of usability' and has published a number of books on the subject.

Getting more from design agencies (including web design)

Here is a set of questions that you should ask designers:

- ▶ *Can I see your portfolio?*
- ▶ *What's so great about you? (Look for a proven track record in understanding your sector.)*
- ▶ *Will the team working on the design pitch also work with us long-term?*
- ▶ *What's the line of command? (Who can we talk to if things go wrong?)*
- ▶ *Is the proposal off-the-shelf or bespoke?*
- ▶ *What are your payment terms?*
- ▶ *Can I speak to your existing clients?*
- ▶ *What does your designer expect from me:*
  - ▷ *full copy?*
  - ▷ *concepts?*
  - ▷ *pictures?*
- ▶ *Who owns the site/designs?*
- ▶ *You may outgrow the site/agency. Can you leave the building?*

- ▶ *Who owns the code, scripts, pictures, etc?*
- ▶ *Are there costs for transferring the site?*

In addition to these questions, make the following checks also:

- ▶ *In the case of web design agencies, don't stop at the front page of sites you review.*
- ▶ *Check the navigation. (Novice designers tend to over design and so slow the pace of websites.)*
- ▶ *Be wary of cheap deals.*
- ▶ *Keep a back-up of the entire site – including coding – on file.*

Apply and adapt this web marketing brief to help plan your online design strategy and approach.

The formal web marketing design brief

General
- ▶ *Who is your organization?*
- ▶ *Mission and vision: brand e-experience (what do you want the web design to achieve that offline design alone cannot fully accomplish?)*
- ▶ *Key audiences (stakeholders, customers, clients, and/or markets).*

Website role
- ▶ *Identify what the website will achieve for each key audience. For example, provide services such as e-learning, online tutorials, generate (customized) documents, etc.*
- ▶ *Assign a priority rating to each role from 1 (essential) to 5 (nice-to-have).*

(Contd)

Measures of success
- ▶ *Public awareness*
- ▶ *Website accesses*
- ▶ *Customer/client/stakeholder enquiries*
- ▶ *Sales*
- ▶ *Email subscriptions*
- ▶ *Bookings/reservations*

Maintenance
- ▶ *How often will the website need to be updated?*
- ▶ *What website maintenance expertise does your organization have in-house?*
- ▶ *Which website maintenance programs or platforms do you currently use or prefer? For example, FrontPage, Dreamweaver?*
- ▶ *Will staff require website content and/or maintenance training?*

Constraints
- ▶ *Development timeframe – is the website launch to coincide with an event or promotional campaign?*

(You can read more about how to write for the web and improve web search optimization in the Teach Yourself title *Improve your Copywriting*.)

> **Did you know?**
> Many logos feature wildlife (Esso is an example). You can imaginatively capitalize upon this by donating some of your profits to the chosen animal's wildlife fund. This shows you care as much for your environment as your image.

It looks great on paper

Printing can be an expensive business. It needn't be. There are ways to cheat the colour process. The most commonly used method is to print a tint of the full colour. Just use your corporate colour and a tint of it (provided you don't feature too many tints as it can look a total mess!). This said, I believe that design is too important to cheat on colour, just for the sake of saving a few pennies here and there.

Another thing to bear in mind is to consider how your colour(s) reproduce on different formats, including on PDFs when downloaded via the web. Check with your printer to see how it looks on standard letter headed paper and on laser copy paper. You'll be amazed by the difference. Also ask to see how it reproduces on a business card. Whenever possible show your company's sense of corporate social responsibility by printing on recycled paper and if possible, with vegetable dye inks. Finally, consider how it will reproduce on the side of delivery vans, on stickers, boxes, labels, signs, forms, clothing, exhibition boards, advertisements, and so on.

Nine deadly printing sins

1 *Over/under printing quantities.*
2 *Printing on the wrong material. (Always keep a box full of samples – and ask to see more. Many pay a high price when they attempt to be too clever with paper sizes and weights.)*
3 *Overlooking how print is finished – do you want it laminated, stitched, folded...?*
4 *Assuming any photograph can be reproduced simply.*
5 *Not budgeting for proofs.*
6 *Under-estimating print/delivery times.*
7 *Not checking mailing restrictions if posting business reply coupons.*
8 *Opting for the first quote that comes through the door.*
9 *Not printing on environmentally friendly paper.*

Perfectly packaged communication

Packaging is the tactile manifestation of your brand. It gives your product substance. It imbues independence and instils confidence. Logos and other printed corporate identity provide a sense of feeling for a brand. Like love at first sight, packaging takes those emotions on to the next stage in a relationship. It is the sensuous moment, when your customers reach out, hold and experience the feel, texture and shape of a marketing 'promise' for themselves.

A classic example of packaging is the Coca-Cola bottle. The original straight-sided bottle design was introduced around 1910. By 1915, the company needed a distinctive corporate identity. It is thought that the familiar curvaceous bottle was based on one of the drink's main ingredients – the cola nut. Around the time, *Life* magazine featured an article about the bottle which said of the packaging… 'It remains the queen of the soft drink container… Its shape is aggressively female – a quality that, in merchandise as in life, sometimes transcends functionalism.'

Together with Coca-Cola's dynamic contour curve introduced in 1970, today's Coke is one of the most recognized symbols on the planet.

Did you know?

The grandfather of Lana Turner (the 1940s Hollywood star) invested in Coca-Cola, but he didn't think the name would ever catch on so he withdrew his investment and instead chose what he felt would be a much shrewder option – The Raspberry Cola Company.

Perfume companies have long recognized that the sweet aroma of success depends, to a large extent, on the style and design of the container. Similarly, alcoholic drink companies invest as much time in perfecting the shape of a bottle as balancing the flavours. The style of that packaging, like all aspects of great design, is interpreted throughout their marketing communications.

This was illustrated when an executive of an alcoholic brand confided in me that, except for the addition of fruit juice flavourings, many alcoholic drinks aimed at the young were designed to be virtually tasteless. After all, he explained, youngsters want to drink as much as possible without a lingering bitter taste in their mouths. So, whilst there may not be that taste inside the bottle, the outer shell tells another story. Go along to any trendy night club and you'll see fashionable drinkers – especially men, clasping bottles of designer beer and lager to their chests. It's as if they are visually 'saying' 'love me, love my choice of brand'.

I call this clique-specific marketing Tribal Branding. It hearkens back to when we lived in caves, hunted in groups and based ideals on peers. (See also, 'The evolution of marketing', page 2.)

This packaging philosophy is also practised in retail outlets. For example, many consumers will buy clothes not just because of how comfortably they fit but because they are attracted to the lifestyle depicted on the packaging, even extending to graphics on in-store posters. Lifestyle marketing as a concept explains the feeling and what can't be sensed by words alone.

Another element of responsible design is the training of your teams who provide a service. Here, the importance of business grooming and developing your people within the service sector assumes equal ranking to the way you package manufactured goods.

Nothing to be sniffed at

An up-and-coming stratagem takes creative design into a new dimension beyond sight, sound and touches. Smell is one of the most provocative of all sensations. A scent can remind you of a holiday or childhood. Just like a holiday memory often relates to lazy summer days, so smells have their seasons. Rich, spicy smells like mulled wine have winter flavours perhaps suitable for marketing woollen clothing. Floral fragrances and citrus bouquets are worth considering for marketing fresh environmental products.

Charities for the blind have been known to successfully impregnate their mailings with scent. Pass by a coffee shop brewing freshly ground coffee and the temptation to treat yourself to a cup of coffee becomes virtually irresistible. Fresh bread can have a similar effect.

Too much of a smell can put off prospective buyers. Too little and you irritate as they try to pinpoint the aroma's source. Some airlines have corporate scents. They subtly pump the smell of fresh leather into the first-class cabin. Others develop a certain sweet perfume that captures the freshness and vitality of a service. (Typically, long-haul coach operators wishing to keep passengers relaxed and sickness-free, or nightclubs that prefer that customers smell invigorating aromas rather than sweat can also adapt this technique.)

If you venture into the area of odour marketing, do so at your peril. For heavenly smell is in the nose of the beholder. Remember, take responsibility for your design at every level of implementation and you can secure the lead within your sector.

ESSENTIALS FROM THIS CHAPTER

▶ *Marketing design includes everything from the mechanisms of a product or service to corporate literature, packaging and even online brand experiences (e-experiences).*

▶ *Design is the planning, decision-making and management of activities which determine the function and characteristics of a finished product or service.*

▶ *Perceivable Branding Properties (PBPs) make an immediate comforting brand impact which reaches deeply into the subconscious of consumers.*

▶ *Remember the nine deadly sins of printing.*

▶ *Logos are not just painting the face of a company simply for the sake of it – through their design, they make visible the strategy and aspirations of a company.*

11

....

Generating demand

In this chapter you will learn:

- *how to plan a written as well verbal marketing presentation*
- *classic tips to help you deliver your marketing plan with confidence*
- *a checklist of things to watch out for before and during your marketing presentation*

At some point, unless selling online or over the phone, you'll come face-to-face with prospective consumers. This can feel daunting (no reflection on any of your current charming customers!). However, it needn't be so – the more you understand consumers by meeting and listening to them, the better your marketing campaigns. (The markets, rather than theories alone, lead all marketing.) In management, getting involved with people throughout the entire business process is called Managing by Walking Around (MBWA).

Apart from end-of-year budgeting, one of the things that can make marketers really nervous is making a presentation either on paper or in person.

Written marketing presentations

Let's deal first with being effective on paper. As a lecturer, I am often asked how to prepare successful reports.

Reports come in two main flavours – pure information and informed proposals. A common mistake is getting an informative report mixed up with a proposal.

The word 'report' comes from the French word *reportage*. Pure *reportage* reports all facts without favour or bias. So a report needs to tell the reader everything from the history of a product or service to current state of play – including information on marketing projects and on the various departments within the organization.

On the other hand, a proposal needs to propose – based on favour and of course bias. Unlike writing a report, a proposal allows for added imaginative insights. This includes predicting events and opportunities and hopefully persuading the reader to take action.

FOUR STEPS FOR A THOROUGH PROPOSAL

1 **The scenario** – *in this first section you detail the overall situation regarding the background to a project.*
2 **The enigma** – *in this part you highlight the immediate needs arising from the situation to be resolved before addressing a wider picture.*
3 **The options** *available. Here you closely examine each possibility, weighing up its pros and cons for the reader.*
4 **The recommended course of action** – *this is your final proposition. Having read steps 1–3 the reader should be left feeling that your recommended proposal is both logical as well as ideal.*

Each part of your proposal should be supported by arguments leading to a conclusive recommendation. Additional support – graphs, enclosures, and so forth – should be recorded in the appendix. Then, the main thrust of the argument is not clouded.

This technique works well in most proposal formats (including detailed emails). All proposals should be directed to the reader as distinct from being overly concerned with your organization's concerns. By demonstrating how you can satisfy a prospect's needs you can prove your organization's ability to deliver appropriate proposals.

Personal marketing presentations

Being eloquent on paper is one thing – acting persuasively as a speaker is another. However, both are essential techniques to master, after all, you are in the business of marketing *communications* – that includes all kind of presentations.

When making a personal address, your goal should be to leave an appropriate lasting impression with the audience. Too often the only impression a marketing presentation leaves is the thought that it contained too much hype, too many slides, too many dull data tables and not enough sincerity.

The greater your own knowledge and understanding of your subject and its relationship with a target market, the more pertinent and personal your presentation. When preparing a marketing presentation, before writing a word, keep cross-referring in your mind to how it will benefit the assembly. Consider their situation, interests, ambitions, possible objections, and so on. Also, think about your props such as laptops, and so on. If using PowerPoint, keep your slides to the absolute minimum and never cram them full of words.

Use PowerPoint to *support* rather than *lead* you through the presentation. If possible remove text and add pictures – providing that they are not cliché types of shots that everyone downloads from picture libraries.

As with presenting your ideas on paper, there are two types of oral presentation technique.

The informative approach depicts, defines, demonstrates and corroborates. (Defining issues is a great way to start an informative marketing speech.)

For example, 'Marketing – according to the Chartered Institute of Marketing it means …'

The influential approach appeals to passions tempered by reasoning and logic. Here the aim is to incite action or inspire belief.

Put it to the test

If you are stuck for a title for your speech, try names from famous records or titles from classic books.

YOU'VE FINISHED WHAT YOU WANT TO SAY, BUT ARE YOU STILL TALKING?

Marketing speeches take longer to plan than to write. Avoid speaking for more than 20 minutes. This equates to 2,000 words, allowing you to pace your talk comfortably to 100 words per minute. If you are a novice at delivering marketing speeches, why not try writing the speech in its entirety? The downside of reading a speech is that it can sound staccato. Worse still, you may lose your place. You can avoid both hurdles by rehearsing either to a mirror or to colleagues, typing the script with double-line spacing and underlining key words or sentences that help you to keep track as well as emphasize points.

Index cards can be helpful if you want to improvise on key points – one per card, as you go along, However, if this kind of delivery is new to you, be careful not to ramble on too much.

Once you have outlined your marketing presentation you need to add practical substance. It's this substance that provides insight and integrity to what you have to say. Below are two popular marketing-speech delivery structures.

Step-by-step
This is the basic method, whereby you state a problem then follow with the issues caused by the problem (or situation) and then wrap it up with a viable, rather than mealy-mouthed, solution.

Miss Marple
State the obvious – '*Make a Difference with Your Marketing* explains invaluable marketing techniques'. Then carry out a little detective work on your statement: 'This book is crammed with career-boosting tips.' Therefore 'reading this book will provide you with techniques to enhance your marketing career'.

Marketing presentation structure

Section	Possible 'hooks'
Intro (establish rapport and credibility)	Ask a question. If to a small audience – directly – allowing for no more than two answers, if any. Better still, rhetorically.

Refer to a date and its significance.

Show key statistics and describe why and how they are relevant.
Tell an amusing story related to your subject.
Relate to a piece of news or recent event.
Quote someone famous.
(Providing your interpretation of the quote is of greater relevance than the original quote.)
For example, in a marketing speech to the agricultural community: 'George Orwell said: "advertising is the rattling of a stick inside a swill bucket". I say that's great if you're advertising buckets to pig farmers.'

Main body of presentation

Overview what has occurred. Where do you currently stand and where could you go? (This is particularly effective if you want to put across a new marketing direction.)

Interpret a situation.
Explain what it is, what it does, how it directly affects the audience, where it's going and why they should care.

Bust a scandal.
Often used if your organization suffers a public relations disaster or is subject to malicious industry gossip.
- *Face the accusation head on, describing it in full – no holds barred.*
- *Counter the rumour or accusation with hard facts – not hearsay. Feel it.*

(Contd)

	Selectively repeat a key 'power' word to re-enforce an objective, (e.g. IF it were better, IF it were clear. IF we went further...) Other typical power phrases include: ▶ Read my lips... ▶ No pain, no gain ▶ We haven't even started, yet; we're at the start of a new kind of marketing thinking. ▶ I'd rather run towards an opportunity now, than run away from a disaster later. ▶ We need to offer marketing credibility – not promises. So here is the offer: credible campaigns rather than marketing promises.
Close Reverse mapping. (Hammer home the core message)	That is where we were; this is where I recommend we should be.

Things to watch

▶ *Arrive on time.*
▶ *Never criticize your audience.*
▶ *Don't skip slide details.*
▶ *Allow time for questions and answers.*
▶ *Avoid UFOs – Un-Funny Observations.*
▶ *Practise and be familiar with your slides.*
▶ *Spell-check your slides.*
▶ *Switch off mobiles.*
▶ *Look confident. Think confidently.*
▶ *Don't apologize for your presentation or lack of preparation.*

- *Don't talk to one person – address the entire audience personally-embellishing your talk with relevant anecdotes.*
- *Don't keep looking at your wrist watch.*
- *Pre-check that everything works/carry a spare plug and be ready to talk unaided by slides.*

Put it to the test

Debate the following with your colleagues: The art of public oration is dead. Then deliver a five-minute speech supporting your point of view.

ESSENTIALS FROM THIS CHAPTER

▶ *In management – getting involved with people throughout the entire business process is called MBWA – Managing by Walking Around.*

▶ *Remember the four stages towards writing a thorough proposal.*

▶ *Remember the Corporate Social Responsibility Report or case study considerations.*

▶ *Use PowerPoint to support rather than lead you through the presentation.*

▶ *Marketing speeches take longer to plan than to write. Avoid speaking for more than 20 minutes. This equates to 2,000 words, allowing you to pace your talk comfortably to 100 words per minute.*

12

Some inspire naturally, the rest use PR

In this chapter you will learn about:
- *what the press need to tell your story*
- *what to include and exclude from a good PR story*
- *key PR indicators*
- *news vs. propaganda*
- *types of news letter (including online)*
- *stories for blogs and newsletters*
- *using celebrities in PR*
- *PR and exhibition tips*

Public relations (PR) is an essential part of your communications mix. It provides a strong voice in a sea of noise crowded by advertising message – the so called, 'clutter effect'. Effectively implemented, PR generates awareness, creates need and influences decision makers. In doing so, it builds bridges of understanding between you and all who deal with you.

Who are your ideal PR audiences?

Common news contacts	Typical end external audience	Typical internal audiences
Editors	Buyers	Employees
Journalists	Government	Trade bodies/unions

(Contd)

Common news contacts	Typical end external audience	Typical internal audiences
Reporters	Institutions	Shareholders
Feature writers	Customers and consumers	Investors (potential)
Researchers	Competitors	Partners
Bloggers	Public authorities	Suppliers
Web content managers	International influencers	Channel
Press photographers	Stock market	Sales
News desk editors	Industry bodies	Distribution
Radio editors		Admin

PR is not simply a matter of dealing with the press. Every aspect of relationship-building is touched by PR: from encouraging and cajoling investors at special events and via newsletters to working with the local community, lobbying parliament or launching a new trade marketing initiative. In this way, PR addresses general perceptions of an organization through its public persona as well as through direct personal relationships. Which is why PR plays such a vital role within your total marketing relationships programme.

Put it to the test

Audience (public)	Potential for organization to influence (Scale 1–10) +	Vulnerability of your organization to that public (Scale 1–10) =	Importance of public to you (Scale 1–10) =

Use this guide to assess the importance of your potential PR audiences to your organization.

To be memorable – for the right reasons! – planned PR should always be cost effective – typically, PR accounts for around 10 per cent of your marketing budget. Just as there is no free advertising, so there are no free PR lunches – even with members of the press. PR takes time, a labour resource and, therefore, money.

At all times, PR must be honest. Think about what you want to achieve (e.g. influence, alter conceptions, develop alliances.)

Consider where your publicity appears. If in print, then your comments should be in-depth. On TV, radio and the web, in general your comments should be short, incisive and precise. In the case of television, appearances often take precedence over profundity of comment.

Your message should always remain tactically clear (short term) and strategically consistent (long term).

What the press want to know about your product or service

▶ *What's so different?*
▶ *Who is likely to want it?*
▶ *What are the benefits?*
▶ *How best can it be used?*
▶ *What kind of problems does it address?*
▶ *How does it compare?*
▶ *How does it perform?*
▶ *Who does the editor contact for further information?*

SIX FAULTS TO WATCH OUT FOR IN ANY PR STORY

1 *Irrelevant to their interests*
2 *No story or weak story*
3 *Self-promotion or puffery*
4 *Poor English*
5 *Confusing jargon*
6 *Too long*

FIVE INDICATORS THAT YOU HAVE A GREAT PR STORY

1 *Relevant to your audience*
2 *Timeliness*

3 *Readable (story is hidden)*
4 *Focused on concerns of publication or broadcaster*
5 *Presentable*

From PRessure to pleasure

You can gauge public perceptions through opinion polls or press coverage. (Without company stories, the trade press in particular would have little news to report.) Try to plan where you would like your story to appear. Could it be a main news-grabbing article, in-depth feature or perhaps hidden elsewhere as a 'filler'?

Key PR indicators

Television Rating Points (TVR) – each TVR compares to reaching 1 per cent of the population using a 30-second commercial.

Opportunities To See (OTS) – the number of occasions that your item is seen.

Gross Rating Points (GRP) – the total number of people reached by a medium at one time. (One GPR is the equivalent of 1 per cent of the population.)

Compare your PR communication channels. Was a Business Briefing Breakfast with key influencers more valuable than say, sending a press release alone? What feedback did you get from publicity on the Internet? Have you earned media respect? Which medium delivers best results, advertising or PR? Draw on the parts rather than sum total of your efforts. Exploit and make PR work even harder for you.

'The most dangerous untruths are truths moderately distorted.'

George Christoph Lichtenberg

PR falls or wins on truth, timing and appropriateness. If you have to wait around for too long to get your press release approved, it will probably become too late to get it considered by the news press. (PR tends to deal with active news, rather than passive history.)

Just as importance as timing is truth. Check and double check all your facts. If you have to address a bad news story – do it openly – show you have nothing to hide and everything to gain from dealing with a difficult issue – not just for you – but for all concerned.

Familiarize yourself with the Economy of Truth scale. Depending on how much you wish to reveal or defend, your position on the scale alters. Anything approaching the absolute line of truth needs serious consideration. Anything below this point should be avoided at all costs.

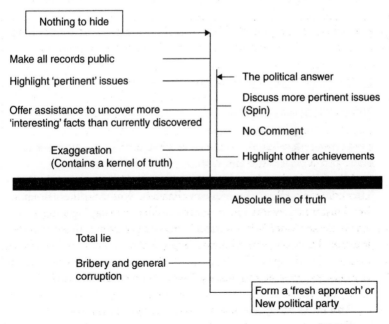

Economy of Truth scale.

Crisis – what crisis?

Issues to consider in a PR crisis:

▶ **Statement:** *Clear and concise press release that highlights a company's position in a particular situation.*
▶ **Media Q&A:** *A series of questions most likely to be asked by members of the media, customers and employees regarding the issue/crisis at hand. This is usually the first document provided in a crisis situation.*
▶ **Employee Communication:** *Your employees can be your best spokespeople, clearly articulating the company's position or statement regarding the crisis at hand is instrumental to any well-managed crisis communication plan.*
▶ **Regulatory Communication:** *Depending upon the size and scope of the crisis at hand, communication with various regulators such as FSA.*
▶ **Customer Service Phone Scripts:** *In times of crisis, customers call.*

News or propaganda?

Concerning newsletters – are you writing about news or promoting sales? If it is purely the latter, then it shouldn't be called a newsletter but something like a 'sales update', 'bulletin' or 'sales letter'. If it is none of these sales variations, you should consider the newsletter's style and format. Here, design, again, plays a key role. A badly produced/designed newsletter adds no substance to your organization's marketing values.

The most important thing about a newsletter is that it should explain (tell) rather than exclaim (sell). In fact, the same goes for all PR content.

Handle with care: watch out for the following overt 'sell' words in your newsletters and press releases:

LEADING / LEADER	BEST / MOST / FASTEST / LARGEST / BIGGEST / etc.	INNOVATIVE / INNOVATION	REVOLUTIONARY
AWARD- WINNING	DISRUPTIVE / DISRUPTION	CUTTING / BLEEDING EDGE	NEXT-GENERATION
STRATEGIC PARTNER- SHIP	SYNERGY	FUTUREPROOF	ENTERPRISE- GRADE
PARADIGM SHIFT	UNQUE SERVICE	UNPARALLELED	INTEROPERABILITY

Types of newsletter

Standard A3, folded down to A4 flyer. Used as an updating device rather than a substantial magazine discussion format.

E-zine. Either a PDF version of a printed newsletter, or an online version published on its own micro-site page. E-zines are typically distributed via e-shots. The email copy features headlines from the e-zine with short introductory overviews of individual stories. The surfer 'clicks' on the headline which takes them to the full story on the micro-site. (A variation of this is a section on a company intranet.)

Poster newsletter. Up to A2 size which is a cross between a general information board and a promotional poster pinned to company notice boards, such as in the coffee room.

News-sheet. Follows the same standards as a traditional newspaper format. This includes sections for different parts of your organization as well as reports or stories. Just as newspaper stories are listed in terms of newsworthiness starting from the front and back and working towards the centre, so there should be space allocated for more trivial pursuits such as crosswords, births, deaths and retirement as well as social matters. As with all newsletters, it is essential that you are sure of your audience type. Just because Mary in Accounts is pregnant, that may not be 'newsworthy' to customers – unless, of course, one of them is responsible!

Company magazine. Contract magazine publishing covers everything from pop music fanzines to in-store magazines and glossy lifestyle publications. All enhance customer care, thereby loyalty, through making individuals feel valued. Some include tailored sections which address individual interests such as skiing supplements for trendy winter sports seekers or antiques supplements for discerning investors.

FOUR THINGS TO COMMUNICATE OTHER THAN NEWS IN A NEWSLETTER

1 *Encourage sales (through explaining rather than extolling) – including cross selling.*
2 *Increase awareness.*
3 *Promote a sense of a company's character.*
4 *Act as a research vehicle.*

STORY COMPONENTS

A good newsletter story is divided into components:

▶ *The headline – captures the subject's spirit and account.*
▶ *The lead – picks up the relevant issues.*
▶ *The body – details those issues.*
▶ *The support – draws on expert opinion and public reaction.*
▶ *The conclusion – summarizes the findings.*

POSSIBLE NEWSLETTER AND BLOG STORIES

Product stories:
Improvements
New models
New applications

News:
Joint ventures
New departments
EventsTrends

People:
Promotions
Awards
New hires
Hobbies
'Day in the life'

Milestones:
Anniversaries
Target reaching
Products shipped

Sales news:
New clients
Bids accepted
Contracts reviewed

How to articles:
Detailed
instructions
with case studies

Previews and reports:
Special events
Conferences
Sales meetings
Seminars

R&D:
New technologies
New internal
systems
Awards

Customer stories:
Customer interviews
Guest articles
Case studies

Financial news:
Quarterly
and annual
report highlights
Shareholder news

Photo captions:
People
Facilities
Products
Events

Columns:
MD's view
Q&As
Technical questions
HR highlights

Gimmicks:
Quiz
Trivia
Puzzles
Cartoons
Recipes
Invite 'how I fixed it'
articles – good for IT

Overseas activities:
Profiles of
subsidiaries,
branches, people

Community affairs:
Fundraisers
Special events
Regional and
national events

A 'classic' marketing cautionary tale relating to pop bands involves Geri Halliwell formerly 'Ginger' Spice who left the once world-famous Spice Girls and their sponsors with a potential dilemma when she decided to drop out of the band especially as some sponsors like Sony had invested in a software game called Spice World.

At the other end of the sponsorship age spectrum, in their time, Castrol Oil, Budweiser and Volkswagen have kept the bands like Rolling Stones rolling. It's all a question of appropriate markets for your brand.

Charity sponsorship

TIPS FOR CHARITIES INVOLVING CELEBRITIES

1 *Ensure the celebrity is well briefed and made to feel important.*
2 *A personality should be looked after throughout and kept happy at all times.*
3 *Pay basic expenses. Send a car or forward a cheque if they are driving themselves, send train tickets, or pay for air fares if they are on an overseas visit.*
4 *'Thank yous' are important. Birthday cards, flowers, get well cards, short notes and telephone calls are significant, too.*
5 *Sometimes invite celebrities to important functions without asking them to do anything! Just their presence at an annual meeting, at a celebration party, or even just to see work is appreciated.*

6 *Involve celebrities in the planning decisions. Ask what they would like to do. They must not feel that they are being given orders. Their knowledge of fund-raising and publicity opportunities is a great asset.*

7 *Keep on the right side of secretaries, personal assistants, or celebrities' spouses. Celebrities rarely manage their own diaries. If you need a favour, consult assistants whose support is vital.*

8 *Monitor the media for anything that may affect your celebrity supporters. If they have received an honour or suffered a sad loss, appropriate letters are important.*

9 *Don't worry about public opinion concerning whether today's celebrity may be tomorrow's has-been. They may make a 'comeback,' and contribute a valuable endorsement. Besides, how will other celebrities feel if they see you drop a contemporary like a hot potato?*

10 *Above all, treat celebrities as your best friends.*

Put it to the test

There's another drought in Africa. Yet although up to 1 million may perish, the public is apathetic towards charitable appeals. Should you consider launching an emergency lottery-ticket promotion or should you use a high-profile celebrity to highlight your cause? Why?

Steps towards a perfect press release

Step 1: The outline
Write down all the components of your story, including quotes from named people, before you start to write your actual press release.

Step 2: The headline
GRAB 'EM'. You have up to eight words here to get their attention – if you miss this opportunity you may never get them to read on. Editors have seconds to decide if the story is of interest.

When appropriate, make them giggle, smirk, or even get their blood boiling a bit. (Exceptions to this should be in the case of hard news or something serious, life-threatening or of worldly concern.)

The best headlines are to the point rather than 'flowery' or clever. Where possible, write in in the present tense. Always be precise about people, dates and titles, and places.

Step 3: The preview points
Include up to three bullet points which preview the key issues covered in your press release. (This helps attract or retain the Editor's interest.)

Step 4: The whole story in one
Encapsulate your whole story in two paragraphs of two sentences comprising up to 16 words for each sentence.

Step 5: The main body
This covers what are known as the 'six journalist's friends': who, what, why, where, when and how.

Step 6: The quote
Incorporate a quote from a user of a service rather than just provider. (This adds credibility.) Whenever possible, add the person's name and ensure that the quote sounds as if someone actually said it, rather than propaganda. If a quote is long-coming, write it yourself and get it approved.

Step 7: Call to action
Note how the press can contact you – including out of office hours.

Step 8: Almost the end...
Add the word 'ENDS' at the foot of your press release, as well as number of words in the release.

Step 9: Notes to Editors
Add two paragraphs of two sentences each, providing background information on the company in general.

Endeavour to get your whole press release down to one side of A4. When sending it, email a PDF as well as .doc version. This shows how it should appear formally as well as makes it easy for the press to cut and paste it. A summary version of the whole story should be included within the main body of your email.

NB: Try, whenever possible to align your story with a wider news event. Also, call journalists on the phone and 'pitch' the merits of your story, followed by sending out the release, which can be archived on your website.

Twitter™ and blogs

Websites and techniques such as Twitter and blogs are ideal PR tools. They are often the first places people look for an immediate response or reaction to a breaking story. In the case of Twitter, short (140 character) updates can be posted over the web to provide a rolling news headline service or sharp insights from a company that would otherwise be overlooked. Equally Twitter can help organizations show a more 'human' side of their personality through revealing personal insights behind public headlines. Blogs too help bridge the gap between an organization and its publics by offering opinions on key issues affecting a business or sector. Such blogs can dovetail with instant messaging sites, including Twitter to add further substance to short updates.

Originally micro-blog sites like Twitter were aimed at the under-30 age group. However, eventually 35–54-year-olds also started to use such sites as communication opportunities.

Notable early PR users of Twitter (collectively known as Twitterati) included Stephen Fry, John Cleese and President Obama. Another business social networking communication site, LinkedIn, grew in 2009 by 63 per cent.

The real danger of micro-sites like Twitter is that marketers may overuse them for 'selling' as opposed to 'telling' purposes, and so alienate users.

The authors of Ofcom's Communications Market Report of 2009 noted:

As the social networking phenomenon has begun to mature, it has started to develop in a different way. In particular, social networking appears to be growing more popular among older age groups. Conversely, there are signs that use of social networking sites may already have peaked among younger adults.

The consultancy firm Deloitte, suggested that the younger age group might be moving on because their parents are beginning to move into this corner of the Internet: 'Young people are saying, "Now that Mum and Dad are on Facebook, do I really want to be there?"'

In 2009 Facebook's audience grew by 73 per cent to 19 million people (almost a third of the total UK population).

A word from our sponsors

You can sponsor anything from your local school team to cricket club or a special event. It shows that your organization shares the values of spectators/participants and is part of, and cares for, the community. By doing so, your brand improves image, integrity and name recall value. This generates a sponsorship aurora where consumer sensitivity is shifted on to your brand.

In the United States, drinks companies battle for exclusive rights to have their vending machines in schools. Marketers have long recognized the playground currency of Pester Power, that is when children harass parents to buy a product. However, children are 'advertising aware', never to be under-estimated in their power to 'filter' messages. Act responsibly and your integrity will return handsome dividends.

Make an impression – not an exhibit of yourself (event planning)

Successful exhibitions depend on planning as far ahead as a year before the event. Check your budget, space allocation and anticipated appropriate attendance.

At least six months prior to the event, ensure you have the materials for your set – either kit form or bespoke, as well as uniforms, give aways and so on. Also pre-book any overnight accommodation. When designing your set, keep in mind your brand image as well as the overall theme of the show. Stands should be 'open' with maximum access to visitors. Keep copywriting on your display boards to a minimum, the objective of all displays being to explain who you are, what you do and why you do it better. If you use video, make sure the programme is subtitled, short – no more than three minutes – and continuously looped. If exhibiting abroad, double check aspects like height of rooms (so your set fits in) and power points (so it all works).

Did you know?

Reserve your stand near the dining area. You'll significantly increase visitor traffic. More if it's also near the toilets. Additionally, security guards often converge in the restaurant area. If this is opposite to your stand, you'll have extra security at no cost (people pilfer from stands).

Three months – Prepare pre-event publicity such as advertising, direct-mail invitations and press releases. Also a good time to arrange special client hospitality, reservations at local restaurants, and so on.

Six weeks – Brief staff. Re-check all your materials, including stock of business cards, brochures, display units, order pads, and so forth. (At the event, make sure you distribute your brochures to the on-site press office.)

Three to two weeks – Send reminder email invitations to key prospects and guests.

One week before – Check documentation (including credit cards and passports if travelling overseas).

The day before – It's all panic stations! Anticipate things not being properly connected, flooring needs to be put down, extra flowers are needed to conceal wiring... Provided you are prepared, you'll take it all in your stride.

At the show – RELAX. Let the event work for you. People attend to pick up information and network. For your part, meet and greet visitors with open-ended questions not 'Can I help you?' – the answer is usually – 'No'. Find time to chat with other exhibitors.

Following the show – Distribute sales leads (followed up within ten days – leads cool by about 12 per cent every three days), thank everyone who helped make the event a success and learn for next time.

Put it to the test

Referring to the newsletter story format formula, devise a story about your latest trade fair event.

ESSENTIALS FROM THIS CHAPTER

▶ *Every aspect of relationship-building is touched by PR: from encouraging and cajoling investors at special events and via newsletters to working with the local community, lobbying parliament or launching a new trade marketing initiative.*

▶ *Typically, PR accounts for around 10 per cent of your marketing budget.*

▶ *Compare your PR communication channels. PR falls or wins on truth, timing and appropriateness.*

▶ *Issues to consider in a PR crisis:*
  ▷ **Statement:** *Clear and concise press release that highlights a company's position in a particular situation.*
  ▷ **Media Q&A:** *A series of questions most likely to be asked by members of the media, customers and employees regarding the issue/crisis at hand.*
  ▷ **Employee communication:** *Your employees can be your best spokespeople.*
  ▷ **Regulatory communication:** *Depending upon the size and scope of the crisis at hand, communication with various regulators such as the Financial Services Authority.*
  ▷ **Customer service phone scripts:** *In times of crisis, customers call.*

▶ *The most important thing about a newsletter is that it should explain (tell) rather than exclaim (sell).*

▶ *Your newsletter story is divided into components:*
  ▷ **The headline** – *captures the subject's spirit and account.*
  ▷ **The lead** – *picks up the relevant issues.*
  ▷ **The body** – *details those issues.*
  ▷ **The support** – *draws on expert opinion and public reaction.*
  ▷ **The conclusion** – *summarizes the findings.*

▶ *Aligning your brand with a celebrity often pays large dividends – provided the celebrity is suitable and cost effective.*

▶ *Twitter and blogs are ideal PR tools. They are often the first places people look for an immediate response or reaction to a breaking story. Twitter can help organizations show a more 'human' side of their personality through revealing personal insights behind public headlines.*

▶ *Successful exhibitions depend on planning as far ahead as a year before the event. Check your budget, space allocation and anticipated appropriate attendance.*

13

From d-mail to email and online

In this chapter you will learn about:
- *how to improve your traditional direct mail*
- *spam dos and don'ts*
- *personalizing your direct marketing*
- *planning an effective email campaign*
- *improving Search Engine Optimization*
- *measuring e-marketing success*
- *viral marketing*
- *marketing and Web 2.0*

Direct marketing – sometimes called 'integrated', 'quantitative', 'one-to-one', 'database', 'relationship' or 'through-the-line' marketing – measures success by response. Used imaginatively, it supports your brand values as well as tactical objectives. As discussed previously and contrary to popular belief, direct marketing is not solely concerned with direct mail. It encompasses the full gambit of the communications mix including loose inserts, advertisements, e-shots, radio commercials, direct response television and the Internet.

Whichever medium is chosen, by being personal, direct marketing makes your communication relevant, clear, intriguing (illustrating the key benefits of a product or service) ... and so establishes the basis for a dialogue. Like meeting people for the first time, the better pre-informed you are, the more is likely to be gained from the developing relationship.

Searching for clues

From a sales perspective, the whole world is your oyster. But valuable pearls are rare. If your direct marketing lands in the wrong hands, irrespective of its content or design, it's a waste of money and your efforts have simply produced junk mail. What's needed is a communication that makes a prospect jump up and pay attention to what you have to say. This is where profiling enters into the scenario.

Irritating junk mail

When it comes to consumer direct mailing, be wary of poor personalization and lack of relevance of your offer to the recipient. Your aim is to match prospects with existing customers. Commercial listings include consumer based information – such as where people live, what they enjoy and so on, to business listings which segment according to job titles, geographic areas, types of companies. Additionally, you can target directors at home, Small Office, Home Office businesses and members of trade organizations.

Comprehensive consumer lists include: postcode data available as software for simple identification of an entire address by house number alone (ideal for telemarketing); geodemographic classifications; subscriptions to magazines; lifestyle club membership; propensity to donate to a charity; credit card ownership – the list is forever growing. Make sure your list is 'clean', in other words, up to date with no 'gone-aways' or deaths.

Royal Mail research pointed to UK small businesses losing over £3bn a year through poor communication. You can often negotiate net name agreement discounts for names which have been disregarded after cleaning against other lists as well as through profiling.

Spam – is it all just junk?

According to the Messaging Anti-Abuse Working Group (2009) almost one third of consumers questioned admitted answering emails they suspected were spam. Among those who responded to spam, 17 per cent said they clicked on it by mistake, 13 per cent said they sent a note to the spammer to complain, whilst amazingly 12 per cent said they were interested in the product or service!

SPAM DOS AND DON'TS

▶ *Make sure your email's message is as focused on your surfer as possible.*
▶ *Don't over-send emails. If you email more than once a week you better have a good reason for them to want to hear from you and so open the email.*
▶ *If someone requests you to stop sending emails – stop! (If you don't stop – most surfers will simply add you to a 'blacklist' so automatically bin your emails.)*
▶ *Ensure that email content is still relevant to people. (Such people are called 'emotionally subscribed'. The dormant affiliates of an email list are known as the 'emotionally unsubscribed'. Unsubscribe rates are typically low c. < 0.1% per campaign. However, there's in excess of 50% of a list who are 'emotionally unsubscribed' and hardly ever open or click.)*
▶ *Invite people to 'opt into' your email.*
▶ *Offer a genuine 'unsubscribe' option on all emails – and honour it. Sometimes dormant customers can still be converted to active customers simply by sending them direct mail or giving them a call. The main thing is to make them feel engaged and connected.*

Did you know?

To increase awareness of postcodes, the UK Post Office once promoted a quiz featuring just one question – what's your postcode? Only a few responses were received – it was discovered that in furnishing their address details, the Post Office had printed the wrong postcode!

Finding your list

List brokers are go-betweens who source lists and assess results on your behalf. They usually earn their keep on commission from list managers and owners. (List managers market lists for list owners.)

Other considerations include:

- ▶ *How was the list compiled?*
- ▶ *Is there a sample list print-out available?*
- ▶ *Who else has used the list and how?*
- ▶ *Does the list have unlimited usage or is it rented on a single-use basis?*
- ▶ *If your direct mailing is to more than 5,000, can you use a mailing house to print, package and send? (If it is an emailing, can you use an e-broker?)*
- ▶ *Include your name as a 'seed' on the list to assess how long it takes to receive the mailing.*
- ▶ *Advise the mailing house in which order a mailing should be inserted in the envelope. (Usually letter then working 'in' to flyers and coupons.) Provide a finished sample to check and print more than you need – just in case.*
- ▶ *Numerically code every returnable part of the mailing. This lets you keep track.*
- ▶ *Anticipate late deliveries.*
- ▶ *Check if suppliers belong to a trade organization like the Direct Marketing Association.*
- ▶ *For emails, measure the broad performance of your list. For example, who opens emails and when? How many emails have never been opened, against those which haven't been opened in two weeks, one month, one quarter and so on?*

THIS TIME, IT'S PERSONAL

Whichever list you choose, where appropriate, feature a personalized name and even a different colour signature on your letters. This leaves an indelible impression of integrity as opposed to uncaring mass-mailed insincerity. It is accountable. However, it also means that your mailing is competing against scores of others. It is why your mailing has to appear appealing from the envelope inwards. In *Teach Yourself Copywriting* (see 'Taking it Further', p. 340), I detail creative techniques to power-charge your mailings and e-shots. In the meantime, it is interesting to consider some points to improve your general mailings.

Of the letters that get opened in the morning, up to a quarter are not read until later in the day. Those, which look personal and relevant, are read first. Elaborate prize draw promotions are read last – if at all. The more financially biased your mailing, such as investments, insurance and banks, the less the likelihood that the mailing will be retained for future reference. This is probably down to so many companies within the financial services sector using direct mail.

Every mailing must be carefully planned from concept to response device with maximizing return uppermost in mind. Therefore, offer an easy method for people to contact you. Think about the sensitivity of a form or coupon. If you are asking for personal details, always provide a reply envelope. Don't just rely on forms or coupons, test responses against telephone numbers, email and fax options. As with all correspondence, faxes must be decent and lawful, clearly showing contact details.

Just as you invest in setting the right tone of voice and selecting the right mailing list, so offer a premium response device. By providing first-class return postage you appear serious when your brochure urges RESPOND TODAY.

Did you know?
More than 60 per cent of people read the PS part of a letter.

In telemarketing terms, opportunities are plentiful. Depending upon your budget, you can offer free calls, pay for local charges – even if the call is received at a national level. And, of course, you can provide a standard telephone number – marketed as a Hotline, Order line, Care line… and so on.

Is anybody out there?

The first indicator of a successful mailing is the extent of responses received. Many assume average response rates of around two per cent but I have found that this rate is contrived. (See 'Made-to-measure costs', page 99.)

To win greater response, consider:

- ▶ *Accuracy of your data.*
- ▶ *Perceived value and relevance of your promotional offer.*
- ▶ *Scheduling of your mailing (I normally send 'anniversary' reminders no later than three months before the expiration of, say, a magazine subscription, home insurance, etc.)*
- ▶ *Creative rationale behind your mailings contents.*
- ▶ *Creative design – especially the look, feel and copy style of the entire mailing.*
- ▶ *Ease of response.*

The appeal of direct mail is that all these factors can be tested in groups or individual components. Don't assume because a mailing failed that you should re-start from scratch. Like a molecular structure, examine each element and you'll discover ample opportunities otherwise destined for the dustbin (literally).

Put it to the test

What is the difference between a list broker and list manager?

Integrated solution providers

Direct marketing isn't simply direct mail. Through a broad mix of communications, including sales promotion, press, direct response television and the Internet, direct marketing provides the appropriate conduit to 'manage' customers at every stage of the buying life cycle.

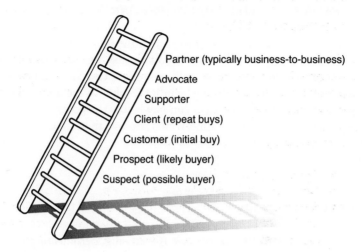

The loyalty ladder.

Through integrated media and messages, direct marketing turns a casual sale into a long-term relationship.

CONSUMER-AWARE ADVERTISING

Above-the-line marketing originally referred to 'the line' above which agencies received a commission from suppliers. (Below-the-line services like sales promotion, direct mail and printing didn't pay agencies a fee.) Through-the-line encompasses awareness media such as television, radio, the www, cinema or publishing media. And commission is a matter of negotiation between the agency and its suppliers.

Through-the-line, integrated marketing combines 'above' and 'below-the-line' marketing. Above-the-line establishes awareness; below-the-line, targets prospects directly. That requires extensive data, via lists – hence it is sometimes called database marketing.

You could pay agencies a percentage of the total value of advertisements placed on your behalf but most prefer straight fees such as for design implementation and extra for disbursements like postage. (Few opt for payment by results.) Whichever route you choose, remember that if you pay below the going rate for work, agencies will be less motivated to serve than if you are 'above board'.

Customer loyalty

You manufacture mobile phones. Advertising, perhaps on the radio, in the cinema, on television ... raises the notion that rather than watching TV at home, someone could watch television while on the move. This establishes a brand positioning which strengthens the motive that watching on a mobile is worth pursuing. Next, you need to establish preference for your particular brand. So you further explain – by direct mail or e-shots perhaps – why your mobile phone is particularly appropriate. Following this, you persuade the person that having opted for a mobile phone, yours has the edge over the competition. This could be demonstrated by a promotion through a discount or value-added campaign – a great way of dispelling any 'last minute' change of mind on the part of your customer.

Your customer buys the mobile and is happy – but it's not enough for you as an imaginative direct marketer. You want to encourage loyalty to your brand; even recommending your company to other music lovers at large. So you may follow the purchase with incentives rewarding continued allegiance. Once all done, thanks to the recommendations by your existing customers, prospects for mobiles are better targeted. Plus, in recognition of your awareness advertising, you are already further up the list of a customer's preferred brand. This integrated approach adjusts itself to the age and reputation of your brand. The greater market maturity, the less need to invest in the awareness and positioning – and the greater the need to invest in loyalty (unless of course you are re-positioning your brand).

Five steps for planning an effective email campaign

1 **Don't rush in.** *Don't overwhelm your recipients and only send appropriate emails, rather than unfocused offers.*
2 **Integrate rather than 'bolt-on'.** *Time your emails to coincide with key promotions and events. This includes dovetailing your email campaign to complement other promotional activities.*
3 **Get your dates right.** *If you have the recipient's birthday details and your email is* not *for business-to-business purposes, then show that you have them in mind by sending an e-card. Likewise, remind people six weeks prior to anniversary renewal that it is time to re-subscribe to your service or product. (Avoid sending business-to-business emails just prior to public holidays or weekends.)*
4 **Be prepared.** *Allow up to eight weeks prior to an email campaign to finalize your creative designs and copywriting.*
5 **A/B Testing.** *Conduct split tests – 'A' example versus 'B' example – (at least once each quarter) to determine which email approach works best. Such tests make you consider your subject line, copywriting, design, reason for someone to act, landing page and so on.*

Time before renewal	Offer	Support
Six weeks	Reminder	
Five weeks	Reminder and discount reward	
Three weeks	Reminder	Press/direct mail
Ten days	Reminder	
24 hours	Reminder and last chance to take discount offer.	

Timetable for renewal reminders.

Measuring e-marketing success

1 *Open rate?*
2 *Click-through rate?*
3 *Conversion rate?*
4 *Website traffic?*
5 *Inbound sales calls/emails*

Put it to the test
Organize a through-the-line media schedule for a new
combined You Tube and TV-friendly mobile.

Is it a bird or a plane? – no, it's advertising!

When the citizens of Metropolis in the 1950s television series
looked up and saw Superman flying, it was a visual manifestation
of the 'American Way'. Similarly, advertising is the most commonly
used way to pursue your imaginative strategy and make it leap up
so that your audience takes note – and, hopefully, is persuaded
to respond. Mass-market advertising revolves around what the
Oxford English Dictionary describes as the most significant word
of the twentieth century – Television.

Integrated advertising, including television marketing, doesn't have
to be handled by one type of agency. Instead, integrate a compelling
message, simply and clearly explained, which works creatively across
every medium. In this way, your marketing communications mix will
be driven by the creative proposition aiming for results rather than
the channels used to feature the basic proposition.

The more integrated your communications, the less fragmented
your message:

Establish desire
Draw attention to a need. 'I knew I wanted something, but until
now, I didn't know what I actually needed.'

Support it through placing your proposition in the public conscious. This often features broad awareness in television or targeted interest press. (With multi-channel digital television it means that, as an integrated medium, television can be better targeted than ever.) Irrespective of the medium, deliver a singularly creative persuasive message.

Focus on your brand
Establish an argument why your brand should be considered first. Use appropriate media such as sales leaflets and direct mail, and win brand preference.

Drive purchase
Including a further compelling reason for someone to buy... Our brand delivers more than the nearest competitor – often features discounts and value-added promotions.

Reward loyalty
Bolster long-term and repeat purchases. This can include in-store marketing theatre (sales promotion techniques) such as, buy this product, get that one free.

From zero to unlimited customer potential – thanks to integrated advertising.

Put it to the test

List four considerations when selecting a direct mailing list.

Marketing objectives for websites

Marketing-led websites must be accessible, useful and offer an experience beyond offline (the e-experience).

Surfers should feel that through using your site they can achieve their goal quickly and efficiently. Right from the homepage, they must understand the structure and purpose of your site, value the ease (navigation) of finding information or making a purchase and sense that the site gives the impression that it is inclusive of their personal needs – including offering the option to be personalized in some way. (Also see 'The three Cs of homepage design', page 245.)

As people are judging sites on impulse, less copy but more substance is called for when designing a homepage. Some web designers interpret this as featuring a large oblong image towards the top half of the page which, through choice photography, shows at a glance what the site is about. Others suggest incorporating multi-media on homepages (mash-ups) that link videos to more in-depth written blogs and articles on subjects.

Beyond meta-tags

With millions of sites to choose from, finding yours is a matter of promotion – including using offline promotions. Online, promotion depends in a great part on either search engine optimization (SEO), pay per click (PPC) and paid inclusion.

Traditionally search engines like Google would list and rank sites according to number of hits and the description words listed as 'meta-tag' keywords. Around 14 words (separated by commas) per page were provided in the html coding of a specific page. This together with a two-sentence description of the site (meta-description) would, in most parts, be enough for Google to set to work with ranking a site.

Today, such SEO can be boosted with pre-purchased words using Google Ad words as well as ensuring that words in hypertext links are relevant to the overall content of the page and the page it is being linked to, equally ensuring that words within headings are content appropriate.

Tools which help optimize your choice of promotional description words are available from:

- ▶ *www.abakus-internet-marketing.de/tools/topword.htm (estimates traffic to your site).*
- ▶ *www.google.com/trends (highlights peaks and long-term trends in how your users search for you or your products in different countries).*
- ▶ *www.google.com/webhp?complete=1&hl=en (offers keyphrase suggestions according to the number of pages on that topic).*

The more genuine (rather than contrived) links you have to and from your site, the better for SEO. 'Backlinks' or 'inbound links' to your site help generate interest in your site. This tool checks for such backlinks: https://siteexplorer.search.yahoo.com/mysites

Try it for yourself and then approach the sites to improve the backlink value. Also see *Improve Your Copywriting (Teach Yourself)* for a much more detailed explanation of SEO.

Psst ... keep this between you me and a million others – viral marketing

Just as with any human tragedy, when Michael Jackson died at first there was shock, then questions but then ... a viral campaign.

Viral marketing relies on individuals within a group to voluntarily pass on a message. If the message makes a person believe that his or her peers will respect them for taking the time to act as a messenger they feel empowered. Self- and collective respect is boosted for passing on something that is funny, useful, insightful, surprising... and always relevant.

Society has always taught by example and demonstration. Through experience, we learn what makes people retain information and repeat it to others. For example, religious leaders passed on stories through scriptures retold throughout generations.

The web simply makes the process more efficient and timely. Videos on YouTube clarify rumours with moving images. Blogs offer opinions and insights. Emails incorporate attachments such as PowerPoint (PPT) to illustrate messages. Twitter delivers instant messages that invite 'followers' to either pause and think or join like-minded people who in turn recruit more 'followers'.

A relevant message causes people to feel that the messenger deserves their recognition. Respect comes from the value of the information contained within the message. That core value could be presented as a joke with an unexpected tag-line or video showing what authorities would prefer the general public not see, or PPT offering a brief diversion from mundane office life, or a tip-off directed at groups looking for 'inside knowledge'.

However, even if the message has value, the right messenger must also deliver it. This is illustrated by the true story of two men: William Dawes and Paul Revere.

THE BRITISH ARE COMING

In 1775 on the night of April 18, Joseph Warren, an American doctor learnt that British soldiers planned an invasion. Warren passed on the news to a young tanner called William Dawes Jr. as well as Paul Revere, a respected silversmith.

Dawes set off in one direction out of Boston through the Boston Neck, whilst Revere rowed across the Charles River in the other.

Revere had always been involved with the local community. He had connections in several business sectors beyond jewellery, for example, dentistry.

When Revere alerted people of the assault, they listened and warned others to prepare themselves. The not so well connected Dawes delivered the same message but initially had greater difficulty getting people to heed his warnings.

IT'S NOT WHAT YOU KNOW – IT'S WHO TOLD YOU

For a relevant message to spread quickly, it has to come from a respected character rather than official mouthpiece.

Influential groups of like-minded people spread valued messages to others wishing to be associated with the source of their news. Eventually the sheer numbers of 'links' create a validated, invincible chain.

Such endorsers want more than just hearsay – they demand authentic insights which resonate throughout their closely-knit community of compatible souls. In fact, genuine authenticity often presents itself as a double-edged sword for viral marketers. Good news spreads fast; bad even faster. United Airlines discovered this when baggage handlers damaged the guitar of musician Dave Carroll. After receiving no compensation from United, Carroll posted a music video on YouTube called 'United Breaks Guitars' (http://www.youtube.com/watch?v=5YGc4zOqozo). To date it has had more than 3 million views.

THE COLLECTIVE CONSCIOUSNESS OF CROWDS

One viral off-shoot being employed by viral marketers is 'viralsourcing'. Using social networking sites like Facebook, LinkedIn or Twitter, viralsourcing invites informed crowds to suggest ideas for products or services. For example, recently in America the CMO of Best Buy wanted to recruit an 'emerging media marketing expert'. He asked Twitterers to help write the recruitment advertisement. In addition to saving on recruitment agency costs he received an avalanche of suitable applications from thousands of candidates.

Another example is from Peugeot Citroën that regularly holds design competitions with cash and prizes for new car model ideas. In addition to receiving groundbreaking design suggestions from a worldwide group of enthusiastic collaborators, the competitions help boost the car manufacturer's online brand to auto fans.

WALKING ON THE MOON – A GIANT STEP FOR VIRAL CAMPAIGNS

Which brings me back to Michael Jackson's tragic death. Millions watched Jackson's bizarrely moving official memorial service. As in life, rumours about everything from the cause of his death to his strange lifestyle abounded. But for the real fans, a web viral was created and spread. www.eternalmoonwalk.com invited devotees to film themselves performing Jackson's classic Moonwalk. The clips were added to each other – creating an eternal viral tribute of Jackson's signature routine.

SIX TIPS FOR VIDEO WEB VIRAL MARKETING

1 **Plan your plot and keep it short.** *Your YouTube video should be under five minutes long, probably three minutes. Like all great promotions with a central message it should have a beginning, middle and end.*

2 **Understand your brand image.** *Your production must come across as authentic. In certain cases that may even mean having a 'homemade' feel. Remember, your job is to 'tell' rather than overtly 'sell'.*

3 **Start a series of viral pieces.** *YouTube prefers videos to be under ten minutes long – so do most viewers. This offers you the opportunity to produce a series of mini-videos that, through being a series, become collectable – and so viral!*

4 **Tag it carefully.** *People can only find your video masterpiece through its title and description. Include your company name and something that will intrigue. Good examples are the compelling 'will it blend' series of videos. In them a 'mad' scientist blends well-known products in a food mixer. Crazy – but he actually has brand names knocking on his door to have their products blended to bits in a Blendtech blender, and so made viral – see www.willitblend.com.*

5 **Make it real.** *Wherever possible, avoid using 'wooden' actors in your viral videos. Cheesy B celeb television stars are just so 1980s… Today people are interested in real people – just like them.*

6 Get your customers to make their own virals. *Don't be afraid to ask for feedback. Your honesty will be rewarded. Encourage customers to view your viral video and produce one of their own. (In the US alone, there are 100 million YouTube downloads a day.) Through participation, viral marketing builds communities.*

LINK SATELLITES (LINK BAITS)

One highly effective way to encourage hits to your site is to create satellite links. (Not to be confused with 'link farming' which exchanges reciprocal links with sites to increase SEO. Search engines such as Google view link farming as a form of spam so throw out known sites participating in link farming.) On the other hand, with satellite linking you invite a number of totally independent influential with a specialist interest in an aspect of your product or service to become noted commentators about your organization. They are not compelled to link back to you directly but instead discuss your organization on their site. Their reward is to be part of a network given exclusive and advanced notification about any new developments occurring at your organization. This encourages people to check their site in order to get 'the inside view' of a subject.

Providing the chosen influencers are not simply paid affiliates and are allowed total autonomy and freedom of speech, link satellites tend to generate not simply more hits but more valuable visits to your own site.

Web 2.0

The term, 'Web 2.0' was devised by Tim O'Reilly. Originally Web 2.0 was the 'web as a platform'.

Instead of thinking of the web as a place where browsers viewed data through small windows on screens, the web was actually the platform that allowed people to get things done. Today Web 2.0 encourages amateur developers and contributors to create applications and sites that get more credibility than traditional news sources and software vendors. Such applications and sites include social networking sites, podcasts, blogs and tools which help people collaborate with organizations rather than be dictated by them.

With Web 2.0. markets become conversations between companies and their public. Once that conversation gets underway, it spreads between audiences through techniques such as video on YouTube or Vimeo (viral marketing). The key to all Web 2.0 success is the accessibility and usefulness of the original marketing companies resources. So for example, a Google interactive map will be more Web-2.0 friendly than a static one. Allow surfers to add their own details to that map and it becomes even more compelling. The more compelling something becomes the greater the chance that it is also trusted.

As more traditional companies look for greater profits from web-based resources, so those resources have to become faster, relevant and of course useful. That requires more sophisticated technologies such as the 'semantic web' described by the originator of the original world wide web, Tim Berners Lee, as a common framework that allows data to be shared and reused across application, enterprise and community boundaries. This will lead to the future of marketing on the web: a completely seamless and integrated experience that combines the intuitiveness of human contact with the speed, connectivity and efficiency of a globally efficient, network available on a variety of formats and devices anywhere and anytime.

PC era
80s–90s

• Windows
• Mac Os

Web 1.0
90s–00s
Database
Groupware

Web 2.0
0010
Keyword
search
Wikis
Portals
Mash-ups
Socialnet
working
Widgets

Web 3.0
2010–25
Semantic search
Mash-ups (combined
media on the same site)
Virtual worlds
(for example, virtual
focus groups)
Social media,
sharing-combining
integrated email with
rich media and social
networking

Web 4.0
2025+
Intelligent
personal
agents
Mind-activated
content

ESSENTIALS FROM THIS CHAPTER

▶ *Direct marketing measures success by response.*

▶ *When emailing, make sure your message is focused and the content is relevant. Don't over-send emails. If someone requests you to stop sending emails – stop! Invite people to 'opt into' your email, or offer a genuine 'unsubscribe' option. Avoid sending business-to-business emails just prior to public holidays or weekends.*

▶ *List brokers are go-betweens who source lists and assess results on your behalf.*

▶ *To win greater response, consider:*
  ▷ *Accuracy of your data.*
  ▷ *Perceived value and relevance of your promotional offer.*
  ▷ *Scheduling of your mailing.*
  ▷ *Creative rationale behind your mailings contents.*
  ▷ *Creative design.*
  ▷ *Ease of response.*

▶ *Through-the-line, integrated marketing combines 'above' and 'below-the-line' marketing. Above-the-line establishes awareness; below-the-line, targets prospects directly.*

▶ *Measure email marketing success by: open rate?; click-through rate?; conversion rate?; website traffic?; inbound sales calls/ emails.*

▶ *Marketing-led websites must be accessible, useful and offer an experience beyond offline (the e-experience). The more genuine (rather than contrived) links you have to and from your site, the better for SEO. 'Backlinks' or 'inbound links' to your site help generate interest in your site.*

▶ *Viral marketing relies on individuals within a group to voluntarily pass on a message. If the message makes a person believe that his or her peers will respect them for taking the time to act as a messenger they feel empowered.*

▶ *The key to all Web 2.0 success is the accessibility and usefulness of the original marketing companies resources.*

14

Which agency is right for you?

In this chapter you will learn about:
- *how to select a communications agency*
- *questions to ask a new agency*
- *paying agencies*

An enthusiastic agency can ease your workload, save on costs when buying media and, of course, gain a 'buffer-zone' between you and what at times appears to be the multitude who want to sell you media, design, PR, Internet and so forth.

Just like in a personal relationship, opposites attract. Balancing strategic skills with creative know-how isn't a case of opting for an agency biased towards one or the other. Ideally, you want them to excel equally.

As in dating, ideal partnerships are usually through introduction via a mutual acquaintance. Failing this, seek recommendations from trade associations or perhaps other marketers who may well appreciate your wanting an agency that understands your needs rather than just aims for their own rewards.

Would you like an army working for you or just one specialist officer providing the same service without the extra costs to feed the troops? The decision to opt for a large or small agency boils down to whether you want to benefit from the substantial resources available at larger companies yet remain a small fish in a large pond – or enjoy the more personal service of a smaller agency. In the latter case, agency staff members probably have a stake in the agency so will want you to be especially satisfied. However, they won't be able directly to offer the services of the larger agency.

Before agencies can communicate the brilliant aspects of your product or service, they have to understand more about you, where you want to be, what you offer and why someone would want to deal with you. This requires a brief, influenced by your positioning statement/platform (see 'Quick, what's your position on this?', page 54).

Who's who at the typical large creative agency

The Chairman
Usually has money in the company
Networker
'Media Front' person

Managing Director
▶ Top new sales person
▶ Top Account Director
▶ Your port of call if things really go wrong
▶ Background usually in account management

Account Director
▶ Overall project co-coordinator
▶ Ensures campaign objectives are being met
▶ Works with entire project team to keep everything on track and within budget

Account Manager
▶ Middle Manager
▶ Your main contact for more important regular work
▶ Liaises between creative team and management

Account Executive
▶ No real management power – but aims to serve
▶ A co-coordinator

(Contd)

- ▶ Tries to please everyone
- ▶ Wants to be an Account Director
- ▶ Takes contact report notes (abridged minutes of a meeting)

Creative Director
- ▶ Ensures the campaign is 'creatively' sound
- ▶ Usually either art or copy biased
- ▶ Either loves the creative side or has aspirations of joining management to show 'them' how it should really be done
- ▶ Often expected to be slightly eccentric

Copywriter
- ▶ Wants to get under the skin of your company message
- ▶ Interested in what makes people tick
- ▶ Makes creative connections
- ▶ Frustrated author

Art Director
- ▶ Understands all aspects of graphic design
- ▶ If really good, can work without an Apple Mac
- ▶ Often has pretensions of being a writer
- ▶ Thinks in metaphors
- ▶ Often works in a writer/designer team

Account Planner
- ▶ Takes a more strategic approach to work
- ▶ Works alongside market researchers
- ▶ Maps out plans for domestic and international markets
- ▶ More of a consultant

Mac Designer
- ▶ Puts it all together
- ▶ Sometimes works to 'agency style' templates (depending on approach by Creative Director)
- ▶ Has a good eye for detail
- ▶ Wants to be an Art Director
- ▶ Appreciates the nuances of graphic design

Getting an agency pitch in tune with your needs

The two-part agency audit below can be adapted according to your required communications discipline.

PART ONE – QUESTIONS THE AGENCY SHOULD ANSWER

▶ *How many clients have you lost in the last three years?*
▶ *What are you proud of? Include communication examples.*
▶ *Will the team working on the pitch also work long term on our behalf?*
▶ *How are your teams structured? What's the line of command? (Know where the 'buck stops' at each point of the communications journey.)*
▶ *What are your payment terms? Are you willing to tell us about your financial stability?*
▶ *What are your reporting procedures and what kind of a response do you expect? (This covers everyday details like paperwork. Ignore this now and you could regret it later.)*
▶ *If we can't initially decide between you and another agency, why should we choose you? (Their positioning statement.)*
▶ *Would you mind if we speak to a couple of your existing clients?*

PART TWO – QUESTIONS YOU SHOULD EXPECT TO BE ASKED BY AN AGENCY

▶ *Why do you want an agency? For example, increase franchises, sell more units?… (Include organizational background notes.)*
▶ *Are you looking for only one type of communications solution? (For example, a PR proposal.)*
▶ *Which channels – including online – would you consider?*
▶ *Would you consider an integrated approach?*
▶ *Do you currently use an agency? If 'YES', show recent work. If 'NO' show recent work produced 'in house'.*

- *How do you think your company is perceived and, more importantly, how would you like it to be perceived? (This can be influenced by your mission statement, see page 55.)*
- *What justification exists for it to be perceived in that way? (Your positioning statement/platform.)*
- *Are you selling something – what? List three aspects that the competition either does or doesn't do any better. (Include market share, PODs, positioning and history.)*
- *Who are your customers? (It is not enough to say people aged 50. Assemble an identification kit. List interests, type of work these 'people' do, number of children, type of home…)*
- *What do you believe these people think about your company? (Any supporting research?)*
- *How do you want this market to respond? (Internet, phone, email …)*
- *How much are you prepared to spend? (Agencies tend to cut the cloth to fit a wardrobe rather than suit a tailored need.)*
- *Are there any taboos? (for example, industry regulations).*

PAY ME AND I'LL SELL YOU SOMETHING

If you think it's right that an agency should be compensated for time, materials and labour into convincing you to place your business with them, offer a modest 'pitch fee'.

Within ten days let agencies approached know of your decision and give reasons. The choice is made and the marriage is sealed. Hopefully, the honeymoon will be the start of something great, rather than the calm before the storm. Happy hunting!

Payment options

Fees are the dominant method of payment for marketing suppliers. These can be based on project or time. Agree advance blocks of time month/year/quarter. (Agencies look to make at least 20% margin.)

Commission
Most media agencies traditionally look to earn around 10% to 15% commission from placing advertisements in the media. This covers their administration fees.

Cost-plus
This is hybrid between commission and fee. Cost-plus works well if you are not retaining an agency long-term. The Agency responds to your brief with a proposal, which includes an estimate of the costs for completing the project based on expectation. The Agency then agrees an agreed mark-up on staffing costs etc., plus an allocation for third party costs.

PBR (Payment by Results)
Here you only pay the agency by the results their marketing produce. One agency I knew was paid 40p for every hectolitre (176 pints) of beer sold. Another agency was paid by each car sold by a car-manufacturing client. In all cases – targets were exceeded.

HOW WILL YOU MEASURE PBR SUCCESS?

▶ *Sales*
▶ *Market share*
▶ *Marketing contribution*
▶ *Brand performance*
▶ *Brand recall*

Put it to the test
Imagine you are an external agency pitching for your business. Using the Q&As above, how would you approach the project?

ESSENTIALS FROM THIS CHAPTER

▶ *Before agencies can communicate the brilliant aspects of your product or service, they have to understand more about you, where you want to be, what you offer and why someone would want to deal with you. This requires a brief.*

15

Sales and marketing – made for each other

In this chapter you will learn about:
- *how sales and marketing collaborate*
- *principles of selling*
- *selling to types*
- *defining a win–win sales opportunity*
- *kudzu selling*

There is no such thing as selling – just helping

Imagine taking a prospective buyer out for lunch. Seated at the table are the customer, a salesperson and yourself. The object is to persuade the customer to buy a new car. Your imaginative marketing campaign details strategic issues like the car's brand positioning and PODs. It all helps to establish credibility in the buyer's mind. But it doesn't secure a sale.

The salesperson develops a tactical one-to-one relationship with the prospective buyer. The salesperson can be compared to the buyer's best friend who knows inside facts that you don't, such as the buyer's rival has recently bought a top-of-the-range model from a competitive manufacturer. So when the salesperson approaches the buyer, it is from a position of the prospective customer's self-worth.

So it is that marketing and sales should work in unity. Instead of marketing simply being a department that produces literature and sales being a force driven by targets rather than market awareness, the two work as a team, each undertaking a complementary role.

Raphael Gabay, who runs the world-successful Beacon Group IT dedicated to enhancing performance management for government, corporate, non-profit organizations and NGOs, has devised the following set of powerful sales principles:

The Beacon IT Sales Principles

1 *Listen.*
2 *Add value to your customer's life. Remember that your customer has a customer. In the case of buying a car, those customers may include a spouse and children. So your sales techniques must adapt and so demonstrate how he/she can justify to them buying a more expensive car.*
3 *Ensure your customer perceives a 'win–win' scenario. He/she must not feel vulnerable or that you have been left vulnerable. No one gets a sour deal and so the sale becomes the start of an all-round profitable partnership.*
4 *A sale does not finish when a contract is signed or you get paid. The first sale always costs more than the sales which follow. Aim to develop this cost-effective route.*
5 *Give valued customers your email and mobile number. It creates trust and stops you from being just a sales person but makes you a valued personal contact.*

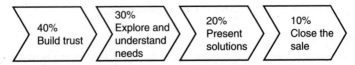

Old sales model.

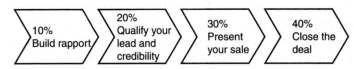

| 10%
Build rapport | 20%
Qualify your
lead and
credibility | 30%
Present
your sale | 40%
Close the
deal |

New marketing supported sales model.

Selling to types

Marketing helps sales people address underlying motives to buy and, through marketing campaigns and support material, including websites, sales aids and so on, drives home a vital sales message with benefits that address a buyer's characteristic motives.

What they buy?

Directors are 'drivers' – they need reassurance that they can accomplish goals.

Sellers are drivers – offer messages highlighting success, recognition...

Engineers are analytical – offer messages highlighting safety and order.

Supporters such as team workers want messages suggesting safety and sense of belonging.

Adapt your message for your audience.

Can you really win–win?

There are two approaches to sales negotiation: 'win at all costs (WAAC)' and 'win–win (WW)'.

The WAAC negotiator sees every negotiation as a struggle between winning and losing.

WAAC negotiators:

▶ *Initially take extreme positions*
▶ *Claim limited authority, so you end up bidding against yourself rather than them!*
▶ *Manipulate emotional tactics*
▶ *From the outset treat you as an adversary*
▶ *View any concessions you make as weaknesses*
▶ *Offer limited concessions*
▶ *Miss deadlines.*

Your options are to:

▶ *Beat them at their own game with the same tactics*
▶ *Walk away*
▶ *Try a collaborative 'win–win' approach.*

WW negotiators:

▶ *Aim to produce acceptable gains for all parties*
▶ *View conflicts as problems to be solved*
▶ *See conflicts as opportunities to be more creative, thus enhancing positions*
▶ *See relationships as being based on respect and trust.*

Kudzu selling™

'Never give up' is key to successful selling. After all, if pioneers had listened to their critics, Columbus would never have discovered America, man would never have gone to the moon and you wouldn't take that important step in your own life... In fact, all potentials would be halted. It takes imagination and perseverance to succeed. Yet endurance is not enough. To be adaptable, you must have vision to see opportunities where others are short-sighted. I call this Kudzu selling™. Kudzu was introduced to the south-eastern United States in 1876. It is a vine native to Japan and can grow 45 cm (18 inches) a day – up to 30 metres (100 feet) in a single growing season. Kudzu has sprouted its own industry comprising anything from kudzu jelly to poetry devoted to the vine. As a salesperson you have to be equally tenacious, drawing on marketing to get to the roots of a project, covering every detail to finding new ways to reach customers and extend values to existing clients. By listening to your prospect's views before 'jumping in' with a sales proposition, you can negotiate a better solution for you, your client and the company. This turns a win–lose sales exercise into a win–win standard.

Did you know?

Whatever your costs to keep an existing customer, you'll spend as much as six times more to secure a new one.

Remember, life's a pitch – and then you buy!

ESSENTIALS FROM THIS CHAPTER

▶ *Marketing and sales should collaborate and work as a team, each undertaking a complementary role.*

▶ *Principles of effective selling are:*
  ▷ *Listen*
  ▷ *Add value*
  ▷ *Offer a win–win scenario.*
  ▷ *Look to win the more cost-effective follow-up sale.*
  ▷ *Create trust by offering access.*

▶ *There are two approaches to sales negotiation: 'win at all costs (WAAC)' and 'win–win (WW)'.*

16

The future: it's in your hands

In this chapter you will learn about:
- *what the future might hold for marketing professionals*
- *how the future might affect the traditional Ps*
- *recognizing your talents to succeed beyond your expectations*

Your world is changing. A marketing job with one company is no longer for life. Instead, your career encompasses many amazing facets. Technology continues to shift market demands. Microchips halve in size and double in capacity every 11 months. Therefore logically, information technology will eventually destroy its own digital age to be replaced by crystal storage, photonics then nanotechnology. Information will be incorporated into chromosomes within DNA cells. Imagine, you'll target people using neural marketing programmes accessed by thought alone.

Place – distribution cycles will be further reduced through borderless currency, telecommunications and working communities.

Promotion – campaigns will be more precision targeted.

Price – less bulky production materials will drive down costs.

Processes – will become more dependent on thinking and design rather than actualization, the easy part.

Physical evidence – will bring brands to 'life' through value added consumer experiences which constantly adapt.

People – will, once again, take centre stage, shaping, managing and manipulating the market.

Planning – the more prepared you become the better: Plan for the best – prepare for the worst.

Planet – material resources will become more sparse – but ingenuity will create potential and that keeps markets turning.

By 2050, the focus may be on issues over data protection and direct access to personal neural networks. Looking further, as the world's population swells and we colonize other planets, so marketing will become even more advanced. Dispersed cliques may connect their minds to brand 'lifestyle spheres' where a brand's values come to life in a virtual setting. Mineral resources on our planet will naturally decrease, yet humankind's natural intellectual resources will be developed to replenish and make what we have go further. The most valued currency will be imagination. The strategy to communicate will continue to be marketing and the market, as always, will create demand to be satisfied by the enterprising few.

However technologically advanced we become, I hope that by acting as your guide around the world of marketing I have demonstrated that every marketing tool supports just one thing – stimulating ways to deal with people – profitably.

However far you venture in your own career, right now, you have the power to change your world and the community around you. It doesn't matter whether you are part of a conglomerate or marketing on your own. It takes only a single idea and persuasive method to kindle the imaginative spirit.

It's a big market out there – have courage and conquer!

Jonathan Gabay (www.brandforensics.co.uk)

ESSENTIALS FROM THIS CHAPTER

▶ *The essentials to make a difference: a great product or service, a considered marketing plan and YOU.*

Appendix

Typical marketing production times

Brochure, including copy, print and design	Six weeks
Business cards	Ten days
Christmas cards	One month
Corporate ID	Six weeks–four months
	Three months–seven months (international)
Direct mail, including copy and design	Four weeks
Newsletters including copy, design and print	Four weeks
Overhead presentation material	One week
Press advertisement – design, copy, photography and placement	Six weeks
Press release	One–seven days
Radio commercial (including planning and production)	One day–ten days
Re-branding	Seven–ten months
TV commercial or corporate video (including planning and production)	Seven weeks–four months
Website, including copy, design and planning	Four months

NB: Always treat a written brief as a legal contract. Never accept to undertake a marketing project without a satisfactory brief which is agreed and signed by all parties.

Marketing jargon buster

....

A/B Testing Testing two versions of a keyword, advertisement, website, web/landing page, banner design or variable to see which performs the best.
....

Ad Groups A group of ads within a Campaign.
....

Advertising effectiveness Targeted audience recall of an advertising message.
....

Advertising funded Media funded totally or partly from advertising.
....

Advertising Standards Authority Promotes and enforces the highest standards in non-broadcast advertisements in the UK and acts independently of the government and advertising industry.
....

Ad Views (Impressions) Number of times an ad banner is downloaded and seen by visitors.
....

Advocacy advertising Corporate advertising highlighting a company's position on a mission-critical question.
....

Affinity marketing Joint sponsorship by broadly un-competitive businesses sharing a common interest in an event (e.g. the soccer World Cup).
....

Affordable Method Advertising budget based upon what can be afforded, rather than needs to be achieved.

Arbitrary Method Advertising budget which doesn't consider basic calculations or even the desired result.

Arena advertising Posters seen at an event as well as wider television and online audience.

ASDL Asymmetric Digital Subscriber Line; transmits digital information at high speed.

Audit Bureau of Circulation Provides the UK's independent system for the validation of circulation and exhibition data.

Back-to-back Commercials broadcast within the same commercial break for the same product or pair of complementary products/services.

Banner ad A graphical (static or video/Java/Flash based web advertising unit).

BBS Web bulletin board system.

Behavioural intent Following a marketing programme, customers' perception awareness and ultimately intent to purchase a product or service.

Best practice An exceptional style of service and process that gives the perception that an organization is the best in class.

Bitmap Dots on web page which make up a picture.

Blitzkrieg advertising see, 'fast marketing'.

Blog A frequent, chronological publication of personal thoughts and web links.

BOGOFF Mnemonic for Buy One Get One Free, i.e. two for the price of one promotions.

Bot Abbreviation for robot (also called a spider). Software programs that scan the web to index web pages for search engines or harvest email addresses for spammers.

Bottom-up planning Plans and suggestions forming an integrated corporate plan. Opposite – top-down planning.

Brand conditioning Campaign which complements a brand impression.

Brand Manager Executive who controls a specific brand's marketing communications.

Brand properties Collective features that shape a brand's personality.

Brand reinforcement Support for customers' beliefs and so disposition towards a brand.

Brand share Percentage of a brand's sales/consumption sales rather than total market. Calculations are based on either levels of units sold, distributed, income or general awareness.

Browser A program which enables you to see web pages.

Calling cycle Average duration between calls to a specific customer.

Canned presentation Standard sales or marketing presentation committed to memory.

Click-Through Rate Percentage of times a surfer responds to an advertisement by clicking on the ad button/banner.

Cognitive dissonance Conflicting ideas and actions (e.g. buying something that you would otherwise never purchase, then justifying to yourself why you made such a purchase).

Commando selling Intensive campaign into a new market with a new product or service using a specially recruited sales force.

Conversion rate The percentage of your clicks which generate sales or leads. (Derived by dividing the number of sale/leads by the number of clicks you send to the offer: 100 clicks generated 100 visitors to your site, and they generate 5 sales/leads. So your conversion rate would be 20%.)

Cost-per-click (CPC) The cost or cost-equivalent paid per click-through.

CPA (Cost Per Action) A form of advertising where payment is dependent upon an action, such as signing up for a newsletter, that a user performs.

Culture Relates to either corporate or consumer beliefs, values and behaviour.

Customized marketing Tailored as opposed to mass-marketed services or products.

CPM Cost per thousand impressions.

CUT Consumer Usage Test.

DAR Day After Recall (market research).

Decay effect The result of a brand being forgotten because of lack of marketing. (During a recession, marketers who fail to continue to market risk the delay effect. This often leads to loss of custom through competitive initiatives conducted during the recessionary period.)

Deep linking Linking to a web page other than a site's home page.

Diadic Two people separately reporting findings on two advertisements or products.

Dirty proof Proof full of amendments.

Dissonance reduction theory A person's need to be convinced that a product or service is worth buying.

Divergent marketing Separate organizations within a company with individual marketing goals and profit centres.

Domain Official Internet address.

Doorway page Web page optimized to rank highly for a given keyword phrase. (Also known as a Hall Way or Tunnel Page.)

Dumping Products sold and distributed overseas for less than they would be marketed locally.

Dynamically continuous Same service or product but technically enhanced and re-marketed for a new audience.

Electronic catalogue Accessible website database, featuring products or services, leading to online shopping.

End values A person's most important values – love, security, welfare...

End-user The consumer who actually uses rather than pays for a product or service.

Engel's Law Theory which suggests that given set of tastes and preferences, as income rises, the *proportion* of income spent on food falls, even if *actual* expenditure on food rises.

EPOs Electronic Point of Sale.

Equivalent advertising value Sum total of publicity and editorial coverage in the press, in terms of space, compared to buying the equivalent space using advertising.

Events marketing Campaign which invites customers or prospects to a venue.

Fag A chosen person highlighted within a database for future testing or re-mailing.

Family life cycle
a) Young, alone living outside parental home.
b) Just married/co-habiting, no children.
c) Married/co-habiting, youngest child under six.
d) Married/co-habiting, youngest child over six.
e) Married/co-habiting, child about to become independent.
f) Children left home, breadwinner still in employment.
g) Children left home, breadwinner retired.
h) Surviving partner is the breadwinner.
i) Surviving partner is retired.

Fast marketing Also **Blitzkrieg advertising** Advertising delivered at once over a relatively short timescale to encourage a high-volume response.

Favicon A small icon that is used by some browsers to identify a branded site.

Filler Prepared advertisement to be used as a last minute 'filler' in the press – often published at cut cost.

Firewall An installed and connected computer (or several) between an Intranet and Internet controlling user access.

First proof Initial proof of promotional material to check for spelling or other errors.

Flanking attack Ambushing a competitor at a weak spot.

Flashpack Packaging with a sales promotion message.

Free continuous premium Coupons redeemed for a gift or concession according to the number of purchases.

Gable end Poster at the end wall of a building.

Generic products Un-branded products aimed at frugal customers.

Generic term Brand name to describe a type of product (e.g. Hoover, Xerox).

Gestation period Elapsed time between an initial product inquiry and order.

Google Sandbox A supposed mechanism that factors a website's age into its ranking on popular keywords.

Government relations PR dealing with local, national and international interests.

Guerrilla marketing Attacks competitive activities through confusion and demoralization techniques with the aim to capture a niche spot in the market.

Hall test Research technique also known as In-Theatre Research ... in which people at a specific location answer questions for a marketing campaign.

Hidden value Initially insignificant value which is later promoted by a supplier.

Housewife time The radio broadcast period between morning rush hour and the early evening drive times.

HTML Hypertext Mark-up Language – basic language for writing sites.

Incentive marketing Added incentives such as prize draws and discount vouchers.

In-home media Any media in the home (e.g. television, lifestyle press, radio and web TV).

In-home use test Pre-product testing in consumer's home.

Institutional advertising Advertising for entire sectors.

Institutional market Community care market – hospitals, schools, prisons...

Intelligent agent Web software which searches the web for information based on your preferences.

Internet relay chat A web system for surfers to see and hear each other in real time.

ISDN Integrated Services Digital Network (for speeding up the production process between studio and printer). See also **ASDL**.

Java A language and platform for distributed network computing.

Joint promotion Co-sponsored and managed promotion aimed at increasing impact whilst reducing marketing costs.

Key success factor The essential element which makes a product or service a market success.

Keyword matching In Google Ad Words, there are four different keyword matching options.

Broad match If your web ad group contained the keyword, marketing expert, consultant, your ad would appear when a surfer's search query contained marketing expert and consultant, in any order. Your web ads could also show for singular/plural forms, synonyms, and other relevant variations.

Phrase match If you enter your keyword in quotation marks, as in "marketing expert", your ad will appear when a surfer searches on the phrase 'marketing expert', in this order. For example, your ad could appear for the inquiry internet 'marketing expert' but not for 'expert for marketing'.

Exact match If you surround your keywords in brackets, such as [marketing expert], your web ad will be eligible to appear when a user searches for the specific phrase 'marketing expert', in this order, and without any other terms in the query.

Negative keyword If your keyword is 'marketing expert' and you add the negative keyword 'internet', your ad will not appear when a user searches on internet for 'marketing expert'. Negative keywords are useful if your account contains lots of broad-matched keywords.

Killer application 'Must have' software (e.g. email).

Law of demand The higher the price, the lower the demand (or vice versa).

Letterbox marketing Hand-distributed marketing promotions – usually with free local newspapers.

Link Bait A type of spam in the mode of editorial content posted on a blog or page and submitted to social networking media sites with hopes of building inbound links from other sites.

Live marketing Management of any situation where a customer interacts face to face with a brand, to ensure a positive brand perception.

Loyalty marketing Brand loyalty programme featuring gifts/financial incentives.

Lumpy demand Lumps in demand due to seasonal variations of consumer tastes.

MAPS Management Analysis and Planning Systems; designed for the measurement and control of critical business functions.

Market reach The maximum number of prospects reached with a marketing campaign.

Market recognition Common brand or product awareness usually gauged in percentage sales.

Micro marketing Marketing tailored to address individual objectives.

Mood advertising Advertising which instils an attitude conducive to a product or service.

Mousetrapping The use of browser techniques to keep a visitor browsing at a site, often by disabling the back button or generated repeated pop-up windows.

Link popularity A measure of the quantity and quality of sites that link to your site.

NABS The only major UK charity that covers the whole of the marketing communications industry.

Neck hanger A sales promotion device like a miniature leaflet affixed to the neck of a bottle.

New media multimedia such as the World Wide Web, Blu-Ray, TV on-demand, video clips via the web.

Nixies Undeliverable addresses.

Noise Over-exposed advertising messages to a wearied audience.

Opt in/Opt out An email marketing promotion offering consumers an opportunity to 'opt in' (taking action to be part of the promotion) or to 'opt out' (taking action to not be part of the promotion).

Pass-on readership Total readership of a publication, including those who didn't actually buy it in the first place (tertiary readership – read publication casually whilst sitting in a waiting room e.g. at the dentist).

Pay per click Online advertising payment model in which payment is based solely on qualifying click-throughs.

Penetration pricing A cut-price strategy to gain quick, wide market penetration.

Permission marketing Marketing centered around obtaining customer consent to receive information from a company.

Plug-ins Web software to run value-added programs such as audio or video. (Also known as Apps.)

Podcast Published audio files to the web for playback on mobile devices and personal computers.

Product clutter Outdated products which hinder innovative marketing management.

Professional services marketing Marketing aimed at professionals such as lawyers, accountants and architects.

Push technology Digitally 'pushing' information based on a consumer's preferences through a computer and thereby creating a tailored, value-added sales channel.

Quasi retailing Retailers selling things apart from core products (e.g. building societies, funeral parlours, hotels).

Quota sample Pre-selected research groups, representative of the larger population.

Rank A web banner or advertisement's standing in comparison to other ads, based on the graphical click-through rate.

Readership profile Segmentation of readership.

Rears Advertising spaces on the back of cars, taxis, buses and trams.

Repositioning A campaign to alter perceived brand values and relevance.

Reputation management The management and tracking of an organization's 'off' or 'online' presence and status.

Rifle approach A targeted message at a targeted audience; opposite – blunderbuss approach.

ROAS Return on Ad Spend. Sales impact measurement of sales activities.

Sales platform Main sales proposition.

Salting Also Seeding, or Sleeper. Name within a mailing or email list charged with monitoring the mailing process.

Search engine An electronic web page location indexing system.

SEM (Search Engine Marketing) Building and marketing a site to develop its position in search engine results. (SEM includes search engine optimization (SEO) and pay per click advertising (PPC)).

Search engine optimization The process of choosing targeted keyword phrases related to a site, and ensuring that the site places well when those keyword phrases are part of a web search.

Semi-solus Advertisement which appears on the same page as another – but not next to it.

SERP (Search Engine Results Page) The page surfers see once they've entered their query into the search box.

Share of voice Percentage of your marketing budget compared to your competitors.

SKU Stock Keeping Units (goods on superstore shelves).

Skyscraper ad An online ad significantly taller than the 120 × 240 vertical banner.

SLP Self Liquidating Promotion (pays for itself).

Starch ratings US advertising effectiveness measurement system.

Stickiness A measure used to determine the value of a site in retaining surfers.

Suit Slang for marketing or advertising, account administrator, manager or director.

Surround session Advertising sequence in which a visitor receives ads from one advertiser throughout an entire site visit.

Tactical pricing Price manipulation to encourage sales.

Tags Individual keywords or phrases for **organizing** content.

TAP Total Audience Package – broadcast spots stretched out over time.

TAT Thematic Apperception Test – consumers artistically describing feelings about a product or service with pen and paper.

Teaser Intriguing advertisement such as a poster or direct mailer.

Tissue First-draft creative concepts presentation.

Top-of-mind Easily recalled brand – not necessarily the brand leader.

Torture test To demonstrate endurance, a product or service is subjected to extremes.

Tracking Domain A domain (denoted by the last letters or a website address to show type or advertised location of the website) to measure traffic delivered to a site.

Unaided brand awareness Number of a research sample who can name a brand after summarizing similar products or services within a sector.

Undifferentiated marketing technique Mass marketing without any distinctive target audience benefits.

Unique Users The total number of different surfers, or computer terminals which have visited a site.

Universe Selection of population used as a research sample.

URL Uniform Resource Locator – expresses the location of a site.

Valid hits Hits to a site which deliver all information to a user. Excludes hits such as redirects, error messages and computer-generated hits.

Vehicle Medium featured in a marketing communications programme.

Vertical market Services or products segmented within a single market classification.

Video on demand Videos, such as those used in promotions, stored on a central server and run on request, exclusively for an individual via a PC, network computing device or television.

Viral marketing Encouragement of market to 'push' a marketing message throughout a community, and in doing so enhance reputations within communities.

Virtual agency network Creative suppliers collaborating to provide a marketing communications service either nationally or globally.

Vlog A video blog.

Vortal A site that provides information and services to specialist markets.

Voucher copy Complimentary edition of newspaper or magazine – usually to see a published advertisement in situ.

Waste circulation Percentage of published circulation which has no value to a marketer but still needs to be bought.

Webcasting Broadcasting over the Internet.

White goods Consumer durables such as microwave ovens, fridges and washing machines.

Widget A live update or surfer chosen content or applications on a website, webpage, or desktop.

Wobbler Adhesive sales promotion display device which 'wobbles' when pushed.

X-bar Statistical symbol which represents an average.

X-factor The inexact marketing aspect within a person or a company that can't be copied but equals success.

YES bias A respondent's tendency to complete the YES boxes in a coupon.

Z-card Miniature brochure folded into a credit-card sized format.

Z-chart A chart showing values over a period of time such as a year whilst providing daily, weekly or monthly figures to support the sum total.

Zine Magazines or newsletters which are published digitally, rather than on paper.

Zone plan Marketing test for a new product or service using advertising in a highly targeted, small geographic area.

Taking it further

Useful contacts

Advertising Association www.adassoc.org.uk

Advertising Standards Authority www.asa.org.uk

Copy rules advice on advertising and promotions
Tel: +44 (0)20 7580 4100

Audit Bureau of Circulation www.abc.org.uk

Beacon Group IT www.beaconit.com.au

British Market Research Association (BMRA) www.bmra.org.uk

Broadcast Advertising Clearance Centre www.bacc.com.uk

Broadcasters' Audience Research Board Tel: +44 (0)20 7741 9110

Broadcasting Standards Council Tel: +44 (0)20 7233 0544

Chartered Institute of Marketing www.cim.co.uk

Design Council www.design-council.org.uk

Direct Marketing Association www.dma.org.uk

Gabay – marketing resources including education
www.gabaynet.com

Incorporated Society of British Advertisers www.isba.org.uk

Independent Television Commission www.itc.org.uk

Institute of Direct Marketing www.thidm.co.uk

Institute of Directors www.iod.co.uk

The Institute of Packaging www.info@iop.co.uk

Institute of Practitioners in Advertising (IPA) www.ipa.co.uk

Institute of Public Relations www.ipr.press.net

Institute of Sales Promotion (ISP and SPCA) www.isp.org.uk

Mailing Preference Service www.dma.org.uk

Market Research Society www.marketresearch.org.uk

NABS www.nabs.org.uk

The Newspaper Society www.newspapersoc.org.uk

NOP Research Group Tel: +44 (0)20 7890 9439

Public Relations Consultants Association www.prca.org.uk

Complaints about premium rate telephone lines, call 0800 500 212
or go to www.icstis.org.uk

THE NETHERLANDS

Esomar www.esomar.nl

AUSTRALIA

Australian Association of National Advertisers

Sydney Tel: +61 2 9221 8088

Australian Direct Marketing Association Ltd

Sydney Tel: +61 2 247 7744

Australian Federation of Advertising

North Sydney Tel: +61 2 957 3077

Australian Marketing Institute

Melbourne Tel: +61 3 820 8788

Council of Sale Promotional Agencies Tel: +61 203 325 3911

Public Relations Institute of Australia (New South Wales)

North Sydney Tel: +61 2 369 2029

Public Relations Institute of Australia Tel: +61 2 369 2029

PRIA (Queensland)

Tel: +61 7 368 3662

PRIA (South Australia)

Marden South Australia 5070 Tel: +61 8 362 1559

PRIA (Tasmania)

Tel: +61 0 233 4439

PRIA (Western Australia)

East Perth Tel: +61 9 421 7555

Promotion Industry Club (Sales)

Naperville Tel: +61 708 369 3772

CANADA

Canadian Direct Marketing Association

Toronto, Ontario Tel: +1 416 391 2362

Canadian Public Relations Society Inc. (CPRS)
Tel: +1 613 232 122

Institute of Canadian Advertising

Toronto, Ontario Tel: +1 416 482 1396

UNITED STATES

Advertising Council Inc.

New York Tel: +1 212 922 1500

American Advertising Federation

Washington DC Tel: +1 202 898 0089

American Association of Advertising Agencies

New York Tel: +1 212 682 2500

American Marketing Association

Chicago Tel: +1 312 648 0536

Business Professional Advertising Association

Alexandria VA Tel: +1 703 683 2722

Direct Marketing Association

New York Tel: +1 212 768 7277

International Advertising Association

New York Tel: +1 212 557 1133

Marketing Research Association

Connecticut Tel: +1 203 257 4008

Point-of-Purchase Advertising Institute

Englewood NJ Tel: +1 201 894 8899

Public Relations Society of America

New York Tel: +1 212 995 2230

HONG KONG

Public Relations Association of Hong Kong Limited (PRAHK)

GPO Box 1264, Hong Kong

Further recommended reading

Gabay's Copywriters' Compendium by Jonathan Gabay, Hodder Education, 2010 ISBN 9781444110920

Improve Your Copywriting by Jonathan Gabay, Hodder Education, 2010 ISBN 9781444102956

Soul Traders by Jonathan Gabay, Marshall Cavendish, 2009 ISBN 9781905736515

Reinvent Yourself by J. Jonathan Gabay, Momentum, 2002
ISBN 1840304015 8

Trade Name Origins – NTC Publishing Group,
ISBN 0-8442-0904-X

RECOMMENDED MARKETING COURSES

Brand Forensics – Led by author, Jonathan Gabay –
www.brandforensics.co.uk

Chartered Institute of Marketing www.cim.co.uk

Institute of Direct Marketing Tel: +44 (0)20 8977 5705

Institute of Sales Promotion Tel: +44 (0)20 7837 5340

Marcus Evans www.marcusevanspt.com

Capita Learning and Development www.capita-ld.co.uk

Index

Reference should also be made to the Marketing Jargon Buster on pages 319–334